THE WORLD OF FARLEY MOWAT

ABOUT THE AUTHOR

FARLEY MOWAT, author of such distinguished books as *People of the Deer, Never Cry Wolf, A Whale for the Killing, The Snow Walker,* and *Sea of Slaughter,* has long been eloquent in his indictment of man's exploitation of human and non-human life on this planet. He was born in Belleville, Ontario, in 1921 and began writing for a living in 1949 after spending two years in the Arctic. He has lived in or visited almost every part of Canada and many other lands. More than ten million copies of Farley Mowat's books have been translated and published in hundreds of editions in over forty countries.

THE
WORLD OF
FARLEY
MOWAT

A SELECTION FROM HIS WORKS

EDITED AND WITH AN
INTRODUCTION BY
PETER DAVISON

SEAL BOOKS
McClelland-Bantam, Inc.
Toronto

*This edition contains the complete text
of the original hardcover edition.*
NOT ONE WORD HAS BEEN OMITTED.

THE WORLD OF FARLEY MOWAT: A SELECTION FROM HIS WORKS

*A Seal Book / published by arrangement with
McClelland & Stewart Limited*

PRINTING HISTORY
*McClelland & Stewart edition published October 1980
A Selection of Book-of-the-Month Club February 1981
Seal edition / April 1982
2nd printing . . . December 1988*

ISBN 0-7704-1736-1

PRINTED IN CANADA

U   11   10   9   8   7   6   5   4   3   2

CONTENTS

The World of Fantasy Mount

MOWAT COUNTRY
An Introduction

◆

For nearly thirty years Farley Mowat has been writing about the way men live at the top of the world, that part of the globe above 46 degrees north latitude, the cosmopolis of cold. Through these regions man first arrived on the American continent, in prehistoric times travelling eastward by land from Eurasia, and in historical times travelling west by sea from the Old World. In terms of nationhood, this vast region has been dominated through recorded history by the Norse people, the Russians, and the Canadians. During the recent volatile decades, Mowat has spoken perhaps more eloquently and certainly more consistently than any other writer in our language for the equipoise between man and nature in our northern latitudes.

No region of the earth contains so much residual wealth of minerals and protein; nor has any other seen man give freer rein to his greed for gold, fish, furs, oil, whales, and that most elusive of mother-lodes, glory. Mowat's compilations of texts about the top of the world (*Coppermine Journey, Ordeal by Ice, The Polar Passion,* and *Tundra*) record not only his profound knowledge of the literature of the North, but a tragic spectacle of man consuming himself in pursuit of chimeras. What could be more abstract, more certifiably insane, than the nineteenth century's chauvinistic struggle to be the first man, the first nation, to stand at the imaginary point of 90 degrees north latitude, in the dead center of the frozen Arctic Ocean? Yet man performed some of his most noble gestures, and some of his basest trickeries, to attain that literal end. Hundreds of men and perhaps thousands of animals perished in the attempt.

Farley Mowat's own writings, as distinguished from those he has collected from other pens, have been largely unconcerned with adventure as such. Polar passions do not ultimately interest him, nor the attainment of death-defying stunts or earth-girdling explorations. Such activities set man at unnatural hurdles. It is the "natural" order, in which man lives in harmony with his surroundings, that Mowat finds to characterize the Golden Age — no age that ever was on sea or land, but an age that can blossom into being at any time, and even at the corners of the earth. Cold, hunger, storm, arduous extremity, none of these interferes with the attainment of harmony in the world — as long as man is willing to live with such forces and recognize that they are part of his destiny. "Ah, me son," Mowat quotes a Newfoundlander, "we don't be *taking* nothing from the sea. We sneaks up on what we wants — and wiggles it away."

Mowat is not a religious man or a religious writer, but he can read what is written in Nature's book and understand, with Rousseau, that "Nature never deceives us; it is always we who deceive ourselves." No, Mowat would not join the meliorative chorus in praise of human nature. He finds more harmony in humor than he finds satisfaction in denunciation, though he indulges in both.

In *Survival*, a tendentious but perceptive study of Canadian literature, Margaret Atwood generalizes that if the central symbol of English literature can be identified as the island, and of American literature the receding frontier, the comparable symbol in Canadian writing is survival, with the victim as its ruling self-image. If *Survival* had dealt with Farley Mowat's writings alone, few would question its validity, for both in their serious and in their humorous aspects, Mowat's twenty-five books all deal with endurance, with man's role among the animals and with his inhumanity to his fellows; and they give as much attention to the victims of inhumanity as to man's ability to survive long enough for laughter. Survival, in Mowat Country, comes mostly in the face of blizzard on land or tempest by sea.

Rain lashed into his face with the strength of driven shot. His hastily donned slicker whipped against his body. Shielding his face with one hand, he gripped a stanchion with the other and peered out into the roaring night. It was almost impossible to distinguish sea from air. The storm waves now rose to fearful heights but, as they lifted, so were their tops blown clean away — blown away in great streaks of foaming scud which mingled with the almost horizontal blasts of rain.

(The Serpent's Coil, p. 54)

In the face of such harrowing, men are more alike than different, whether they be salvage-tug mariners, Siberian reindeer-herdsmen, cod fishermen on the Grand Banks, seal-hunters on the spring ice, or soldiers in a front-line foxhole. Mowat Country is not much of a place for women, who mostly stay home or under cover. It is a place of robust appetites for raw meat and strong red rum, for oil-skins, mukluks, and parkas lined with the fur of wolverines. It is a land for dogs but not for horses: the symbols of life include not the plow or the wagon but the sled and the dory or, for errands of mercy, the bush plane. Mowat Country is a land of isolated men and tiny settlements, and of entertainments and laughter as predatory as the need for food.

I was so elated by the realization that I had not only located a pair of wolves, but by an incredible stroke of fortune had found their den as well, that I forgot all caution and ran to a nearby knoll in order to gain a better view of the den mouth.

The male wolf, who had been loafing about the foot of the esker after the departure of his wife, instantly saw me. In three or four bounds he reached the ridge of the esker, where he stood facing me in an attitude of tense and threatening vigilance. As I looked up at him my sense of exhilaration waned rapidly. He no longer seemed like a playful pup, but had metamorphosed into a magnificent engine of destruction which impressed me so much that the neck of my flask positively rattled against my teeth.

(Never Cry Wolf, p. 66)

Such humor, like such country, is distinctively northern, not to say Canadian. Those of us who have become used to Canadian humor realize how much it has to do with survival-connected emotions — surprise, defense, ridicule, and danger. Stephen Leacock, the great Canadian humorist, once described the perfect Canadian joke as the episode in a cowpasture baseball game when a showoff steals second base with a terrific slide, only to discover that the base had been deposited by a cow. Such, in domesticated terms, are the delights of Mowat Country. When, in the mock-idyll, *The Boat Who Wouldn't Float*, the leaky craft sailed by Farley and his publisher finally fetches up in a safe harbor, dawn discovers it to be moored beneath the waste-pipe of a fish-processing factory. The tempest may be rough but it is at least clean. Civilized life tends to corrupt; high civilization corrupts absolutely.

It is no coincidence, then, that Mowat Country extends to the cold air north of where most of us live, and that Mowat's books do not ever concern themselves with metropolitan life. At an early age Mowat shook off — or had stripped from him — the inhibitions and the manners of civilized society. This selection from his work aims to trace the way Farley has chosen to spend his life, and my choices from his books are arranged roughly in the order of his actual experiences: not in the order in which he chose to write about them, but in the best order to read them.

Farley Mowat was born in Belleville, Ontario, on May 12, 1921, and his childhood followed the peregrinations of his colorful father, Angus Mowat, whose life I predict Farley will one day write. Angus Mowat was a writer and librarian, an Anglo-Canadian of fierce passions and loyal prejudices. Having lost the use of one arm in World War I, Angus Mowat, a dapper, bristling man, wrote novels, kept bees, sailed boats, and managed libraries in various Ontario towns, and ultimately, beginning when Farley was twelve, in Saskatoon, Saskatchewan.

It was the Saskatoon landscape, rich with bird and beast, that first attracted the teen-age birdwatcher in Farley, whose early ambition it was to be a biologist. The rascally adventures of this boy and his dog Mutt and their friends the owls are recounted in *The Dog Who Wouldn't Be* (1957), in which the virtues of animality — and of an aspiration higher than an animal's fate — are recounted. (They also recur in the children's book *Owls in the Family*, 1961, which, with Mowat's three other children's books, is excluded from this collection.) Mowat was not beyond his teens when World War II broke out, but he soon volunteered for military service, the partial story of which is recounted in *And No Birds Sang* (1979) as well as in the earlier, less personal *The Regiment* (1955). On his return from wartime service in Europe, Mowat returned to Saskatchewan for several months, where it became clear to him that his professional interest in biology was gone, and where he began to think of his wartime writing efforts (mostly poetry, but also including early sketches for *The Dog Who Wouldn't Be*) as a possible prelude to a writing career. He became an impatient student at the University of Toronto in the fall of 1946 and began making plans to visit the Arctic. His two extended Arctic visits in 1947 and 1948 paid dividends in three books: *People of the Deer* (1952), *The Desperate People* (1959), and *Never Cry Wolf* (1963), as well as in *The Snow Walker* (1975).

People of the Deer, serialized in *The Atlantic Monthly* and first published in the United States by the Atlantic Monthly Press, made a great sensation in Canada and launched Mowat's reputation as well as winning him the Anisfield-Wolf Award. But Mowat's footloose days were at an end for a while. Having married Frances Thornhill in 1949, he bought some land in Palgrave, north of Toronto, and built himself a log house with outbuildings, where he wrote his first ten books, published between 1952 and 1960. The Palgrave log house would prove to have been Mowat's place of longest residence, and the place where his two sons were reared. But the restless student turned out to be a restless husband, and in 1961 he went to England, where he spent the winter doing research for his most complex and scholarly (and, as it proves, his least excerptible) book, *Westviking* (1965), a study of the Norse voyages in the North Atlantic and Norse settlements in the New World.

During the 1950's Mowat had already turned his attention from the barren lands of the North to the Atlantic Ocean. Retained as early as 1955 by the Foundation Company to write a history of their marine salvage operations in the North Atlantic, Mowat became absorbed in the life, the language, and the courage of the seafaring man in this most dangerous and altruistic of callings: the saving of life and property threatened by shipwreck. It was a range of subject matter fitting to a student of survival. In 1958 he published *The Grey Seas Under*, the first of two books on the subject; *The Serpent's Coil* followed in 1961.

His own survival as an artist took Mowat to a new residence, the outport town of Burgeo, on the south coast of Newfoundland. Ever since 1960, when he had first begun cruising the Newfoundland shores in a notoriously unseaworthy little fishing schooner named *Happy Adventure*, the bluff, salty ways of the dory fishermen had attracted him to the codfish civilization of the North Atlantic, to those broad shoal waters that had carried the fishing fleets of the new and the old worlds for centuries, from Bilbao, Reykjavik, and Whitby to St. John's, Halifax, Gloucester, and Boston. In 1962, already the author of three books about the sea and its coasts, he settled in Burgeo, after completing his first "outport" book, the children's story *The Black Joke*.

It is characteristic of the writer's imagination that the first book Mowat actually wrote in Newfoundland, the comic yet elegant *Never Cry Wolf* (1963), should return to the Arctic setting and refer to experiences fifteen years old. The next, transitional volume, *Westviking*, was not finished or published till 1965. It received not only the support but the participation (as illustrator) of his second wife, Claire Mowat, whom he had originally met in the island port of St. Pierre, and who now shared his life in Newfoundland. Burgeo provided a rich, crowded, and, despite its isolation from urban centers, a far-from-private existence, for it laid the Mowats on the pulse of a delicately balanced community — not, this time, as visitors but as participants. Yet writers have impulses stronger than wishing to belong to communities: the impulse to lyrical evocation, the impulse to indignation and outcry.

Mowat's three Newfoundland books, in addition to his travel book *Sibir* or *The Siberians* (1970), are *This Rock Within the Sea*, illustrated by the chiaroscuro photographs of John de Visser (1968), *The Boat Who Wouldn't Float* (1969), and *A Whale for the Killing* (1972). The first, written before the tragic whale episode of 1967, evinces Mowat's love for the villagers, tucked in their fingerhold at the edge of the howling ocean; the second, after the Mowats' disenchantment, tries to make light of the discovery that inhumanity was not exclusive to city folk; and the third, written in 1971 after several years had passed, attempts to recount both the human and the elemental tragedy of the stranded whale that happened to be trapped in a Burgeo tidal pond in 1967.

The "whale episode" would prove to be a pivotal incident, a turning point in Mowat's career as a writer. It deepened his sense of mystery about the animal world and darkened his disenchantment with his fellow man. That book moves between the echoing depths in which whales swim and the surface antipathy in which men quarrel. After those experiences, Mowat could no longer live in Newfoundland, and he and his wife soon found another home in Ontario. Port Hope would be his base in the 1970's as Palgrave had served for the 1950's and Burgeo for the 1960's.

The middle 1970's were not Mowat's most productive period. Separated from the elementals of outports and the Arctic, he found less material to draw upon. For a few years he maintained a summer residence on the Magdalen Islands, moored in the middle of the Gulf of St. Lawrence halfway between Prince Edward Island and the Gaspé Peninsula; but the half-French, half-English society did not retain its appeal for him, and several writing projects undertaken in that beautiful, windswept island setting came to nothing. But *Wake of the Great Sealers*, illustrated by David Blackwood (1973), drawing on the seal-hunting tradition of Newfoundland and the Magdalen Islands alike, is one of Mowat's starkest and most striking writing achievements.

Retreating again to Port Hope, the Mowats moved into a different house, and in the late 1970's Farley found another house in remoter country, between the Bras d'Or Lakes and the sea in Nova Scotia's Cape Breton Island, a site fertilized by fresh and salt water equally. No sooner had this new location been settled than Mowat began to hark back once again (as he had in *The Dog Who Wouldn't Be* and *Never Cry Wolf*) to memories, to refreshed awakening of old territories of the psyche. Though in the early 1970's he had published books on the Arctic (*The Snow Walker*, 1975, and *Canada North Now [The Great Betrayal]*, 1976), these books were revisions of old material. *And No Birds Sang* (1979), however, reopened old wounds to the point of bleeding. This account of Mowat's wartime life as a soldier breaks off almost in mid-sentence, as if the agony of remembered war became intolerable.

It is worth it, when an author has given us so copiously of his experience as Mowat has, to look at the quality of understanding that his experience has won from him. Mowat's work is full of a compassion for the victims of modern life — the displaced outport fisherman, the dispossessed Eskimo, the ravaged animal species of the North like whale and wolf and caribou. But as his career goes on, Mowat's writings take us deeper into the general human condition. The misery of the human situation becomes less easy to laugh off, the failures of love and understanding become harder to explain. In the 1980's and after, as Mowat casts aside some of the exaggerations of his youthful behavior and takes on the task of facing what it is that has driven him as a writer, he may find how lucky he has been in his human and animal relations on this planet and begin celebrating the high quality of those powerful encompassments that Edwin Muir refers to as "the archaic companionship" — that of parents, lovers, beloved animals. There was reason, in ancient times, for emperors to be buried with their wives, their dogs, their horses. Barbaric as the practice was, it paid homage to what binds us to life. Though we are obliged to survive, it is only for love that we do so. In one of Mowat's books after another we hear his favorite words — "existence," "elemental," "unbelievable," "superhuman," "irresistible," "struggle" — repeating themselves in the rhythm of insistence on what it is that holds us together in the companionship of animals. It is part of being animals that enables us to feel the tie between Kikik and her children, between the dying whale and her sentinel at the edge of the sea, between husband and wife, between a son and his father, a boy and his dog, even between a writer and his friends. We do not survive in order to die as victims but to live as companions.

Peter Davison
Gloucester, Massachusetts
January 1980

I.
SASKATCHEWAN

FROM

THE DOG WHO WOULDN'T BE, 1957

THE
COMING OF MUTT

An oppressive darkness shadowed the city of Saskatoon on an August day in 1929. By the clock it was hardly noon. By the sun — but the earth had obliterated the sun. Rising in the new deserts of the southwest, and lifting high on autumnal winds, the desecrated soil of the prairies drifted northward; and the sky grew dark.

In our small house on the outskirts of the city my mother switched on the electric lights and continued with the task of preparing luncheon for my father and for me. Father had not yet returned from his office at the Public Library, nor I from school. Mother was alone with the somber day.

The sound of the doorbell brought her unwillingly from the kitchen into the hall. She opened the front door no more than a few inches, as if expecting the menace of the sky to thrust its way past her into the house.

There was no menace in the appearance of the visitor who waited apologetically on the step. A small boy, perhaps ten years of age, stood shuffling his feet in the grey grit that had been falling soundlessly across the city for a day and a night. He held a wicker basket before him and, as the door opened, he swung the basket forward and spoke in a voice that was husky with the dust and with the expectation of rebuff.

"Missus," he asked in a pale, high tone, "would you want to buy a duck?"

3

Mother was a bit nonplussed by this odd echo of a catch phrase that had already withered and staled in the mouths of the comedians of the era. Nevertheless, she looked into the basket and to her astonishment beheld three emaciated ducklings, their bills gaping in the heat, and, wedged between them, a nondescript and bedraggled pup.

She was touched, and curious — although she certainly did not want to buy a duck.

"I don't think so," she said kindly. "Why are you selling them?"

The boy took courage and returned her smile.

"I gotta," he said. "The slough out to the farm is dry. We ate the big ducks, but these was too small to eat. I sold some down to the Chinee Grill. You want the rest, lady? They're cheap — only a dime each."

"I'm sorry," Mother replied. "I've no place to keep a duck. But where did you get the little dog?"

The boy shrugged his shoulders. "Oh, *him*," he said without much interest. "He was kind of an accident, you might say. I guess somebody dumped him out of a car right by our gate. I brung him with me in case. But dogs is hard to sell." He brightened up a little as an idea struck him. "Say, lady, you want him? I'll sell him for a nickel — that way you'll *save* a nickel for yourself."

Mother hesitated. Then almost involuntarily her hand went to the basket. The pup was thirsty beyond thirst, and those outstretched fingers must have seemed to him as fountains straight from heaven. He clambered hastily over the ducks and grabbed.

The boy was quick to sense his advantage and to press it home.

"He likes you, lady, see? He's yours for just *four* cents!"

Less than a month had elapsed since my parents and I had come out of the verdant depths of southern Ontario into the arid and dust-shrouded prairies.

It had seemed a foolhardy venture then, for those were the beginnings of the hard times, even in the east; while in the west the hard times — the times of drought and failure — were already old. I do not know what possessed my father to make

4

him exchange the security of his job in Windsor for a most uncertain future as Saskatoon's librarian. It may be that the name itself, Saskatoon, Saskatchewan, attracted him irresistibly. It may have been simply that he was tired of the physical and mental confines of a province grown staid and stolid in its years.

In any case he made his decision in the fall of 1928, and the rest of us acquiesced in it; I, with a high heart and bright anticipation; Mother, with grave reservations and gloomy prophecies.

Father spent that winter building a caravan, a trailer-house which was destined to carry us westward. It was a long winter for me. On Saturdays I joined my father under a shed and here we hammered and sawed industriously, and the caravan took shape. It was an unconventional shape, for my father was a sailor at heart and he had had but little experience in the design of land conveyances. Our caravan was, in reality, a household perched precariously on the four thin wheels of an old Model T chassis. Her aspect was bluff and uncompromising. Her sides towered straight from the frame a full seven feet to a gently cambered deck (which was never referred to as a roof). She was big-boned and buxom, and she dwarfed poor Eardlie — our Model A Ford convertible — as a floating derrick dwarfs the tug which tows it.

I had my choice of riding in Eardlie's rumble seat, where I became the gunner in a Sopwith Camel; or I could ride in the caravan itself and pilot my self-contained rocket into outer space. I preferred the caravan, for it was a private world and a brave one. My folding bunk-bed was placed high up under the rear window, and here I could lie — carefully strapped into place against the effect of negative gravity (and high winds) — and guide my spaceship through the void to those far planets known as Ohio, Minnesota, Wisconsin, Michigan, and North Dakota.

When we reached Saskatchewan, I no longer needed to exercise my imagination by conjuring up otherworldly landscapes. The desolation was appalling, and it was terrifyingly real. The dust storms had been at work there for several years and they had left behind them an incipient desert. Here and there the whitening bones of abandoned buildings remained to mark the death of hopes; and the wind-burnished wood of engulfed fences protruded from the drifts of subsoil that were overwhelming the works of man.

EARLY DAYS

During his first few weeks with us Mutt astonished us all by his maturity of outlook. He never really was a puppy, at least not after he came to us. Perhaps the ordeal with the ducks had aged him prematurely; perhaps he was simply born adult in mind. In any case he resolutely eschewed the usual antics of puppyhood. He left behind him no mangled slippers, no torn upholstery, and no stains upon the rugs. He did not wage mock warfare with people's bare feet, nor did he make the night hideous when he was left to spend the dark hours alone in the kitchen. There was about him, from the first day he came to us, an aura of resolution and restraint, and dignity. He took life seriously, and he expected us to do likewise.

Nor was he malleable. His character was immutably resolved before we ever knew him and, throughout his life, it did not change.

I suspect that at some early moment of his existence he concluded there was no future in being a dog. And so, with the tenacity which marked his every act, he set himself to become something else. Subconsciously he no longer believed that he was a dog at all, yet he did not feel, as so many foolish canines appear to do, that he was human. He was tolerant of both species, but he claimed kin to neither.

If he was unique in attitude, he was also unique in his appearance. In size he was not far from a setter, but in all other respects he was very far from any known breed. His hindquarters were elevated several inches higher than his forequarters; and at the same time he was distinctly canted from left to right. The result was that, when he was approaching, he appeared to be drifting off about three points to starboard, while simultaneously giving an eerie impression of a submarine starting on a crash dive. It was impossible to tell, unless you knew him very well indeed, exactly where he was heading, or what his immediate objective might be. His eyes gave no clue, for they were so close-set that he looked to be, and may have been, somewhat cross-eyed. The total illusion had its practical advantages, for gophers and cats pursued by Mutt could seldom decide where he was aiming until they discovered, too late, that he was actually on a collision course with them.

An even more disquieting physical characteristic was the fact that his hind legs moved at a slower speed than did his front ones. This was theoretically explicable on the grounds that his hind legs were much longer than his forelegs — but an understanding of this explanation could not dispel the unsettling impression that Mutt's forward section was slowly and relentlessly pulling away from the tardy after-end.

And yet, despite all this, Mutt was not unprepossessing in general appearance. He had a handsome black and white coat of fine, almost silky hair, with exceptionally long "feathers" on his legs. His tail was long, limber, and expressive. Although his ears were rather large and limp, his head was broad and high-domed. A black mask covered all of his face except for his bulbous nose, which was pure white. He was not really handsome, yet he possessed the same sort of dignified grotesquerie which so distinguished Abraham Lincoln and the Duke of Wellington.

He also possessed a peculiar *savoir-faire* that had a disconcerting effect upon strangers. So strong was Mutt's belief that he was not simply "dog" that he was somehow able to convey this conviction to human onlookers.

One bitterly cold day in January Mother went downtown to do some post-Christmas shopping and Mutt accompanied her. She parted from him outside the Hudson Bay Department Store, for Mutt had strong antipathies, even in those early months, and one of these was directed against the famous Company of Gentleman Adventurers To Hudson's Bay. Mother was inside the store for almost an hour, while Mutt was left to shiver on the wind-swept pavement.

When Mother emerged at last, Mutt had forgotten that he had voluntarily elected to remain outside. Instead he was nursing a grievance at what seemed to him to be a calculated indifference to his comfort on my mother's part. He had decided to sulk, and when he sulked he became intractable. Nothing that Mother would say could persuade him to get up off the frigid concrete and accompany her home. Mother pleaded. Mutt ignored her and fixed his gaze upon the steamed-up windows of the Star Café across the street.

Neither of them was aware of the small audience which had formed around them. There were three Dukhobors in their quaint winter costumes, a policeman enveloped in a buffalo-skin coat, and a dentist from the nearby Medical Arts Building. Despite the cold, these strangers stood and watched with growing fascination as Mother ordered and Mutt, with slightly lifted lip and *sotto-voce* mutters, adamantly refused to heed. Both of them were becoming exasperated, and the tone of their utterances grew increasingly vehement.

It was at this point that the dentist lost touch with reality. He stepped forward and addressed Mutt in man-to-man tones.

"Oh, I say, old boy, be reasonable!" he said reproachfully.

Mutt replied with a murmur of guttural disdain, and this was too much for the policeman.

"What seems to be the matter here?" he asked.

Mother explained. "He won't go home. He just won't go!"

The policeman was a man of action. He wagged his mittened paw under Mutt's nose. "Can't you see the lady's cold?" he asked sternly.

Mutt rolled his eyes and yawned and the policeman lost his temper. "Now, see here," he cried, "you just move along or, by the gods, I'll run you in!"

It was fortunate that my father and Eardlie came by at this moment. Father had seen Mutt and Mother in arguments before, and he acted with dispatch, picking them both up almost bodily and pushing them into Eardlie's front seat. He did not linger, for he had no desire to be a witness to the reactions of the big policeman and of the dentist when they became aware of the fact that they had been arguing with a dog upon a public street.

Mutt had another exasperating habit that he developed very early in life, and never forgot. When it was manifestly impossible for him to avoid some unpleasant duty by means of argument, he would feign deafness. On occasions I lost my temper and, bending down so that I could lift one of his long ears, would scream my orders at him in the voice of a Valkyrie. But Mutt would simply turn his face toward me with a bland and interrogative look that seemed to say with insufferable mildness, "I'm sorry — did you speak?"

We could not take really effective steps to cure him of this irritating habit, for it was one he shared with my paternal grandfather, who sometimes visited us. Grandfather was stone deaf to anything that involved effort on his part, yet he could hear, and respond to, the word "whiskey" if it was whispered inside a locked bedroom three floors above the chair in which he habitually sat.

It will be clear by now that Mutt was not an easy dog to live with. Yet the intransigence which made it so difficult to cope with him made it even more difficult — and at times well-nigh impossible — for him to cope with the world in general. His stubbornness marked him out for a tragicomic role throughout his life. But Mutt's struggles with a perverse fate were not, unfortunately, his alone. He involved those about him, inevitably and often catastrophically, in his confused battle with life.

Wherever he went he left deep-etched memories that were alternately vivid with the screaming hues of outrage, or cloudy with the muddy colors of near dementia. He carried with him the aura of a Don Quixote and it was in that atmosphere that my family and I lived for more than a decade.

MUTT MAKES
HIS MARK

It all began on one of those blistering July days when the prairie pants like a dying coyote, the dust lies heavy, and the air burns the flesh it touches. On such days those with good sense retire to the cellar caverns that are euphemistically known in Canada as beer parlors. These are all much the same across the country — ill-lit and crowded dens, redolent with the stench of sweat, spilled beer, and smoke — but they are, for the most part, moderately cool. And the insipid stuff that passes for beer is usually ice cold.

On this particular day five residents of the city, dog fanciers all, had forgathered in a beer parlor. They had just returned from witnessing some hunting-dog trials held in Manitoba, and they had brought a guest with them. He was a rather portly gentleman from the state of New York, and he had both wealth and ambition. He used his wealth lavishly to further his ambition, which was to raise and own the finest retrievers on the continent, if not in the world. Having watched his own dogs win the Manitoba trials, this man had come on to Saskatoon at the earnest invitation of the local men, in order to see what kind of dogs they bred, and to buy some if he fancied them.

He had not fancied them. Perhaps rightfully annoyed at having made the trip in the broiling summer weather to no good purpose, he had become a little overbearing in his manner. His comments when he viewed the local kennel dogs had been acidulous, and scornful. He had ruffled the local breeders' feelings, and as a result they were in a mood to do and say foolish things.

The visitor's train was due to leave at 4 P.M., and from 12:30 until 3 the six men sat cooling themselves internally, and talking dogs. The talk was as heated as the weather. The local men immediately began telling tales of Mutt, and if they laid it on a little, who can blame them? But the more stories they told, the louder grew the visitor's mirth and the more pointed his disbelief. Finally someone was goaded a little too far.

"I'll bet you," Mutt's admirer said truculently, "I'll bet you a hundred dollars this dog can outretrieve any damn dog in the whole United States."

Perhaps he felt that he was safe, since the hunting season was not yet open. Perhaps he was too angry to think.

The stranger accepted the challenge, but it did not seem as if there was much chance of settling the bet. Someone said as much, and the visitor crowed.

"You've made your brag," he said. "Now show me."

There was nothing for it then but to seek out Mutt and hope for inspiration. The six men left the dark room and braved the blasting light of the summer afternoon as they made their way to the public library.

The library stood, four-square and ugly, just off the main thoroughfare of the city. The inevitable alley behind it was shared by two Chinese restaurants and by sundry other merchants. My father had his office in the rear of the library building overlooking the alley. A screened door gave access to whatever air was to be found trapped and roasted in the narrow space behind the building. It was through this rear door that the delegation came.

From his place under the desk Mutt barely raised his head to peer at the newcomers, then sank back into a comatose state of near oblivion engendered by the heat. He probably heard the mutter of talk, the introductions, and the slightly strident tone of voice of the stranger, but he paid no heed.

Father, however, listened intently. And he could hardly control his resentment when the stranger stooped, peered beneath the desk, and was heard to say, "*Now* I recognize the breed — Prince Albert rat hound did you say it was?"

My father got stiffly to his feet. "You gentlemen wish a demonstration of Mutt's retrieving skill — is that it?" he asked.

A murmur of agreement from the local men was punctuated by a derisive comment from the visitor. "Test him," he said offensively. "How about that alley there — it must be full of rats."

Father said nothing. Instead he pushed back his chair and, going to the large cupboard where he kept some of his shooting things so that they would be available for after-work excursions, he swung wide the door and got out his gun case. He drew out the barrels, fore end, and stock and assembled the gun. He closed the breech and tried the triggers, and at that familiar sound Mutt was galvanized into life and came scuffling out from under the desk to stand with twitching nose and a perplexed air about him.

He had obviously been missing something. This wasn't the hunting season. But — the gun was out.

He whined interrogatively and my father patted his head. "Good boy," he said, and then walked to the screen door with Mutt crowding against his heels.

By this time the group of human watchers was as perplexed as Mutt. The six men stood in the office doorway and watched curiously as my father stepped out on the porch, raised the unloaded gun, leveled it down the alley toward the main street, pressed the triggers, and said in a quiet voice, "Bang — bang — go get 'em boy!"

To this day Father maintains a steadfast silence as to what his intentions really were. He will not say that he expected the result that followed, and he will not say that he did not expect it.

Mutt leaped from the stoop and fled down that alleyway at his best speed. They saw him turn the corner into the main street, almost causing two elderly women to collide with one another. The watchers saw the people on the far side of the street stop, turn to stare, and then stand as if petrified. But Mutt himself they could no longer see.

He was gone only about two minutes, but to the group upon the library steps it must have seemed much longer. The man from New York had just cleared his throat preparatory to a new and even more amusing sally, when he saw something that made the words catch in his gullet.

They all saw it — and they did not believe.

Mutt was coming back up the alley. He was trotting. His head and tail were high — and in his mouth was a magnificent ruffed grouse. He came up the porch stairs nonchalantly, laid the bird down at my father's feet, and with a satisfied sigh crawled back under the desk.

There was silence except for Mutt's panting. Then one of the local men stepped forward as if in a dream, and picked up the bird.

"Already stuffed, by God!" he said, and his voice was hardly more than a whisper.

It was then that the clerk from Ashbridge's Hardware arrived. The clerk was dishevelled and mad. He came bounding up the library steps, accosted Father angrily, and cried:

"That damn dog of yours — you ought to keep him locked up. Come bustin' into the shop a moment ago and snatched the stuffed grouse right out of the window. Mr. Ashbridge's fit to be tied. Was the best bird in his whole collection. . . ."

I do not know if the man from New York ever paid his debt.
I do know that the story of that day's happening passed into the
nation's history, for the Canadian press picked it up from the
Star-Phoenix, and Mutt's fame was carried from coast to coast
across the land.

That surely was no more than his due.

VIGNETTES
OF TRAVEL

I n examining my memories of our family excursions I am
struck by the way Mutt looms so large in all of them. There
was our journey to the Pacific, for example. Looking back on
it now, I can recall a string of vignettes in each of which Mutt
was the center of attention — while for the rest, there is nothing
but an amorphous blur.

We began that journey on the June day in 1934 when I finished
my last school examination paper. I still possess a snapshot
taken of us as we pulled away down River Road, and when I
look at it I am appalled at the manner in which we burdened
Eardlie. None of your pregnant glass-and-chrome showcases of
today could have carried that load for a single mile. Eardlie
could do so only because he was the ultimate result of five
thousand years of human striving to devise the perfect vehicle.
For there is no doubt at all but that the Model A stands at the
apex of the evolution of the wheel. And it is a matter of sorrow
to me — as it should be to all men — that this magnificent
climax should have been followed by the rapid and terrible
degeneration of the automotive species into the effete mechanical
incubi which batten off human flesh on every highway of the
world today.

The load that Eardlie shouldered when he set bravely forth
to carry us across far mountains to the sea almost defies belief.
There was a large umbrella tent tied to the spare tire; there was

Concepcion, our sixteen-foot canoe, supported high above us on a flimsy rack; there were three folding wooden cots lashed to the front mudguards; on the right-hand running board (an invaluable invention, long since sacrificed to the obesity of the modern car) were two wooden crates of books — most of them about the sea; on the other running board were two trunk-suitcases, a five-gallon gasoline can, and a spare spare-tire. In addition, there were the canoe masts, sails, and leeboards; Father's Newfoundland-pattern oilskins and sou'wester; a sextant; a schooner's binnacle compass; Mother's household implements, including pots and pans and a huge gunny sack containing shreds of cloth for use in making hooked rugs; and, not least, a canvas bag containing my gopher traps, .22 rifle, and other essential equipment.

As Eardlie arched his back under the strain and carried us out of the city past the town slough, where the ducks were already hatching their young, we would have done justice to Steinbeck's descriptions of the dispossessed.

Mutt enjoyed travelling by car, but he was an unquiet passenger. He suffered from the delusion, common to dogs and small boys, that when he was looking out the right-hand side, he was probably missing something far more interesting on the left-hand side. In addition, he could never be quite sure whether he preferred the front seat — and looking forward — or the rumble seat — and looking backward. Mutt started out up front with Mother and Father, while I had the rumble seat; but we had not gone five miles before he and Mother were at odds with one another. They both wanted the outside berth, and whichever one was temporarily denied it would growl and mutter and push, until he or she gained his or her ends.

Before we had been driving for an hour Mother lost her patience and Mutt was exiled to the rumble seat.

Riding in the rumble did strange things to him, and I have a theory that his metabolism was disturbed by the enforced intake of air under pressure from the slip stream, so that he became oxygen drunk. He would grow wild-eyed and, although not normally a drooling dog, he would begin to salivate. Frequently he would stand up with his front feet on the back of Mother's neck, and he would drool on her until, driven to extremes, she would poke him sharply on the chin, whereupon he would mutter, and come back to drool on me.

But his favorite position, when he became really full of oxygen, was to extrude himself gradually over one of the rear mudguards until there was nothing of him remaining in the car except his hind feet and his tail. Here he would balance precariously, his nose thrust far out into the slip stream and his large ears fluttering in the breeze.

The prairie roads were indescribably dusty, and his nose and eyes would soon become so clogged that he would be almost blind, and incapable of smelling a dead cow at twenty paces. He did not seem to mind, but like a misshapen and misplaced figurehead he would thrust farther outward until he passed the point of balance. Then only my firm grip on his tail could prevent disaster, and on one occasion, when my grip relaxed a little, he became air-borne for a moment or so before crashing to the road behind us.

When this happened we thought we had lost him forever. By the time Father got the car stopped, Mutt was a hundred yards in the rear, spread-eagled in the center of the road, and screaming pitifully. Father assumed the worst, and concluded that the only thing to do was to put the poor beast out of his misery at once. He leaped out of the car and ran to a blacksmith's shop that stood by the roadside, and in a few minutes returned waving the blacksmith's old revolver.

He was too late. While he had been out of sight, Mutt had spotted a pair of heifers staring at him over the fence, and had hastily picked himself up to give vociferous chase.

Although he suffered no lasting injuries from this mishap, there was one minor consequence that allowed me to make a place for myself in the family annals by subsequently reporting that "Mutt was so scared he went to the bathroom in his pants."

Because of the dust, we three human travellers were equipped with motorcyclists' goggles. Father decided one evening that this was favoritism, and that Mutt should have the same protection. We were then entering the outskirts of a place called Elbow, a typical prairie village with an unpaved main street as wide as the average Ontario farm, and with two rows of plank-fronted buildings facing each other distantly across this arid expanse. The drugstore was the only place still open when we arrived.

Father, Mutt, and I entered the shop together, and when an aged clerk appeared from the back premises, my father asked him for driving goggles.

The old fellow searched for a long time and finally brought us three pairs that had been designed and manufactured in the first years of the automobile era. They seemed to be serviceable and without more ado Father began trying them on Mutt.

Happening to glance up while this was going on, I met the clerk's gaze. He was transfixed. His leathered face had sagged like a wet chamois cloth and his tobacco-stained stubs seemed ready to fall from his receding lower jaw.

Father missed this preliminary display, but he was treated to an even better show a moment later when he got briskly to his feet, holding the second pair of goggles.

"These will do. How much are they?" he asked. And then suddenly remembering that he had forgotten to pack his shaving kit before leaving Saskatoon, he added, "We'll want a shaving brush, soap, and a safety razor too."

The old man had retreated behind his counter. He looked as if he was going to begin weeping. He pawed the air with one emaciated hand for several seconds before he spoke.

"Oh, Gawd!" he wailed — and it was a real prayer. "Don't you tell me that dawg *shaves,* too!"

We had to improvise a special harness for the goggles because of the unusual shape of Mutt's head, but they fitted him tolerably well, and he was pleased with them. When they were not in use we would push them up on the lift of his brow, but in a few days he had learned how to do this for himself, and he could pull them down again over his eyes in time of need. Apart from the effect they had on unimaginative passers-by, Mutt's goggles were an unqualified success. However, they did not give him protection for his nose and one day he met a bee at forty miles an hour. The left side of Mutt's already bulbous nose swelled hugely. This did not inconvenience him too severely, for he simply moved to the other side of the car. But luck was against him and he soon collided with another bee, or perhaps it was a wasp this time. The total effect of the two stings was bizarre. With his goggles down, Mutt now looked like a cross between a hammerhead shark and a deep-sea diver.

Our second night on the western road was spent at Swift River in southern Saskatchewan. Swift River was almost the center of the dust-bowl country and it had a lean and hungry look. We were very hot, very dusty, and very tired when we drove into its northern outskirts and began searching for the municipal tourist camp — for in those times there were no motels, and the only alternative to a tent of one's own was a tiny cubicle in a crematorium that bore the sardonic title of "hotel."

Swift River was proud of its municipal tourist camp, which was located in a brave but pathetic attempt at a park, near the banks of an artificial slough.

We set about pitching the tent, which was a patented affair and not easily mastered. Soon a policeman came along and eyed us suspiciously, as if convinced that we were undesirable vagrants masquerading as bona fide tourists. He became quite grumpy when called upon to help with the tent.

We were all in a taut temper when we finally crawled into our blankets that night. It did not ease our mood that the night's rest was fragmentary due to the influx of clouds of mosquitoes from the nearby slough, and due also to the sad moanings of a pair of emaciated elk who lived in a nearby wild-life enclosure.

We tossed and muttered in the hot and crowded tent, and were not disposed to rise with the dawn. We were still abed, still partly comatose, when voices near at hand brought us unwillingly back to the new day.

The voices were feminine, spinsterish, and indignant. I was too drugged with fatigue to catch the gist of the conversation at first, but I was sufficiently conscious to hear Father's sudden grunt of anger, and Mother's whispered attempts to soothe him. Things seemed interesting enough to warrant waking fully, so I sat up in bed and gave the voices my attention.

The dialogue went like this:

From outside: "It's a shame — that's what it is. A regular public nuisance! I can't imagine what the officials are thinking of to allow it."

Mutterings from Father, who seemed to know what this was

all about: "Old harridans! Who the devil do they think they are?"

Mother, soothingly: "*Now*, Angus!"

Outside again: "What a perfectly *poisonous* smell. . . . Do you think it really *is* a dog?"

At this my father jerked convulsively, and I remembered that Mutt had abandoned the dubious comforts of the tent in the early dawn and had walked all over me, seeking the doorway. I began to share my father's annoyance. No stranger had the right to speak of Mutt in terms like these. And they were growing worse.

"It looks like a dog — but how it stinks!" the disembodied and waspish voice continued. "Phew! Whoever owns it should be put in jail."

This was more than Father could bear. His bellow shook the tent.

"*I* own that dog," he cried, "and what do you intend to do about it?"

He had already begun to stumble about, looking for his clothes, when one of the voices responded in a manner that unhinged him completely.

"Well!" it said scathingly. "Why don't you bury it — or is that too much to expect from — from drifters!"

It was at this point that Father burst out of the tent, clad only in his pajama tops, and so angry that he was incoherent. Wordless he may have been, but his tone of voice was sufficient to send the two bird watchers — for that is what they were — skittering to their car. They vanished with a clash of gears, leaving us alone with the unhappy elk — and with a dog.

It was not Mutt. It was a strange dog, and it floated belly up in a backwater of the slough not more than twenty feet away. It had been dead a long, long time.

Mother was triumphant. "There, you *see?*" she told my father. "You never *look* before you leap."

She was undeniably right, for if Father had looked we would have been spared the half hour that followed when the grumpy policeman returned and demanded that we haul our dog out of the slough and bury it at once. He was really more truculent than grumpy, and he did not have a sympathetic ear for our attempts at explanation. It would perhaps have been easier to convince him that the whole affair was a misunderstanding had Mutt been present, but Mutt had gone off in the early dawn to examine the quality of Swift River's garbage cans, and he did not return until Eardlie stood packed and ready to flee. Mutt never understood why Father was so short with him for the rest of the day.

The remainder of our journey through the prairies passed without undue excitement, and this was well, for it was a time of mounting fatigue, and of tempers strained by days of heat, by the long pall of dust, and by the yellowed desert of the drying plains. The poplar bluffs were few and far between, and their parched leaves rustled stiffly with the sound of death. The sloughs were dry, their white beds glittering in the destroying heat. Here and there a tiny puddle of muck still lingered in a roadside ditch, and these potholes had become death traps for innumerable little families of ducks. Botulism throve in the stagnant slime, and the ducks died in their thousands, and their bodies did not rot, but dried as mummies dry.

It was a grim passage, and we drove Eardlie hard, heedless of his steadily boiling radiator and his laboring engine. And then one morning there was a change. The sky that had been dust hazed for so long grew clear and sweet. Ahead of us, hung between land and air, we saw the first blue shadows of the distant mountains.

We camped early that night and we were in high spirits at our escape from drought and desert. When the little gasoline stove had hissed into life and Mother was preparing supper, Mutt and I went off to explore this new and living land. Magpies rose ahead of us, their long tails iridescent in the setting sun. Pipits climbed the crests of the high clouds and sang their intense little songs. Prairie chickens rose chuckling out of a green pasture that lay behind a trim white farmhouse. We walked back to the tent through a poplar bluff whose leaves flickered and whispered as live leaves should.

We crossed through most of Alberta the next day, and by evening were climbing the foothills. It had been a day for Mutt to remember. Never had he suspected that cows existed anywhere in such vast numbers. The size of the herds bewildered him so much that he lost all heart for the chase. He was so overwhelmed (and so greatly outnumbered) that he stayed in the car even when we stopped for lunch. In the evening we made our camp near a little roadside stand that sold gasoline and soda pop, and here Mutt tried to recover his self-respect by pursuing a very small, very lonely little cow that lived behind the garage. His cup of woe was filled to overflowing when the little cow turned out to be a billy goat — Mutt's first — and retaliated by chasing him back to the tent, and then attempting to follow him inside.

One day, after we had entered the mountains, we paused for a drink of spring water near the face of a forbidding cliff, and of course Mutt was unable to resist the challenge. We did not notice that he was gone until a large limousine drew up alongside us and from it four handsome women and two well-fed men emerged. They were all equipped with movie cameras and binoculars, and some of them began staring at the cliff with their glasses, while the rest levelled their cameras. The whirr of the machines brought me over to see what this was all about. I asked one of the women.

"Hush, sonny," she replied in a heavy whisper, "there's a real live mountain goat up there!" And with that she too raised her camera and pressed the button.

I spent a long time looking for that goat. I could see Mutt clearly enough, some three hundred feet up the cliffside; but no goat. I supposed that Mutt was on the goat's trail, and it irked me that I was blind while these strangers were possessed of such keen eyes.

After some ten minutes of intent photography the tourists loaded themselves back into the limousine and drove away, engaging in much congratulatory backslapping at their good luck as they went.

I had caught on by then. That night we discussed the anomaly of a piebald mountain goat with long black ears, and I am afraid we laughed outrageously. Yet in point of fact no genuine mountain goat could have given a more inspired demonstration of mountaineering techniques than could Mutt.

Leaving the mountains temporarily, we descended into the Okanagan valley, where we hoped to see a fabulous monster called the Ogo Pogo that dwells in Lake Okanagan. The monster proved reluctant, so we solaced ourselves by gorging on the magnificent fruits for which the valley is famous, and for which we had often yearned during the prairie years. To our surprise — for he could still surprise us on occasion — Mutt shared our appetites, and for three days he ate nothing at all but fruit.

He preferred peaches, muskmelon, and cherries, but cherries were his undoubted favorites. At first he had trouble with the pits, but he soon perfected a rather disgusting trick of squirting them out between his front teeth, and as a result we had to insist that he point himself away from us and the car whenever he was eating cherries.

I shall never forget the baleful quality of the look directed at Mutt by a passenger on the little ferry in which we crossed the Okanagan River. Perhaps the look was justified. Certainly Mutt was a quaint spectacle as he sat in the rumble seat, his goggles pushed far up on his forehead, eating cherries out of a six-quart basket.

After each cherry he would raise his muzzle, point it overside, and nonchalantly spit the pit into the green waters of the river.

SQUIRRELS, UNCLES, AND OTHER BEASTS

Shortly after I fell under the influence of my Great-uncle Frank I began to be something of a trial to my parents. Frank laid his hand upon me when I was five years old, and I have not completely evaded his shadowy grip even to this day.

He was a naturalist and collector, of the old school, who believed that everything in nature from eagles' eggs to dinosaur bones deserved house room. He also insisted that the only way to know animals was to live with them. He impressed upon me that, if it was impossible actually to live among them in the woods and fields, then the next best thing was to bring the wild folk home to live with me. I proceeded to follow his advice and on my first expedition as a budding scientist I collected, and brought home, a cow's skull and two black snakes, for which I found quarters underneath my bed.

Mother said that snakes were not fit companions for a five-year-old, but Frank — who had a good deal of authority in the family — took my side and the snakes remained with us for some weeks, until the landlord of our apartment heard about them.

Those snakes were only the first of an interminable procession of beasts, furred, feathered, and finned, which I inflicted upon my parents. It is to their eternal credit that they managed somehow to bear with most of my house guests, nor did they attempt to discourage my bent toward practical zoology. I think Mother had some hope that I would become another Thoreau; or it may be that she simply preferred to have me declare my pets openly, rather than have me secrete them against the inevitable, and startling, moment of discovery.

There were a few such moments anyway. There was the time I kept rattlesnakes in a bookcase — but that incident passed off harmlessly enough. Then there was the time when I was six years old and was staying for a week with my paternal grandmother. One afternoon I went fishing with another lad and we caught half a dozen mud pouts, or catfish, as some people call them. I brought the fish home so that I could live with them.

Grandmother Mowat was an immensely dignified and rather terrifying old lady who did not easily tolerate the pranks of youth. Yet it was with no intention of playing a practical joke on anyone that I placed my mud pouts in the toilet bowl. I had no other choice, since there were no laundry tubs in the house, and the bathtub drain leaked so badly that you had to keep the tap running when you took a bath.

I was honestly and tearfully penitent when the mud pouts were discovered — and penitence was needed. Grandmother made the discovery herself, at a late hour when the rest of the household was fast asleep.

She forgave me, for she had a knowing heart. But I doubt that she ever fully forgave my parents.

All through the early years before we moved to Saskatoon, our rented homes and apartments housed not only us three, but a wide variety of other beasts as well. In Trenton I had a Blanding's tortoise — a rare terrestrial turtle of which I was immensely proud, and which one day distinguished itself beyond all other turtles by talking. True, it spoke but once, and then under unusual circumstances. Nevertheless, it actually did speak.

Some of my parents' friends were visiting our house, and they were kind enough to humor me and ask to see my turtle. Proudly I got it out of the box of sand where it normally lived, and released it on the dining-room table. I was chagrined when it refused to poke so much as a leg out of its shell. In exasperation I prodded it with a pencil.

Slowly it protruded its head, peered sadly up at us out of its old-woman's face, and then in the clearest, but most despondent tones imaginable it spoke a single word.

"Yalk!" it said — as distinctly as that — and without further preamble laid an egg upon the tabletop.

I kept that jelly-bean-shaped leathery object on top of the stove for seven months, but it never hatched. I suppose my turtle must have been a virgin.

We left Trenton not long afterwards and moved to Windsor. Point Pelee National Park was only thirty miles away, and we used to drive to it on week ends so that I could do field work in natural history. One day I spied what looked like a crow's nest in a tall pine, and I climbed up to investigate. It turned out to be a black squirrel's nest containing three young squirrels.

Naturally I brought one of them home with me, carrying it inside my shirt. Without really meaning to I rather overdid Great-uncle Frank's precept, for I spent the next few days living very close to a band of several hundred fleas.

The little squirrel took readily to captivity. We called him Jitters, and Father built a cage for him that hung over the kitchen sink. It had a door that he could open and shut by himself, and he had the run of the house, and later of the neighborhood. He was an ingratiating little beast and one of his favorite diversions was boxing. He would sit on the back of a chair and box with us, using his front paws against our forefingers.

Jitters liked people, but he hated cats and he waged a bitter vendetta against them. Our own cat, whose name was Miss Stella (after our landlady of the moment), became incurably neurotic as a result of the torment inflicted on her by the squirrel, and eventually she left home forever. The cats of our neighbors suffered severely too.

It was Jitters's delight to seek out an unwary cat sunning itself beneath a tree, or under the lee of a house wall. Jitters would then quietly climb high above his victim and launch himself into space like a diving sparrow hawk. Since these leaps were often made from twenty or thirty feet up, the impact when he struck was sufficient to leave the poor cat breathless. By the time it recovered, Jitters would have scampered to a safe vantage point from which he could taunt his enemy.

We had Jitters for over a year, and in the end it was his cat baiting that killed him. He died rather horribly. One afternoon he launched himself from halfway up the wall of our three-story apartment building and landed, not on what he had supposed was a sleeping cat, but upon a foxskin neckpiece laid to air on a concrete balustrade.

By the time we moved to Saskatoon my parents tended to take my interest in natural history for granted. Yet even they were startled one night shortly after we arrived in Saskatoon.

Mother was having a dinner party that evening for a number of local people whom we had only recently met. When dinner was ready she called to me up the back stairs, and I came down to join the party, a little dreamily, for my mind was filled with the thrill of a great discovery.

I had just begun to practice dissections, and that day I had found a dead gopher that proved to be an ideal subject for experiment. When Mother called me I had just completed my preliminary work. I had removed most of the internal organs and placed them in a saucer of formaldehyde solution. The problem of identifying all these parts was a nice one, and I was so preoccupied with it that I brought the saucer with me to the dinner table.

It was a candle-lit dinner, and no one noticed my saucer until after soup had been served. I finished my soup before anyone else and decided to employ the waiting moments by continuing with my investigations. I was so lost in them that I was not aware of the peculiar dying away of conversation on either side, until my father's voice aroused me.

"What in heaven's name have you got there, Farley?" he demanded sharply.

I answered eagerly — for I had just that instant made a momentous discovery and one that I was anxious to share.

"Dad," I cried, "you'll never guess. I've got the uterus of a gopher *and she was pregnant!*"

OWLS UNDERFOOT

W hen the owls first joined our family they were less than six weeks old, but already giving promise that their ultimate size would be impressive. My parents, who had never seen a full-grown horned owl, had no real idea as to just *how* impressive they could be, and I preserved a discreet silence on the subject. Nevertheless, Mother vetoed my plan for keeping the two newest, and youngest, members of the family in my bedroom, even though I pointed out to her that the birds might get lost, and in any case they would be in considerable danger from cats and dogs if they were kept outside.

Mother looked speculatively at the talons which the unhappy fledglings were flexing — talons already three quarters of an inch in length — and gave it as her considered opinion that the cats and dogs would have a thin time of it in a mix-up with the owls. As to their getting lost — my mother was always an optimist.

Eventually my father solved the housing problem by helping me build a large chicken-wire enclosure in the back yard. This enclosure was used only a few months, for it soon became superfluous.

In the first place, the owls showed no disposition to stray from their new home. Each day I would take them out for a romp on the lawn and, far from attempting to return to their wild haunts, they displayed an overwhelming anxiety to avoid the uncertainties of freedom. Once or twice I accidentally left them alone in the yard and they, concluding that they had been abandoned, staged a determined retreat into the house itself. Screen doors were no barrier to them, for the copper mesh melted under the raking impact of their talons as if it had been tissue paper. Both owls would then come bursting through the shattered screen into the kitchen, breathing hard, and looking apprehensively over their shoulders at the wide outer world where their unwanted freedom lay.

Consequently the back-yard cage became not so much a means of keeping the owls with us, as a means of keeping them from being too closely with us.

The two fledglings were utterly unlike in character. Wol, the dominant member of the pair, was a calmly arrogant extrovert who knew that he was the world's equal. Weeps, on the other hand, was a nervous, inconsequential bird of an unsettled disposition; and plagued by nebulous fears. Weeps was a true neurotic, and though his brother learned to be housebroken in a matter of a few weeks, Weeps never could be trusted on the furniture and rugs.

When they were three months old, and nearly full grown (although tufts of baby down still adhered to their feathers), Wol confirmed Mother's first impression as to his ability to defend himself. At three months of age he stood almost two feet high. His wingspread was in the neighborhood of four feet. His talons were an inch in length and needle sharp, and, combined with his hooked beak, they gave him a formidable armament.

One summer night he was in a huff as the result of a disagreement he had had with Mutt. When darkness fell he refused to come down from a high perch in a poplar tree in order to go to bed in the safe refuge of the cage. Since there was nothing we could do to persuade him, we finally left him in his tree and went to bed ourselves.

Knowing something of the ferocity of the night-stalking cats of Saskatoon, I was uneasy for him and I slept lightly, with one ear cocked. It was just breaking dawn when I heard the sound of a muffled flurry in the back yard. I leaped from my bed, grabbed my rifle, and rushed out of the front door.

To my horror there was no sign of Wol. The poplar trees were empty. Suspecting the worst, I raced around the corner of the house, my bare feet slipping in the dew-wet grass.

Wol was sitting quietly on the back steps, his body hunched up in an attitude of somnolent comfort. The scene could hardly have been more peaceful.

It was not until I came close, and had begun to remonstrate with him for the chances he had taken, that I saw the cat.

Wol was sitting on it. His feathers were fluffed out in the manner of sleeping birds so that only the cat's head and tail were visible. Nevertheless, I saw enough to realize that the cat was beyond mortal aid.

Wol protested when I lifted him clear of his victim. I think he had been enjoying the warmth of his footrest, for the cat had been dead only a few moments. I took it quickly to the foot of the garden and buried it circumspectly, for I recognized it as the big ginger tom from two doors down the street. It had long been the terror of birds and dogs and fellow cats throughout our neighborhood. Its owner was a big man with a loud and raucous voice who did not like small boys.

The ginger tom was the first, but not the last, feline to fall into error about Wol. In time the secret cemetery at the bottom of the garden became crowded with the remains of cats who had assumed that Wol was just another kind of chicken and therefore easy meat.

Nor were dogs much more of a problem to the owls. Rather grudgingly, for he was jealous of them, Mutt undertook to protect them from others of his own race. Several times he saved Weeps from a mauling, but Wol did not really need his protection. One evening a German shepherd — a cocksure bully if ever there was one — who lived not far from our house caught Wol on the ground and went for him with murder in his eye. It was a surprisingly one-sided battle. Wol lost a handful of feathers, but the dog went under the care of a veterinary, and for weeks afterwards he would cross the street to avoid passing too close to our house — and to Wol.

Despite his formidable fighting abilities, Wol was seldom the aggressor. Those other beasts which, like man, have developed the unnatural blood lusts that go with civilization would have found Wol's restraint rather baffling, for he used his powerful weapons only to protect himself, or to fill his belly, and never simply for the joy of killing. There was no moral or ethical philosophy behind his restraint — there was only the indisputable fact that killing, for its own sake, gave him no pleasure.

Although perhaps, if he and his descendants had lived long enough in human company, he might have become as sanguinary and as cruel as we conceive all other carnivores — except ourselves — to be.

Feeding the owls was not much of a problem. Weeps ate anything that was set before him, on the theory — apparently — that each meal was his last. The future always looked black to him — such was his sad nature. Wol, on the other hand, was more demanding. Hard-boiled eggs, hamburger, cold roast beef, and fig cookies were his chosen articles of diet. Occasionally he would deign to tear apart a gopher that one of the neighborhood boys had snared on the prairie beyond the city; but on the whole he did not relish wild game — with one notable exception.

It has been said by scientists, who should know better, that the skunk has no natural enemies. It is this sort of smug generalization that gives scientists a bad name. Skunks *have* one enemy in nature — a voracious and implacable enemy — the great horned owl.

There can be few animal feuds as relentless as the one which has raged between horned owls and skunks for uncounted aeons. I have no idea how it originally started, but I know quite a lot about the tenacity with which it is still pursued.

The faintest whiff of skunk on a belated evening breeze would transform the usually calm and benign Wol into a winged fury. Unfortunately our house stood on the banks of the Saskatchewan River, and there was a belt of underbrush along the shore which provided an ideal highway for wandering skunks. Occasionally one of them would forgo the riverbank and do his arrogant promenading on the sidewalk in front of our house.

The first time this happened was in the late summer of Wol's first year. The skunk, cocksure and smug as are all the members of his species, came down the sidewalk just as dusk was falling. Some children who were playing under the poplar trees fled the approaching outcast, as did an elderly woman who was airing her Pekinese. Swollen with his own foolish pride, the skunk strutted on until he came beneath the overhanging branches in front of the Mowat home.

Our windows were open and we were just finishing a late dinner. There was not much breeze, and by the time the first acrid warning came wafting into the dining room, Wol himself was ready to make his entrance. He came through the open window in a shallow dive and fetched up on the floor, depositing the still-quivering skunk beside my chair.

"Hoo-hoohoohoo-HOO," he said proudly. Which, translated, probably meant "Mind if I join you? I've brought my own lunch."

Owls are not widely renowned for their sense of humor, and Wol may have been an exception, but he, at least, possessed an almost satanic fondness for practical jokes, of which poor Mutt was usually the victim. He would steal Mutt's bones and cache them in the crotch of a tree trunk just far enough above the ground to be beyond Mutt's reach. He would join Mutt at dinner sometimes, and by dint of sheer bluff, force the hungry and unhappy dog away from the dish, and keep him away until finally the game palled. Wol never actually *ate* Mutt's food. That would have been beneath him.

His favorite joke, though, was the tail squeeze.

During the searing heat of the summer afternoons Mutt would try to snooze the blistering hours away in a little hollow which he had excavated beneath the hedge on our front lawn. However, before withdrawing to this sanctuary he would make a careful cast about the grounds until he had located Wol, and had assured himself that the owl was either asleep or at least deep in meditation. Only then would Mutt retire to his repose, and dare to close his eyes.

Despite a hundred bitter demonstrations of the truth, Mutt never understood that Wol seldom slept. Sometimes the owl's great yellow orbs would indeed be hooded, but even then — though he might appear to be as insensible as a graven bird — he retained a delicate awareness of all that was happening around him. His eyesight was so phenomenally acute as to completely discredit the old canard that owls are blind in daylight. Often I have seen him start from what appeared to be a profound trance, if not slumber, and, half turning his head, stare full into the blaze of the noonday sky while crouching down upon his roost in an attitude of taut belligerence. Following the direction of his gaze with my unaided eyes, I could seldom find anything threatening in the white sky; but when I brought my binoculars into play they would invariably reveal a soaring hawk or eagle so high above us that even through the glasses it seemed to be no bigger than a mote of dust.

In any event, Mutt's suspicious reconnoitering before he gave himself up to sleep was usually ineffective and, worse than that, it served to alert Wol to the fact that his quarry would soon be vulnerable.

Wol was a bird of immense patience. He would sometimes wait half an hour after Mutt had slunk away to rest before he began his stalk. He always stalked Mutt on foot, as if disdaining the advantage given him by his powers of flight.

Infinitely slowly, and with the grave solemnity of a mourner at a funeral, he would inch his way across the lawn. If Mutt stirred in his sleep, Wol would freeze and remain motionless for long minutes — his gaze fixed and unblinking on his ultimate objective — Mutt's long and silken tail.

Sometimes it took him an hour to reach his goal. But at last he would arrive within range and then, with ponderous deliberation, he would raise one foot and poise it — as if to fully savor the delicious moment — directly over Mutt's proud plume. Then, suddenly, the outspread talons would drop, and clutch. . . .

Invariably Mutt woke screaming. Leaping to his feet, he would spin around, intent on punishing his tormentor — and would find him not. From the branch of a poplar tree well above his head would come a sonorous and insulting "Hoo-HOO-hoo-hoo," which, I suspect, is about as close to laughter as an owl can come.

APRIL PASSAGE

It was raining when I woke, a warm and gentle rain that did not beat harshly on the window glass, but melted into the unresisting air so that the smell of the morning was as heavy and sweet as the breath of ruminating cows.

By the time I came down to breakfast the rain was done and

the brown clouds were passing, leaving behind them a blue mesh of sky with the last cloud tendrils swaying dimly over it. I went to the back door and stood there for a moment, listening to the roundelay of horned larks on the distant fields.

It had been a dour and ugly winter, prolonging its intemperance almost until this hour, and giving way to spring with a sullen reluctance. The days had been cold and leaden and the wet winds of March had smacked of the charnel house. Now they were past. I stood on the doorstep and felt the remembered sun, heard the gibbering of the freshet, watched little deltas of yellow mud form along the gutters, and smelled the sensual essence rising from the warming soil.

Mutt came to the door behind me. I turned and looked at him and time jumped suddenly, and I saw that he was old. I put my hand on his grizzled muzzle and shook it gently.

"Spring's here, old-timer," I told him. "And who knows — perhaps the ducks have come back to the pond."

He wagged his tail once and then moved stiffly by me, his nostrils wrinkling as he tested the fleeting breeze.

The winter past had been the longest he had known. Through the short-clipped days of it he had lain dreaming by the fire. Little half-heard whimpers had stirred his drawn lips as he journeyed into time in the sole direction that remained open to him. He had dreamed the bitter days away, content to sleep.

As I sat down to breakfast I glanced out the kitchen window and I could see him moving slowly down the road toward the pond. I knew that he had gone to see about those ducks, and when the meal was done I put on my rubber boots, picked up my field glasses, and followed after.

The country road was silver with runnels of thaw water, and bronzed by the sliding ridges of the melting ruts. There was no other wanderer on that road, yet I was not alone, for his tracks went with me, each pawprint as familiar as the print of my own hand. I followed them, and I knew each thing that he had done, each move that he had made, each thought that had been his; for so it is with two who live one life together.

The tracks meandered crabwise to and fro across the road. I saw where he had come to the old TRESPASSERS FORBIDDEN sign, which had leaned against the flank of a supporting snowdrift all the winter through, but now was heeled over to a crazy angle, one jagged end tipped accusingly to the sky, where flocks of juncos bounded cleanly over and ignored its weary threat. The tracks stopped here, and I knew that he had stood for a long time, his old nose working as he untangled the identities of the many foxes, the farm dogs, and the hounds which had come this way during the winter months.

We went on then, the tracks and I, over the old corduroy and across the log bridge, to pause for a moment where a torpid garter snake had undulated slowly through the softening mud.

There Mutt had left the road and turned into the fallow fields, pausing here and there to sniff at an old cow flap, or at the collapsing burrows left by the field mice underneath the vanished snow.

So we came at last to the beech woods and passed under the red tracery of budding branches where a squirrel jabbered its defiance at the unheeding back of a horned owl, brooding somberly over her white eggs.

The pond lay near at hand. I stopped and sat on an upturned stump and let the sun beat down on me while I swept the surface of the water with my glasses. I could see no ducks, yet I knew they were there. Back in the yellow cattails old greenhead and his mate were waiting patiently for me to go so that they could resume their ponderous courtship. I smiled, knowing that they would not long be left in peace, even in their secluded place.

I waited and the first bee flew by, and little drifting whorls of mist rose from the remaining banks of snow deep in the woods. Then suddenly there was the familiar voice raised in wild yelping somewhere among the dead cattails. And then a frantic surge of wings and old greenhead lifted out of the reeds, his mate behind him. They circled heavily while, unseen beneath them, Mutt plunged among the tangled reeds and knew a fragment of the ecstasy that had been his when guns had spoken over other ponds in other years.

I rose and ambled on until I found his tracks again, beyond the reeds. The trail led to the tamarack swamp and I saw where he had stopped a moment to snuffle at the still-unopened door of a chipmunk's burrow. Nearby there was a cedar tangle and the tracks went round and round beneath the boughs where a ruffed grouse had spent the night.

We crossed the clearing, Mutt and I, and here the soft black mold was churned and tossed as if by a herd of rutting deer; yet all the tracks were his. For an instant I was baffled, and then a butterfly came through the clearing on unsteady wings, and I remembered. So many times I had watched him leap, and hop, and circle after such a one, forever led and mocked by the first spring butterflies. I thought of the dignified old gentleman of yesterday who had frowned at puppies in their play.

Now the tracks led me beyond the swamp to the edge of a broad field and here they hesitated by a groundhog's hole, unused these two years past. But there was still some faint remaining odor, enough to make Mutt's bulbous muzzle wrinkle with interest, and enough to set his blunt old claws to scratching in the matted grass.

He did not tarry long. A rabbit passed and the morning breeze carried its scent. Mutt's trail veered off abruptly, careening recklessly across the soft and yielding furrows of October's plow, slipping and sliding in the frost-slimed troughs. I followed more sedately until the tracks halted abruptly against a bramble patch. He had not stopped in time. The thorns still held a tuft or two of his proud plumes.

And then there must have been a new scent on the wind. His tracks moved off in a straight line toward the country road, and the farms which lie beyond it. There was a new mood on him, the ultimate spring mood. I knew it. I even knew the name of the little collie bitch who lived in the first farm. I wished him luck.

I returned directly to the road, and my boots were sucking in the mud when a truck came howling along toward me, and passed in a shower of muddy water. I glanced angrily after it, for the driver had almost hit me in his blind rush. As I watched, it swerved sharply to make the bend in the road and vanished from my view. I heard the sudden shrilling of brakes, then the roar of an accelerating motor — and it was gone.

I did not know that, in its passing, it had made an end to the best years that I had lived.

In the evening of that day I drove out along the road in company with a silent farmer who had come to fetch me. We stopped beyond the bend, and found him in the roadside ditch. The tracks that I had followed ended here, nor would they ever lead my heart again.

It rained that night and by the next dawn even the tracks were gone, save by the cedar swamp where a few little puddles dried quickly in the rising sun. There was nothing else, save that from a tangle of rustling brambles some tufts of fine white hair shredded quietly away in the early breeze and drifted down to lie among the leaves.

The pact of timelessness between the two of us was ended, and I went from him into the darkening tunnel of the years.

II.

TIDE
OF WAR

FROM

AND NO BIRDS SANG, 1979

On the second day of September, 1939, I was painting the porch of our clapboard house in the rural Ontario town of Richmond Hill when my father pulled into the driveway at the helm of his red convertible. He looked as if he might have had a drink or two — high-colored and exhilarated.

"Farley, my lad, there's bloody big news! *The war is on!* Nothing official yet, but the Regiment's been ordered to mobilize, and I'm to go back in with the rank of major, bum arm and all. There'll be a place for you too. You'll have to sweat a bit for it, of course, but if you keep your nose clean and work like hell there'll be the King's Commission."

He spoke as if he was offering me a knighthood or, at the very least, membership in some exceedingly exclusive order.

Slim, wiry, and sharply handsome, my father still carried himself like the young soldier who had gone off in 1915 to fight in the Great War, fired by the ideals of Empire — a Soldier of the King — one of those gay young men whose sense of right, of chivalry, was to bait them into the uttermost reaches of hell. Although he had come back from Hades with his right arm made useless by German bullets, he nevertheless remained an impassioned supporter of the peacetime volunteer militia, and in particular of his own outfit, the Hastings and Prince Edward Regiment, an infantry unit composed of countrymen and townsmen

37

from southeastern Ontario, which was familiarly if inelegantly known as the Hasty Pees.

My father's news excited me tremendously, for I had long been inflamed by his fulminations against the Russophobe French, British, and U.S. politicians and industrialists who had connived at the growth and spread of fascism, concealing their real admiration for it beneath the public explanation that it was the only trustworthy "bulwark against communism." I shared my father's conviction that these men had betrayed democracy, and I took the debacle of Munich and the sellout of Czechoslovakia as proof of this. I believed that every healthy young man in the freedom-espousing countries was duty-bound to take up arms against the fascist plague and, in particular, the singularly bestial German brand.

Nevertheless, I had no great inclination to follow my father into the tightly disciplined ranks of the infantry. The kind of independent derring-do which appealed to me seemed best to be found in the fighter arm of the Air Force.

Early in October I presented myself at a Royal Canadian Air Force recruiting station in Toronto . . . together with, it seemed, about half the male population of that city. When I finally stood before a harassed recruiting sergeant, he gave me short shrift.

"The Air Force don't need no peach-faced kids," he told me with disdain. "Shove off! You're in the way!"

In truth, I looked much younger and more fragile than I was. The year I turned ten, and looked a delicate six, my mother was concerned enough to take me to a famous pediatrician — a gruff old man who checked me over then snorted in some irritation at my mother: "If you'd wanted a football player for a son, you should have got yourself sired by a wrestler . . . and married a truck driver."

In public school I was the Shrimp, and in high school it was Baby Face. Unable to compete physically with my peers, I grew up as an essentially solitary youth who, like Kipling's Cat, preferred to walk by his lone. Most of my free time was spent wandering the fields and woods, for I was an avid naturalist. By the time I was thirteen, in Saskatchewan, where we were then living, I was traipsing off alone on thirty-mile snowshoe trips across the frozen plains, sleeping out in haystacks at twenty below zero, and all for the glimpse of a snowy owl or a flock of prairie chicken. Peach-faced I may have been but, appearances to the contrary, I was no sickly kid.

The sergeant was waiting impatiently for me to leave; instead, I pulled out my birth certificate. He glanced at it dubiously.

"Eighteen, eh? Hmmmm. But you still can't go for air crew. Too young, and anyway we got a waiting list ten miles long. You might come back in about six months."

On May 12, 1940, the day after my nineteenth birthday, I returned to the recruiting station and was grudgingly allowed to take a medical. The Air Force doctors could find nothing to fault me with except that I weighed four pounds less than the official minimum. That was enough to fail me. It was: Good-bye, Mr. Mowat, and thanks for trying.

I seethed with fury all during the train trip home to Richmond Hill.

"What do they need pilots built like King Kong *for?*" I demanded bitterly of my father that night. "They figure I might personally have to belt Hitler on the snoot?"

He soothed me with derogatory remarks about the elitist pretensions of the "junior service," then cunningly reminded me that there were still openings for officer candidates in the 2nd Battalion (the militia battalion) of the Hasty Pees.

Since there now seemed nothing else for it, I was persuaded to take an army medical. Before weighing me, the elderly examining doctor, a good friend of my father's, sent me off to drink as much water as I could hold. Well ballasted and gurgling like an overfull bathtub, I passed the examination with flying colors and was duly enlisted as a private soldier destined to spend the next several months serving as a batman (officer's servant) to a number of newly appointed lieutenants of about my own age.

This interlude was deliberately contrived by my father, who held it as an article of faith that any officer who had not served time in the ranks would be useless as a leader of fighting men. And he was determined that this is what I was going to become.

My military future brightened when, one autumn day, I was formally presented with the King's Commission — a sheet of imitation parchment formidably inscribed in flowing script:

George the Sixth, by the Grace of God, of Great Britain, Ireland and the British Dominions Beyond the Seas, Defender, Emperor of India, to our Trusty and Well Beloved Farley Mowat, Greetings. We, reposing especial Confidence and Trust in your Loyalty, Courage and Good Conduct, do by these Presents Constitute and Appoint you to be an Officer of our Active Militia of our Dominion of Canada in the rank of 2nd Lieutenant. . . .

◆

In 1942, after impatiently enduring long months of training in Canada, Mowat went overseas to join the Hastings and Prince Edward Regiment in England. In July 1943 the regiment took part in the invasion of Sicily; shortly thereafter it arrived on the Italian mainland, rapidly advancing north against stiffening opposition, until, in December 1943, it was bloodily halted at the Moro River, on the Adriatic Coast, by fierce German resistance.

◆

For me the valley of the Moro is to be remembered as the lair of the Worm That Never Dies — and of one particular victim. He was a stretcher-bearer, an older man — he might have been all of thirty-five — who had been with the regiment since the autumn of 1939.

By day and by night the bearers had to make their ways across the valley, crawling forward to the lead platoon positions, if necessary. Some of them must have made that agonizing passage a score of times. For them there was no rest and no surcease; no burrowing in a slit trench to escape the sound and fury. For them there was only a journey into the inferno, then the withdrawal to momentary sanctuary, and the return to hell once more.

That was the hardest thing to bear. Those who remained under sustained and unremitting fire could partially armor themselves with the apathy of the half-dead; but those who had to come and go, knowing the searing repetition of brief escape followed by a new immersion in the bath of terror — those were the ones who paid the heaviest price.

On the last night of our ordeal I was descending the north slope, numbed and passionless, drugged with fatigue, dead on my feet, when I heard someone singing! It was a rough voice, husky yet powerful. A cluster of mortar bombs came crashing down and I threw myself into the mud. When I could hear again, the first sound that came to me was the singing voice. Cautiously I raised myself just as a starshell burst overhead, and saw him coming toward me through that blasted wasteland.

Stark naked, he was striding through the cordite stench with his head held high and his arms swinging. His body shone white in the brilliant light of the flare, except for what appeared to be a glistening crimson sash that ran from one shoulder down one thigh and dripped from his lifted foot.

He was singing "Home on the Range" at the top of his lungs. The Worm That Never Dies had taken him.

Securing the Moro bridgehead brought us no respite. Until December 19 we remained in action, first defending what we had taken, then breaking out in an attempt to drive the paratroopers back toward the ramparts of Ortona, which we could now see encrusting a blunt promontory jutting into the leaden waters of the Adriatic. Ambulance jeeps were perpetually on the move, weaving their way along cratered tracks back and forth across the devastated valley through a desultory fall of shells. For the most part they were laden with men who could have served as illustrations for a macabre catalogue of the infinite varieties of mutilation; but for the first time since we had gone to war they also carried casualties who bore no visible wounds.

These were the victims of what was officially termed "battle fatigue" — "shell shock" they called it in the First World War. Both descriptions were evasive euphemisms. The military mind will not, perhaps does not, dare admit that there comes a time to every fighting man (unless death or bloody ruination of the flesh forestalls it) when the Worm — not steel and flame — becomes his nemesis.

My father had warned me of this in a letter I received just before we left Castropignano for the Adriatic sector. It was a letter so unlike his usual robust and cheerful chronicles of trivia at home that I can believe it was dictated by the Celtic prescience which he claimed as part of his inheritance.

Keep it in mind during the days ahead that war does inexplicable things to people, and no man can guess how it is going to affect him until he has had a really stiff dose of it. . . . The most unfortunate ones after any war are not those with missing limbs; they are the ones who have had their spiritual feet knocked out from under them. The beer halls and gutters are still full of such poor bastards from my war, and nobody understands or cares what happened to them. . . . I remember two striking examples from my old Company in the 4th Battalion. Both damn fine fellows, yet both committed suicide in the Line. They did not shoot themselves — they let the Germans do it because they had reached the end of the tether. But they never knew what was the matter with them; that they had become empty husks, were spiritually depleted, were burned-out.

My own understanding of the nature of the Worm, and of the inexorable way it liquefies and then consumes the inner substance of its victims, was chillingly enlarged on the day we broke out of our bridgehead.

Baker Company led the breakout and fought its way for nearly a mile along the coastal road leading toward Ortona before being halted by flanking fire from the far lip of a ravine to the left of the road. Lt. Col. Kennedy took me with him and went forward to assess the situation, and we got well mortared for our pains. The Germans overlooked and dominated our line of advance to such a degree that we could not push past until they were driven off. We assumed that a unit of Third Brigade, which was supposed to be advancing on our flank, would take care of this and so we dug in to await events.

We had not long to wait. Still anxious to divert attention from his main thrust out of San Leonardo and unwilling to reinforce the coastal sector, the divisional commander passed the word that we must take out the enemy position ourselves. Furthermore, we were ordered to attack immediately and in such a way that "the enemy will conclude you are the spearhead of the main assault." Once again we were to be the goat in the tiger hunt.

From an observation post my intelligence section had hurriedly established in the dubious shelter of a collapsed shed, I looked out over a sea of mud dotted here and there with the foundered hulks of shell-shattered farm buildings and strewn with flotsam of broken vineyard posts and twisted skeins of vineyard wire. It was a scene of mind-wrenching desolation, one that seemed doubly ominous beneath the lowering winter sky.

It also seemed grimly lifeless ... except ... something was moving near a ravaged ruin on the valley floor. I focused my binoculars ... stared hard ... and wished I hadn't. Looming large in the circle of my lenses were two huge sows gorging themselves on the swollen corpse of a mule. I knew they would as greedily stuff their gravid bellies with human meat if chance afforded ... and I knew the chance would certainly be afforded — all too soon.

The battle we were about to enter promised nothing but disaster — a frontal attack in daylight over open ground, in full view of determined paratroopers manning prepared and fortified positions and well supported by heavy weapons. Only a massive weight of accompanying armor could have given an infantry attack the ghost of a chance, and we had only a troop — three tanks — in support. Furthermore, it was obvious to all of us, tankers and infantrymen alike, that neither wheels *nor* tracks could move far through the morass of mud in the bottom of the valley.

Shortly before the attack was due to begin, Kennedy, to my belly-quivering dismay, detailed me to accompany the tanks *on foot,* in order to provide liaison between them and the infantry should radio communication fail.

Zero hour came at 1600. There was a brief outpouring of artillery shells and heavy mortar bombs from our supporting guns; and as the far side of the gully began to be obscured by muddy geysers, flame, and smoke, the men of Dog Company started down the slope.

I watched them go from behind the protection of the troop commander's tank, terrified on their behalf and on my own as well. Not more than fifty men remained to the company, an insignificant and pathetically vulnerable handful, thinly dispersed across that funereal waste of mud and wreckage.

As was intended, the Germans did not suspect this attack was only a diversion; and since it seemed to directly threaten Ortona, the coastal anchor of their new defense line, they reacted by flinging everything they had at us. Dog Company and the valley floor itself disappeared under the smoke and fumes of the most concentrated bombardment I had yet seen.

As the enemy barrage thundered up the slope, I plastered

myself against the back of the troop commander's Sherman, desperately wishing I was inside its armored carapace. The din was so tremendous I did not even hear the roar of accelerating engines and, before I knew what was happening, all three tanks were lurching away from me.

Because the Shermans were tightly "buttoned up" — all hatches closed and dogged — the troop commander had been unable to let me know he had received an urgent call for help from Dog. The remnants of that company, having somehow succeeded in reaching the far side of the valley, had been pinned down by machine-gun fire hosing into them from several bunkers which were impervious to anything except point-blank shelling from tank guns. Fully aware of the odds against them, the tankers were gamely attempting to respond to Dog's SOS.

With their abrupt departure I was left nakedly exposed to the tempest of explosions. Wildly I looked about for shelter, but the nearest was a shattered house two hundred yards away, from which I knew Kennedy was watching the battle. I could not go there. There seemed nothing else for it but to fling myself in pursuit of the tanks, impelled by a primal need to interpose their armored bulk between me and the apocalyptic fury of the German guns.

Reaching the bottom of the slope, the Shermans encountered a maze of drainage ditches in which one of them immediately got itself bogged while the other two, slewing helplessly in deepening slime, dared go no farther. I reached the mired tank in a lung-bursting sprint and, so consuming was my need to escape the cataclysmic bombardment, I began beating on its steel flanks with my fists while howling to be taken in.

My voice was lost even to my own ears in a bellowing drumfire of shell bursts. The Germans had spotted the tanks and were now bent on annihilating them. Bombs, shells, and streams of machine-gun bullets converged on the Shermans. The sound and fury rose to a level beyond my powers of description . . . and beyond the limits of my endurance.

Reason abandoned me. I dropped to my belly and, heedless of what must have happened if the bogged tank had tried to move, tried to burrow under it, between its tracks. But it had already sunk so deeply into the mire that I could not force my way beneath it. There was no place to hide.

Then an armor-piercing shell struck the Sherman. I did not hear it hit but felt the massive machine jolt under the impact, and at once my lungs began to fill with raw petrol fumes.

Somewhere inside myself there was a shriek of agony, for I could already feel the searing heat that would engulf me as the tank flamed into a livid torch. There was no brewup — but that I did not know, for I was already in full flight up the slope, churning through the muck like some insensate robot. A salvo of heavy stuff dropped close enough to slap me flat on my face under a living wall of mud. But the robot got to its feet and staggered on.

I did not pause at the ruins where Kennedy was sheltering. Reaching the shell-pocked road, I trotted along at a steady, purposeful lope. God alone knows how far I might have run — perhaps until exhaustion felled me — had I not been intercepted by Franky Hammond, commander of our antitank platoon, who was trying to get forward with one of his 6-pounder guns. He caught my arm as I trotted sightlessly past his halted jeep and spun me up against the little vehicle. Then he shook me until I went limp.

"Drink this!" he ordered, and thrust the neck of his rum-filled water bottle into my mouth.

Then, "Get in the jeep! Now show me the way to B.H.Q."

Franky had saved me from the Worm.

When, a few minutes later, I reported to Kennedy that I had lost contact with the tanks and with Dog Company as well, he seemed too preoccupied to care. Having heard that Dog Company's commander and his entire headquarters group had been wiped out and two of the three platoon commanders had been killed or badly wounded, Kennedy had immediately radioed Brigade for permission to call off the attack. Brigade had replied that, under orders from Division, *we were to renew the battle and keep on renewing it until told to stop.*

I did not remain to witness the ensuing debacle as Able Company was put into the meat grinder. Kennedy sent me back across the Moro in Hammond's jeep on some now-forgotten errand to rear B.H.Q., which by then was out of range of most of the German guns. Presumably I did whatever it was I had been told to do, after which our quartermaster, George Hepburn, found me wandering aimlessly about and took me into his snug retreat in the cellar of an undamaged house, where he plied me with rum until I passed out.

When I woke next morning it was to find a worried Doc Macdonald, my batman/runner, standing over me with a mug of tea in his hand.

"Jeez, boss, I figured you for a goner. You was yellin' and whoopin' like a bunch o' chimpanzees the whole damn night. You gotta take it easy with that issue hooch."

The attack went in next morning behind a massive rolling barrage fired by five artillery regiments. Crouched in an unroofed barn which was serving as advanced Battalion Headquarters, I felt the reverberations of those hundreds of bursting shells as an obbligato to the unsteady pounding of my heart. I thought of my friends in Able and Baker companies leading the battalion into that throbbing void, and my guts contracted with mingled rage and fear.

For a time things went well enough, then both lead companies found themselves pinned down under machine-gun fire and the enemy counterbarrage just short of their objectives. The company commanders reported heavy casualties and Kennedy, as was his habit (one that I dreaded and abhorred), decided to go forward and see for himself what was happening. He beckoned me to follow.

The storm clouds rolling overhead seemed close enough to touch, and the land lay under a leaden obscurity drained of all color and devoid of shape. Ankle-deep in sucking muck, we plodded across a patchwork of little fields and vineyards. The explosions of our own and German shells pounded hideously inside my skull, yet Kennedy seemed unaware. Not once did he dive for cover or even so much as hunch his shoulders when the grating scream of an incoming projectile warned of imminent destruction. Senseless anger boiled up in the quaking bog within me: You goddamn pig-headed idiot! I mouthed in silence. What in hell are you trying to prove? Rage mounted — and sustained me.

A salvo of medium shells plunging through the overcast into the mud a few yards to our flank sent me grovelling. When I raised my head Kennedy was a dim shape in a dimmed world, plodding steadily onward. I scrambled to my feet, shouting aloud now, against the Doomsday roar: "You crazy bastard!"

But still I followed him. I could not break the leash. More than this: when we eventually stumbled into what was left of Charley Company and Kennedy told me to go and find a squadron of Shermans which was supposed to be coming up in support on our right flank, I went without demur, though raging inwardly. *"The bastard's out to get me killed — get us all killed! Well, let him try!"*

False fury . . . but it kept the Worm at bay.

The axis of our attack was along a ridge dotted with farm buildings and dissected by countless drainage ditches. I made my way to the right and to the rear in a series of abrupt dashes from ditch to ditch, taking a swig of rum from my water bottle as I lay gasping in momentary shelter at the conclusion of each dash. Rum served to fuel my rage.

One such dash took me close to a hut whose partly collapsed stone walls still seemed capable of providing some protection, and the banshee screech of Moaning Minnie rockets sent me scuttling frantically toward this ruin. I reached it just as the bombs exploded a few score yards away. The blast flung me through the empty doorway with such violence that I sprawled full-length on top of a prone human figure who emitted a horrid gurgling belch. It was an unconscious protest, for he and two of his three companions — grey-clad paratroopers — were dead, their bodies mired in the muck and goat manure on the floor. The fourth man — dimly seen in that dim place — was sitting upright in a corner of the little unroofed room and his eyes met mine as I struggled to my hands and knees.

In that instant I was so convinced I had had it — that he would shoot me where I knelt — that I did not even try to reach for the carbine slung across my back. I remained transfixed for what seemed an interminable time, then in an unconscious reflex effort to cheat death, I flung myself sideways and rolled to my feet. I was lurching through the doorway when his thin voice reached me.

"Vasser . . . haff . . . you . . . vasser?"

I checked my rush and swung up against the outer wall, knowing then that I was safe, that he posed no threat. And I felt

47

an inexplicable sense of recognition, almost as if I had heard his voice before. Cautiously I peered back through the doorway.

His left hand was clasping the shattered stump where his right arm had been severed just below the elbow. Dark gore was still gouting between his fingers and spreading in a black pool about his outthrust legs. Most dreadful was a great gash in his side from which protruded a glistening dark mass which must have been his liver. Above this wreckage, his eyes were large and luminous in a young man's face, pallid to the point of translucency.

"Vasser . . . please giff . . . vasser."

Reluctantly I shook my head. "Sorry, chum, I've got none. *Nein* vasser. Only rum, and that's no good for you."

The eyes, so vividly alive in the dying body, pleaded with me. Oh, hell, I thought, he's going anyway. What harm!

I held the water bottle to his lips and he swallowed in deep, spasmodic gulps until I took it back and drank from it myself. And so . . . and so the two of us got drunk together. And in a little while he died.

Some time later I found the tanks and managed to hang on to the turret of one of them on the ride back to where Baker Company was forming up to launch a new attack. I remember sliding off the front of the Sherman, and my legs collapsing under me, then there was nothing.

When I woke it was morning of the day before Christmas, 1943. I was lying on a straw pallet in a corner of a lamplit room with vaulted stone ceilings. The place was crowded with sodden and exhausted men, including several company commanders and their radio operators. An O-group was in progress. Once again Doc was shaking my shoulder.

"Colonel says ya gotta get up, boss," he told me sternly. Then his broad face lightened. "Here . . . see what I got for ya! Pair of clean socks. Liberated 'em out of a dead Jerry's kit."

He was as pleased with himself as if he had brought me a captain's promotion, and he had reason to be, for clean, dry socks had become only distant memories to us in that time and place. I pulled them on and was astonished at how good they made me feel.

I found Kennedy in the next room pointing out something on

a map to the company commanders. I listened with a feeling of detachment as he briefed them, but I remained keenly aware of my new socks and I scrunched my toes in them with exquisite pleasure.

The battle had raged all night and was still raging. The rifle companies were only just managing to cling to the mile-long salient which we had rammed through the German defense line; and now we were running out of men. Able was reduced to little more than platoon strength and the other companies were hardly better off. Although a few replacement officers had reached us, we had received no reinforcement drafts of other ranks since early in November.

Kennedy looked up at me from deeply sunken eyes. His voice sounded inexpressibly weary, lacking the bark and bite with which I was so familiar.

"A draft's arrived at San Vito. Supposed to come up tomorrow. I want them here tonight. Go and get them, Squib, and don't let anything or anybody stand in your way."

My fury had long since evaporated . . . and nothing had yet taken its place. My thoughts were still chiefly concerned with my new socks as I pulled on my Castropignano blanket coat and stepped outside. Then it all came back upon me with the smothering impact of an avalanche.

I had emerged into a haze of driven sleet sweeping across a blasted landscape, most of whose inhabitants were huddling unseen in flooded slit trenches or in the gaping ruins of crumbled buildings, like dumb and enduring beasts passively awaiting what was yet to come. The relentless rains and incessant bombardment had turned the whole achromatic wasteland into one enormous wallow through which no mechanical transport, not even the ubiquitous jeeps, could pass. The only movement came from little groups of mules and men laden with food and ammunition, sloshing along tracks that were more like running rivers. Tiny, indistinct figures in a void, men and mules plunged half-drowning into the roadside ditches as new storms of shellfire lashed over them.

A world of shadows, of primordial gloom, of inchoate violence, lay around me . . . *and no birds sang.* Memory jarred convulsively: *O what can ail thee, knight-at-arms/Alone and palely loiter-*

ing?/The sedge has wither'd from the lake/And no birds sing. . . . A moment's respite in the time that was, then I was staring down a vertiginous tunnel where all was dark and bloody and the great wind of ultimate desolation howled and hungered. I was alone . . . relentlessly alone in a world I never knew.

Shaking as if in the grip of a malarial attack, I stumbled back into the building where our new medical officer, a young Syrian named Homer Eshoo, was organizing a stretcher party to carry half a dozen badly wounded men to the rear. Homer gave me a casual glance, looked at me more closely, then came quickly to me. He thrust a mess tin of rum into my hands and let me drink deeply of it before pushing me toward the door. Not a word passed between us, but we both knew.

I walked out of the salient like a disembodied spirit. Presumably there was shellfire, but I do not recall it. My perceptions were not clouded by alcohol but by a mutiny within — by the withdrawal of sensation. I walked in the silence within myself, hearing nothing but an echo of the great wind. . . .

On the south side of the Moro I was picked up by the driver of the commanding officer's jeep. Halfway to San Vito the little car splattered up to a marching column. It was our reinforcement draft on its own way forward, led and impelled by Alex Campbell — Major Campbell now — returning to us from hospital in North Africa.

Alex was striding along like a colossus of old: huge, indomitable, indestructible. When he saw me he gave a great, fond shout of recognition and pulled me out of the jeep into a bear hug. And I hugged him back so desperately and unashamedly that he too must have known.

"Farley!" he cried, his heavy hand on my shoulder. "Still here? And not a general yet? Must be all that verse you write. Bad for promotion. Here, I've been versifying too. Read this when you get time, and tell me what you think."

He pulled an envelope out of his battledress jacket and handed it to me. I tucked it away unread and fell in beside him as the column marched on, and I was like someone brought back to the surface from an abyssal deep . . . brought to the surface, but no shore in sight.

Alex told me that the hundred and forty soldiers following us had arrived in England from Canada only a month earlier. Inadequately trained and unprepared for what awaited them, they had been prematurely shipped to Italy to transfuse our wasted regiment. Marching behind us in their clean, new uniforms, they joked with one another, stared curiously at the debris of war, and sang the brave and foolish songs they had learned in Canada.

The singing faltered as we crossed the Moro and climbed up through the chaos of destruction which was what remained of San Leonardo. It ceased altogether as we entered the salient and passed thirty or forty of Third Brigade's fatal casualties stacked like cordwood by the shattered road where they had been placed to keep them out of the muck . . . until they could be housed in it permanently.

The first warning shells fell close at hand and Alex shouted an order to increase the interval between men to five yards. It was not enough. A few minutes later we were enveloped in a brief but murderous bombardment from 15cm. howitzers. Before it ended, seven of these newcomers to our inferno were dead or wounded. As for the rest, their education had been well begun.

During my absence Battalion Headquarters had moved farther forward and I reported to Kennedy in what had once been a large and prosperous farmhouse. In addition to ourselves, it was giving precarious shelter to several peasant families whose humbler homes had already been destroyed. However, there was not room for all of us, and so my next task was to get these refugees started toward the rear.

Passively they allowed themselves to be herded out into the storm of rain and steel, encumbered by their babies, bundles, and even some wicker baskets full of sodden hens. There was no resistance except from a tall, bent patriarch who, I believe, must have been blind. He sat in a weighty, carved wooden chair, his hands clutching the ornate arms with such strength and tenacity that we would perhaps have had to break his bony fingers in order to release his grip. His aged body trembled violently but he would not be persuaded, and could not be forced to leave.

"Says he was born here," our interpreter told me. "His father's fathers were born here. His children were born here. And the old son of a bitch says he won't leave unless the *Pope* tells him to!"

So the old man stayed to share our Christmas Eve.

In the rain-drenched darkness of that night the Royal Canadian Regiment moved up into the salient to launch an attack. Their intelligence officer came to get the form from me and we stood together in the shelter of a deep, stone doorway watching the infantrymen plod by — a wavering and serpentine frieze of phantasmagoric figures, rainsoaked and black as the night itself. The shelling began again and before I fled to the farm's cavernous wine cellar I saw those dim shapes sinking down into the slime as if they were earth spirits returning whence they came.

The R.C.R. did not — could not — attack. No more could we; but there was to be no peace on Christmas Eve. All night long paratroop patrols fought to penetrate the salient, and the enraged whicker of automatic small arms and the muffled thud of bursting grenades seemed to echo everywhere in a blind confusion of vicious little battles.

Big guns of both sides sought to intervene and the wild, wet night glared with bursts of flame and reverberated to the clangor of explosions. Direct hits on the farmhouse brought heavy roof tiles hailing down and opened the upper stories to an icy blast of wind and rain; but the massive lower walls remained intact and so did the vaulted cellar which now sheltered both the aid post and the I-section, and where I waited for the interminable night to end.

Silent and immobile against the curves of dimly seen wine vats, the old Italian farmer also sat and waited, his dull gaze staring into emptiness. I cannot guess what apprehensions filled his thoughts, but mine were laden with a corrosive dread that Kennedy might order me out of my burrow to take a message to one of the forward companies. I was convinced that if he did, *and if I went* (such was now the magnitude of my fear that it might, paradoxically, have given me the courage to refuse), there would be no return. I could tolerate no greater weight of terror. I knew I would act as the two nameless friends my father had written about had acted in the dark and distant hour of an earlier war.

Black, nauseous dread was the burden of that livid night. After a time I remembered the poem Alex had given me to read; and in an attempt to escape from the abyss, I fished it out of my tunic. It was scrawled in pencil on a soiled sheet of Salvation Army canteen paper and his angular script was difficult to read in the shaky light of a kerosene lantern that jumped and flared whenever a shell exploded near at hand.

> *When neath the rumble of the guns*
> *I lead my men against the Huns,*
> *I am alone, and weak, and scared*
> *And wonder how I ever dared*
> *Accept the task of leading them.*
> *I wonder, worry, then I pray:*
> *Oh God, who takes men's pain away,*
> *Now, in my spirit's fight with fear,*
> *Draw near, dear God, draw near, draw near!*
> *Make me more willing to obey,*
> *Help me to merit my command.*
> *And if this be my fatal day,*
> *Reach out, oh God, thy helping hand.*
> *These men of mine must never know*
> *How much afraid I really am!*
> *Help me to stand against the foe,*
> *So they will say: He was a man!*

How much afraid I really am! I had not known . . . had not even suspected. That scatheless pillar of a man . . . and yet, the Worm was in him too!

There was no comfort for me in that shattering discovery. With something akin to revulsion I stuffed the poem back into my pocket as Corporal Castle appeared with a message in his hand. It was a cipher from Brigade and, with inexpressible relief, I immersed myself in the mundane task of decoding it. Then someone brought around a canister of hot tea. Two German prisoners were brought in to be searched. The explosion of a shell in one of the upper rooms set the dust dancing so thickly that for a time the lamp was only a dim, red glow in a grey murk. Once I tried to sleep in a filthy little funk-hole under a collapsed stairway, but the Worm was there and drove me out of it. Homer Eshoo, who had been tending the wounded almost without a break since the battle began, found a few free moments to share a drink with me. . . . The hours eroded as slowly as granite, but brought no summons to send me out into the sounding night.

Dawn came at last, and it was Christmas Day.

And at 0700 hours Kennedy ordered Able Company to attack and destroy a force of paratroopers that had infiltrated during the night between Able and Baker. Kennedy himself went forward to give Alex his instructions . . . and this time he did not take me with him.

I tried to follow the course of the action through the earphones of the radio set connecting us with Able Company, but Able's set went off the air and I knew little of what was happening until half an hour later the walking wounded began to straggle into our cellar.

One of the first was a sergeant who was suffering from a deep gash in one thigh. Shakily he accepted a cigarette, then told me what he had seen.

Alex had sent what was left of Seven Platoon to launch the initial attack, and Seven had almost immediately been caught by enfilading fire from three machine guns, with the loss of several killed and wounded. The logical course would then have been for Alex to send one of the other platoons to outflank these guns (something that was successfully done later in the day) but he did not choose to do this. Instead he did the unexpected and the inexplicable.

Seizing a Tommy gun, he levered his great bulk to its full height, gave an inarticulate bellow, and charged straight at the enemy.

He could have gone no more than three or four paces before he was riddled by scores of bullets. Crashing into the mud like a falling colossus, he lay there, his body jerking spasmodically until the dead flesh at last lay still. During that timeless interval, both his own men and the Germans were so stunned by his action that not a further shot was fired by either side.

"It was the bravest goddamn thing I ever saw . . . and the craziest!" The sergeant ground out his cigarette and looked into my face with puzzled eyes. "Crazy as hell! But Jesus, what a man!"

The blanket that screened the shattered cellar door was thrust aside and a party of stretcher-bearers pushed in among us. Al Park lay on one of the stretchers. He was alive, though barely so . . . unconscious, with a bullet in his head.

As I looked down at his faded, empty face under its crown of crimson bandages, I began to weep.

I wonder now . . . were my tears for Alex and Al and all the others who had gone and who were yet to go?

Or was I weeping for myself . . . and those who would remain?

III.

THE
NORTHERN
TERRITORIES

FROM

THE SNOW WALKER, 1975
NEVER CRY WOLF, 1963
PEOPLE OF THE DEER, 1952
THE DESPERATE PEOPLE, 1959

◆

After demobilization in 1946, Mowat hurried back to the fondly remembered scenes of his early youth in Saskatchewan, embittered by what "civilized" society had subjected him to, along with much of the rest of the world, during the war. He was desperately anxious to recover the mood of his pre-war life, but it was gone. His long-held dream of becoming a biologist proved hollow, and his mind turned more and more to a vision of the far North engendered by a childhood trip he had taken to the shores of Hudson Bay. After a restless term as a student at the University of Toronto he went in search of his vision of a place where men were in harmony with the natural world.

◆

FROM
The Snow Walker

SNOW

When Man was still very young he had already become aware that certain elemental forces dominated the world womb. Embedded on the shores of their warm sea, the Greeks defined these as Fire and Earth and Air and Water. But at first the Greek sphere was small and circumscribed and the Greeks did not recognize the fifth elemental.

About 330 B.C., a peripatetic Greek mathematician named Pytheas made a fantastic voyage northward to Iceland and on into the Greenland Sea. Here he encountered the fifth elemental in all of its white and frigid majesty, and when he returned to the warm blue Mediterranean, he described what he had seen as best he could. His fellow countrymen concluded he must be a liar since even their vivid imaginations could not conceive of the splendor and power inherent in the white substance that sometimes lightly cloaked the mountain homes of their high-dwelling Gods.

Their failure to recognize the immense power of snow was not entirely their fault. We who are the Greeks' inheritors have much the same trouble comprehending its essential magnitude.

How do *we* envisage snow?

It is the fragility of Christmas dreams sintering through azure darkness to the accompaniment of the sound of sleigh bells.

It is the bleak reality of a stalled car and spinning wheels impinging on the neat time schedule of our self-importance.

It is the invitation that glows ephemeral on a woman's lashes on a winter night.

It is the resignation of suburban housewives as they skin wet snowsuits from runny-nosed progeny.

It is the sweet gloss of memory in the failing eyes of the old as they recall the white days of childhood.

It is the banality of a TV advertisement pimping Coca-Cola on a snowbank at Sun Valley.

It is the gentility of utter silence in the muffled heart of a snow-clad forest.

It is the brittle wind-rush of skis; and the bellicose chatter of snowmobiles.

Snow is these things to us, together with many related images; yet all deal only with obvious aspects of a multi-faceted, kaleidoscopic, and protean element.

Snow, which on our planet is a phoenix continually born again from its own dissolution, is also a galactic and immortal presence. In the nullity of outer space, clouds of snow crystals, immeasurably vast, drift with time, unchanged since long before our world was born, unchangeable when it will be gone. For all that the best brains of science and the sharpest of the cyclopean eyes of astronomers can tell, the glittering crystals flecking the illimitable void are as one with those that settle on our hands and faces out of the still skies of a December night.

Snow is a single flake caught for an instant on a windowpane. But it is also a signboard in the solar system. When astronomers peer up at Mars they see the Red Planet as a monochromatic globe — except for its polar caps from which gleaming mantles spread toward the equatorial regions. As the antelope flashes its white rump on the dun prairies, so does Mars signal to worlds beyond it with the brilliance of our common sun reflected from its plains of snow.

And so does Earth.

When the first star voyager arcs into deep space, he will watch the greens and blues of our seas and lands dissolve and fade as the globe diminishes until the last thing to beacon the disappearing Earth will be the glare of our own polar heliographs. Snow will be the last of the elementals in his distant eye. Snow may provide the first shining glimpse of our world to inbound aliens ... if they have eyes with which to see.

Snow is crystalline dust, tenuous amongst the stars; but on Earth it is, in yet another guise, the Master Titan. To the south it holds the entire continent of Antarctica in absolute thrall. To the north it crouches heavily upon mountain ranges; and the island subcontinent of Greenland literally sags and sinks beneath its weight. For glaciers are but another guise of snow.

Glaciers are born while the snow falls; fragile, soft, and almost disembodied ... but falling steadily without a thawing time. Years pass, decades, centuries, and the snow falls. Now there is weight where there was none. At the surface of an undulating white waste, there seems to be no alteration, but in the frigid depths the crystals are deformed; they change in structure, interlock with increasing intimacy, and eventually meld into black, lightless ice.

Four times during Earth's most recent geological age snow fell like this across much of the northern half of our continent and in Europe and Asia too. Each time, snow altered the face of almost half a world. A creeping glacial nemesis as much as two miles thick oozed outward from vast central domes, excoriating the planet's face, stripping it of life and soil, ripping deep wounds into the primordial rock, and literally depressing Earth's stone mantle hundreds of feet below its former level. The snow fell, softly, steadily, until countless millions of tons of water had vanished from the seas, locked up within the glaciers; and the seas themselves withdrew from the edges of the continents.

There is no natural phenomenon known to us that can surpass the dispassionate power of a great glacier. The rupturing of Earth during its most appalling earthquake cannot compare with it. The raging water of the seas in their most violent moments cannot begin to match it. Air, howling in the dementia of hurricanes, is nothing beside it. The inner fire that blows a mountain to pieces and inundates the surrounding plains with floods of flaming lava is weak by comparison.

A glacier is the macrocosmic form of snow. But in its microscopic forms, snow epitomizes ethereal beauty. It is a cliché to say that no two snowflakes are identical, but it is a fact that each single snowflake that has fallen throughout all of time, and that will fall through what remains of time, has been — will be — a unique creation in symmetry and form.

I know of one man who has devoted most of his adult life to the study of this transient miracle. He has built a special house fitted with a freezing system, instead of heating equipment. It is a house with a gaping hole in its roof. On snowy days and nights he sits in icy solitude catching the falling flakes on plates of pre-chilled glass and hurriedly photographing them through an enlarging lens. For him the fifth elemental in its infinite diversity and singularity is beauty incarnate, and a thing to worship.

Few of us would be of a mind to share his almost medieval passion. In truth, modern man has insensibly begun to develop a schizophrenic attitude toward the fifth elemental. Although we may remember our childhood experience of it with nostalgia, more and more we have begun to think of snow with enmity. We cannot control snow, nor bend it to our will. The snow that fell harmlessly and beneficently upon the natural world our fore-fathers lived in has the power to inflict chaos on the mechanical new world we have been building. A heavy snowfall in New York, Montreal, Chicago, produces a paralytic stroke. Beyond the congealed cities it chokes the arteries of our highways, blocks trains, grounds aircraft, fells power and telephone cables. Even a moderate snowfall causes heavy inconvenience — if smashed cars, broken bodies, and customers for the undertakers are only inconveniences.

We will probably come to like snow even less. Stories about the good old-fashioned winters when snow mounted to the eaves of houses and horse-hauled sleighs were galloped over drifts at tree-top level are not just old wives' tales. A hundred years ago such happenings were commonplace. However, during the past century our climate has experienced a warming trend, an up-swing (from our point of view) in the erratic cyclic variations of the weather. It has probably been a short-term swing and the downswing may soon be upon us. And where will we be then, poor things, in our delicately structured artificial world? Will we still admire snow? More likely we will curse the very word.

However, when that time comes there may still be men alive who will be unperturbed by the gentle, implacable downward drift. They are the true people of the snows.

They live only in the northern hemisphere because the realm of snow in the southern hemisphere — Antarctica — will not permit the existence of any human life unless equipped with a panoply of protective devices not far short of what a spaceman needs. The snow people ring the North Pole. They are the Aleuts, Eskimos, and Athapascan Indians of North America; the Greenlanders; the Lapps, Nensi, Chukchee, Yakuts, Yukagirs, and related peoples of Eurasia and Siberia.

Cocooned in the machine age, we smugly assume that because these people live unarmored by our ornate technology, they must lead the most marginal kind of existence, faced with so fierce a battle to survive that they have no chance to realize the "human potential." Hard as it may strike into our dogmatic belief that technology offers the only valid way of life, I can testify from my own experiences with many of the snow people that this assumption is wrong. They mostly lived good lives, before our greed and our megalomaniac arrogance impelled us to meddle in their affairs. That is, if it be good to live at peace with oneself and one's fellowmen, to be in harmony with one's environment, to laugh and love without restraint, to know fulfilment in one's daily life, and to rest from birth to death upon a sure and certain pride.

Snow was these people's ally. It was their protection and their shelter from abysmal cold. Eskimos built complete houses of snow blocks. When heated only with simple animal-oil lamps, these had comfortable interior temperatures, while outside the wind screamed unheard and the mercury dropped to fifty degrees or more below zero. Compacted snow provides nearly perfect insulation. It can be cut and shaped much more easily than wood. It is light to handle and strong, if properly used. A snowhouse with an inner diameter of twenty feet and a height of ten feet can be built by two men in two hours. On special occasions Eskimos used to build snowhouses fifty feet in diameter and, by linking several such together, formed veritable snow mansions.

All of the snow people use snow for shelter in one way or another. If they are sedentary folk possessing wooden houses, they bank their homes with thick snow walls in wintertime. Some dig a basement in a snowdrift and roof it with reindeer skins. As long as snow is plentiful, the peoples of the far north seldom suffer serious discomfort from the cold.

Snow also makes possible their transportation system. With dog sleds and reindeer sleds, or afoot on snowshoes or trail skis, they can travel almost anywhere. The whole of the snow world becomes a highway. They can travel at speed, too. A dog or reindeer team can move at twenty miles an hour and easily cover a hundred miles a day.

The mobility snow gives them, combined with the way snow modifies the behavior of game animals, ensures that — other, things being equal — the snow people need not go hungry. Out on the Arctic ice a covering of snow gives the seals a sense of false security. They make breathing holes in the ice, roofed by a thin layer of snow. The Chukchee or Eskimo hunter finds these places and waits beside them until, at a signal from a tell-tale wand of ivory or wood inserted in the roof, he plunges his spear down into the unseen animal below.

In wooded country, moose, elk, and deer are forced by deep snow to "yard" in constricted areas where they can be killed nearly as easily as cattle in a pen. Most important of all, every animal, save those with wings and those who live beneath the snow, leaves tracks upon its surface. From bears to hares they become more vulnerable to the human hunter as soon as the first snow coats the land.

The snow people know snow as they know themselves. In these days our scientists are busy studying the fifth elemental, not so much out of scientific curiosity but because we are anxious to hasten the rape of the north or fear we may have to fight wars in the lands of snow. With vast expenditures of time and money, the scientists have begun to separate the innumerable varieties of snow and to give them names. They could have saved themselves the trouble. Eskimos have more than a hundred compound words to express different varieties and conditions of snow. The Lapps have almost as many. Yukagir reindeer herdsmen on the Arctic coast of Siberia can tell the depth of snow cover, its degree of compactness, and the amount of internal ice crystallization it contains simply by glancing at the surface.

The northern people are happy when snow lies heavy on the land. They welcome the first snow in autumn, and often regret its passing in the spring. Snow is their friend. Without it they would have perished or — almost worse from their point of view — they would long since have been driven south to join us in our frenetic rush to wherever it is that we are bound.

Somewhere, on this day, the snow is falling. It may be sifting thinly on the cold sands of a desert, spreading a strange pallidity and flecking the dark, upturned faces of a band of Semitic nomads. For them it is in the nature of a miracle; and it is certainly an omen and they are filled with awe and chilled with apprehension.

It may be whirling fiercely over the naked sweep of frozen plain in the Siberian steppe, or on the Canadian prairies, obliterating summer landmarks, climbing in scimitar drifts to wall up doors and windows of farmhouses. Inside, the people wait in patience. While the blizzard blows, they rest; when it is over, work will begin again. And in the spring the melted snows will water the new growth springing out of the black earth.

It may be settling in great flakes on a calm night over a vast city; spinning cones of distorted vision in the headlights of creeping cars and covering the wounds, softening the suppurating ugliness inflicted on the earth by modern man. Children hope it will continue all night long so that no buses, street cars, or family automobiles will be aale to carry the victims off to school in the morning. But adult men and women wait impatiently, for if it does not stop soon the snow will smother the intricate designs that have been ordained for the next day's pattern of existence.

Or the snow may be slanting swiftly down across a cluster of tents huddled below a rock ridge on the Arctic tundra. Gradually it enfolds a pack of dogs who lie, noses thrust under bushy tails, until the snow covers them completely and they sleep warm. Inside the tents men and women smile. Tomorrow the snow may be deep enough and hard enough so that the tents can be abandoned and the welcome domes of snowhouses can rise again to turn winter into a time of gaiety, of songs, of leisure and lovemaking.

Somewhere the snow is falling.

FROM
Never Cry Wolf

My early years as a naturalist were free and fascinating, but as I entered manhood and found that my avocation must now become my vocation, the walls began to close in. The happy days of the universal scholar who was able to take a keen interest in all phases of natural history were at an end, and I was forced to recognize the unpalatable necessity of specializing, if I was to succeed as a professional biologist. Nevertheless, as I began my academic training at the university, I found it difficult to choose the narrow path.

For a time I debated whether or not to follow the lead of a friend of mine who was specializing in scatology — the study of the excretory droppings of animals — and who later became a high-ranking scatologist with the United States Biological Survey. But although I found the subject mildly interesting, it failed to rouse my enthusiasm to the pitch where I could wish to make it my lifework. Besides, the field was overcrowded.

My personal predilections lay toward studies of living animals in their own habitat. Being a literal fellow, I took the word *biology* — which means the study of life — at its face value. I was sorely puzzled by the paradox that many of my contemporaries tended to shy as far away from living things as they could get, and chose to restrict themselves instead to the aseptic atmosphere of laboratories where they used dead — often very dead — animal material as their subject matter. In fact, during my time at the university it was becoming unfashionable to have *anything* to do with animals, even dead ones. The new biologists were concentrating on statistical and analytical research, whereby the raw material of life became no more than fodder for the nourishment of calculating machines.

My inability to adjust to the new trends had an adverse effect upon my professional expectations. While my fellow students were already establishing themselves in various esoteric specialties, most of which they invented for themselves on the theory that if you are the *only* specialist in a given field you need fear no competition, I was still unable to deflect my interests from the general to the particular. As graduation approached I found that the majority of my contemporaries were assured of excellent research jobs while I seemed to have nothing particular to offer in the biological marketplace. It was, therefore, inevitable that I should end up working for the Government.

The die was cast one winter's day when I received a summons from the Dominion Wildlife Service informing me that I had been hired at the munificent salary of one hundred and twenty dollars a month to take part in a wolf study, and that I "would" report to Ottawa at once.

I obeyed this peremptory order with hardly more than a twitch of subdued rebelliousness, for if I had learned anything during my years at the university it was that the scientific hierarchy requires a high standard of obedience, if not subservience, from its acolytes.

The Air Force transport was a twin-engined plane capable of carrying thirty passengers, but by the time all the "desiderata" supplied by the Wildlife Service were aboard there was barely room left for the crew and me. The pilot, an amiable flight lieutenant wearing a handlebar mustache, watched the load going aboard with honest bewilderment writ large across his brow. His only information about me was that I was some sort of Government man going on a special mission to the Arctic. His expression grew increasingly quizzical as we swung three great bundles of clanking wolf traps into the cabin, following these with the midsection of a collapsible canoe which looked like nothing so much as a bathtub without ends. True to Departmental precedent, the bow and stern sections of this canoe had been shipped to another biologist who was studying rattlesnakes in the south Saskatchewan desert.

My armament was loaded aboard next. It consisted of two rifles, a revolver complete with holster and cartridge belt, two shotguns, and a case of tear-gas grenades with which I was expected to persuade reluctant wolves to leave their dens so that they could be shot. There were also two large smoke generators prominently labelled DANGER, to be used for signalling to aircraft in case I got lost or — perhaps — in case the wolves closed in. A case of "wolf getters" — fiendish devices which fire a charge of potassium cyanide into the mouth of any animal which investigates them — completed my arsenal.

My scientific gear followed, including two five-gallon cans at the sight of which the pilot's eyebrows shot right up under his cap. They were marked: *100% Grain Alcohol for the Preservation of Specimen Stomachs.*

Tents, camp stoves, sleeping bags, and a bundle of seven axes (to this day I do not know why *seven*, for I was going to a treeless land where even one would have been superfluous), skis, snowshoes, dog harness, a radio transceiver, and innumerable boxes and bales whose contents were as inscrutable to me as to the pilot, followed in due course.

When everything was in and securely roped down, the pilot, copilot, and I crawled over the mass of gear and wedged ourselves into the cockpit. The pilot, having been thoroughly trained in the demands of military security, mastered his rampant curiosity as to the nature and purpose of my bizarre outfit and contented himself with the gloomy comment that he "doubted if the old crate could get airborne, with all that lot aboard." Secretly I doubted it too, but although the plane rattled and groaned dismally, she managed to take off.

The flight north was long and uneventful, except that we lost one engine over James Bay and had to complete the journey at an altitude of five hundred feet through rather dense fog. This minor contretemps temporarily took the pilot's mind off the problem of who and what I was; but once we had landed in Churchill he was unable to contain his curiosity any longer.

"I know it's none of my damn' business," he began apologetically as we walked toward one of the hangars, "but for heaven's sake, chum, what's up?"

"Oh," I replied cheerfully, "I'm going off to spend a year or two living with a bunch of wolves, that's all."

The pilot grimaced as if he were a small boy who had been justly rebuked for an impertinence.

"Sorry," he mumbled contritely. "Never should have asked."

◆

Mowat's ultimate destination was a lonely cabin some three hundred miles northwest of Churchill, in the Keewatin Barrenlands, where he took advantage of the temporary absence of a trapper named Mike.

◆

As I was a newcomer to the Barrens, it behooved me to familiarize myself with the country in a cautious manner. Hence, on my first expedition afield I contented myself with making a circular tour on a radius of about three hundred yards from the cabin.

This expedition revealed little except the presence of four or five hundred caribou skeletons; indeed, the entire area surrounding the cabin seemed to be carpeted in caribou bones. Since I knew from my researches in Churchill that trappers never shot caribou, I could only assume that these animals had been killed by wolves. This was a sobering conclusion. Assuming that the density of the caribou kill was uniform over the whole country, the sample I had seen indicated that wolves must kill, on the average, about twenty million caribou a year in Keewatin alone.

After this dismaying tour of the boneyard it was three days before I found time for another trip afield. Carrying a rifle and wearing my revolver, I went a quarter-mile on this second expedition — but saw no wolves. However, to my surprise I observed that the density of caribou remains decreased in an almost geometric ratio to the distance from the cabin.

Meantime spring had come to the Barrens with volcanic violence. The snows melted so fast that the frozen rivers could not carry the melted water, which flowed six feet deep on top of the ice. Finally the ice let go, with a thunderous explosion; then it promptly jammed, and in short order the river beside which I was living had entered into the cabin, bringing with it the accumulated refuse léft by Mike's fourteen Huskies during a long winter.

Eventually the jam broke and the waters subsided; but the cabin had lost its charm, for the debris on the floor was a foot thick and somewhat repellent. I decided to pitch my tent on a gravel ridge above the cabin; and here I was vainly trying to go to sleep that evening when I became aware of unfamiliar sounds. Sitting bolt upright, I listened intently.

The sounds were coming from just across the river, to the north, and they were a weird medley of whines, whimpers, and small howls. My grip on the rifle slowly relaxed. If there is one thing at which scientists are adept, it is learning from experience; I was not to be fooled twice. The cries were obviously those of a Husky, probably a young one, and I deduced that it must be one of Mike's dogs (he owned three half-grown pups not yet trained to harness which ran loose after the team) that had got lost, retraced its way to the cabin, and was now begging for someone to come and be nice to it.

I was delighted. If that pup needed a friend, a chum, I was its man! I climbed hastily into my clothes, ran down to the riverbank, launched the canoe, and paddled lustily for the far bank.

The pup had never ceased its mournful plaint, and I was about to call out reassuringly when it occurred to me that an unfamiliar human voice might frighten it. I decided to stalk it instead, and to betray my presence only when I was close enough for soothing murmurs.

From the nature of the sounds I had assumed the dog was only a few yards away from the far bank, but as I made my way in the dim half-light, over broken boulders and across gravel ridges, the sounds seemed to remain at the same volume while I appeared to be getting no closer. I assumed the pup was retreating, perhaps out of shyness. In my anxiety not to startle it away entirely, I still kept quiet, even when the whimpering wail stopped, leaving me uncertain about the right direction to pursue. However, I saw a steep ridge looming ahead of me and I suspected that, once I gained its summit, I would have a clear enough view to enable me to locate the lost animal. As I neared the crest of the ridge I got down on my stomach (practicing the fieldcraft I had learned in the Boy Scouts) and cautiously inched my way the last few feet.

My head came slowly over the crest — and there was my quarry. He was lying down, evidently resting after his mournful singsong, and his nose was about six feet from mine. We stared at one another in silence. I do not know what went on in his massive skull, but my head was full of the most disturbing thoughts. I was peering straight into the amber gaze of a fully grown Arctic wolf, who probably weighed more than I did, and who was certainly a lot better versed in close-combat techniques than I would ever be.

For some seconds neither of us moved but continued to stare hypnotically into one another's eyes. The wolf was the first to break the spell. With a spring which would have done justice to a Russian dancer, he leaped about a yard straight into the air and came down running. The textbooks say a wolf can run twenty-five miles an hour, but this one did not appear to be running, so much as flying low. Within seconds he had vanished from my sight.

My own reaction was not so dramatic, although I may very well have set some sort of a record for a cross-country traverse myself. My return over the river was accomplished with such verve that I paddled the canoe almost her full length up on the beach on the other side. Then, remembering my responsibilities to my scientific supplies, I entered the cabin, barred the door, and regardless of the discomfort caused by the stench of the debris on the floor made myself as comfortable as I could on top of the table for the balance of the short-lived night.

It had been a strenuous interlude, but I could congratulate myself that I had, at last, established contact — no matter how briefly — with the study species.

The next morning I undertook to clean up the Stygian mess in the cabin, and in the process I uncovered my compass. I set it on the windowsill while I continued with my work, but the sun caught its brass surface and it glittered at me so accusingly that

I resigned myself to making another effort to restore the lost contact between me and the wolves.

My progress on this second safari was even slower, since I was carrying my rifle, shotgun, pistol and pistol belt, a small hatchet, and my hunting knife, together with a flask of wolf-juice in case I fell into one of the icy streams.

It was a hot day, and spring days in the subarctic can be nearly as hot as in the tropics. The first mosquitoes were already heralding the approach of the sky-filling swarms which would soon make travel on the Barrens a veritable trip through hell. I located the wolf tracks and resolutely set out upon the trail.

It led directly across the muskeg for several miles; but although the wolf had sunk in only three or four inches, my steps sank in until I reached solid ice a foot beneath the surface. It was with great relief that I finally breasted another gravel ridge and lost all trace of the wolf tracks.

My attempts to find them again were perfunctory. As I gazed around me at the morose world of rolling muskeg and frost-shattered stone that stretched uninterruptedly to a horizon so distant it might as well have been the horizon of the sea, I felt lonelier than I had ever felt in all my life. No friendly sound of aircraft engines broke the silence of that empty sky. No distant rumble of traffic set the ground beneath my feet to shaking. Only the disembodied whistling of an unseen plover gave any indication that life existed anywhere in all this lunar land where no tree grew.

I found a niche amongst some lichen-covered rocks and, having firmly jammed myself into it, ate and drank my lunch. Then I picked up the binoculars and began to scan the barren landscape for some signs of life.

Directly in front of me was the ice-covered bay of a great lake, and on the far side of this bay was something which at least relieved the somber monochrome of the muskeg colorings. It was a yellow sand esker, rising to a height of fifty or sixty feet and winding sinuously away into the distance like a gigantic snake.

These Barrenland eskers are the inverted beds of long-vanished rivers which once flowed through and over the glaciers that, ten thousand years ago, covered the Keewatin Barrens to a depth of several thousand feet. When the ice melted, sandy riverbeds were deposited on the land below, where they now provide almost the sole visual relief in the bleak monotony of the tundra plains.

I gazed at this one with affection, studying it closely; and as I swept it with my glasses I saw something move at last. The distance was great, but the impression I had was of someone, just the other side of the esker crest, waving his arm above his head. Much excited, I stumbled to my feet and trotted along the ridge to its termination on the shore of the bay. I was then not more than three hundred yards from the esker and when I got my breath back I took another look through the glasses.

The object I had previously glimpsed was still in view, but now it looked like a white feather boa being vehemently waved by persons or person unseen. It was a most inexplicable object, and nothing I had ever heard of in my study of natural history seemed to fit it. As I stared in perplexity, the first boa was joined by a second one, also waving furiously, and both boas began to move slowly along, parallel to the crest of the esker.

I began to feel somewhat uneasy, for here was a phenomenon which did not seem to be subject to scientific explanation. In fact I was on the point of abandoning my interest in the spectacle until some expert in psychic research happened along — when, without warning, both boas turned toward me, began rising higher and higher, and finally revealed themselves as the tails of two wolves proceeding to top the esker.

The esker overlooked my position on the bay's shore, and I felt as nakedly exposed as the lady in the famous brassière advertisement. Hunkering down to make myself as small as possible, I wormed my way into the rocks and did my best to be unobtrusive. I need not have worried. The wolves paid no attention to me, if indeed they even saw me. They were far too engrossed in their own affairs, which, as I slowly and incredulously began to realize, were at that moment centered around the playing of a game of tag.

It was difficult to believe my eyes. They were romping like a pair of month-old pups! The smaller wolf (who soon gave concrete evidence that she was a female) took the initiative. Putting her head down on her forepaws and elevating her posterior in a most undignified manner, she suddenly pounced toward the much larger male whom I now recognized as my acquaintance of two days earlier. He, in his attempt to evade her, tripped and went sprawling. Instantly she was upon him, nipping him smartly in the backside, before leaping away to run around him in frenzied circles. The male scrambled to his feet and gave chase, but only by the most strenuous efforts was he able to close the gap until he, in his turn, was able to nip *her* backside. Thereupon the roles were again reversed, and the female began to pursue the male, who led her on a wild scrabble up, over, down, and back across the esker until finally both wolves lost their footing on the steep slope and went skidding down it inextricably locked together.

When they reached the bottom they separated, shook the sand out of their hair, and stood panting heavily, almost nose to nose. Then the female reared up and quite literally embraced the male with both forepaws while she proceeded to smother him in long-tongued kisses.

The male appeared to be enduring this overt display of affection, rather than enjoying it. He kept trying to avert his head, to no avail. Involuntarily I felt my sympathy warming toward him, for, in truth, it was a disgusting exhibition of wanton passion. Nevertheless he bore it with what stoicism he could muster until the female tired. Turning from him, she climbed halfway up the esker slope and . . . disappeared.

She seemed to have vanished off the face of the earth without leaving a trace behind her. Not until I swung the glasses back toward a dark shadow in a fold of the esker near where I had last seen her did I understand. The dark shadow was the mouth of a cave, or den, and the female wolf had almost certainly gone into it.

I was so elated by the realization that I had not only located a pair of wolves, but by an incredible stroke of fortune had found their den as well, that I forgot all caution and ran to a nearby knoll in order to gain a better view of the den mouth.

The male wolf, who had been loafing about the foot of the esker after the departure of his wife, instantly saw me. In three or four bounds he reached the ridge of the esker, where he stood facing me in an attitude of tense and threatening vigilance. As I looked up at him my sense of exhilaration waned rapidly. He no longer seemed like a playful pup, but had metamorphosed into a magnificent engine of destruction which impressed me so much that the neck of my flask positively rattled against my teeth.

I decided I had better not disturb the wolf family any more that day, for fear of upsetting them and perhaps forcing them to move away. So I withdrew. It was not an easy withdrawal, for one of the most difficult things I know of is to walk backward up a broken rocky slope for three quarters of a mile encumbered, as I was, by the complex hardware of a scientist's trade.

When I reached the ridge from which I had first seen the wolves I took a last quick look through the binoculars. The female was still invisible, and the male had so far relaxed his attitude of vigilance as to lie down on the crest of the esker. While I watched he turned around two or three times, as a dog will, and then settled himself, nose under tail, with the evident intention of having a nap.

I was much relieved to see he was no longer interested in me, for it would have been a tragedy if my accidental intrusion had unduly disturbed these wolves, thereby prejudicing what promised to be a unique opportunity to study the beasts I had come so far to find.

I went completely to the wolves. To begin with I set up a den of my own as near to the wolves as I could conveniently get without disturbing the even tenor of their lives too much. After all, I *was* a stranger, and an unwolflike one, so I did not feel I should go too far too fast.

Abandoning Mike's cabin (with considerable relief, since as the days warmed up so did the smell), I took a tiny tent and set it up on the shore of the bay immediately opposite to the den esker. I kept my camping gear to the barest minimum — a small primus stove, a stew pot, a teakettle, and a sleeping bag were the essentials. I took no weapons of any kind, although there were times when I regretted this omission, even if only fleetingly. The big telescope was set up in the mouth of the tent in such a way that I could observe the den by day or night without even getting out of my sleeping bag.

During the first few days of my sojourn with the wolves I

stayed inside the tent except for brief and necessary visits to the out-of-doors which I always undertook when the wolves were not in sight. The point of this personal concealment was to allow the animals to get used to the tent and to accept it as only another bump on a very bumpy piece of terrain. Later, when the mosquito population reached full flowering, I stayed in the tent practically all of the time unless there was a strong wind blowing, for the most bloodthirsty beasts in the Arctic are not wolves, but the insatiable mosquitoes.

My precautions against disturbing the wolves were superfluous. It had required a week for me to get their measure, but they must have taken mine at our first meeting; and, while there was nothing overtly disdainful in their evident assessment of me, they managed to ignore my presence, and indeed my very existence, with a thoroughness which was somehow disconcerting.

Quite by accident I had pitched my tent within ten yards of one of the major paths used by the wolves when they were going to, or coming from, their hunting grounds to the westward; and only a few hours after I had taken up residence one of the wolves came back from a trip and discovered me and my tent. He was at the end of a hard night's work and was clearly tired and anxious to go home to bed. He came over a small rise fifty yards from me with his head down, his eyes half-closed, and a preoccupied air about him. Far from being the preternaturally alert and suspicious beast of fiction, this wolf was so self-engrossed that he came straight on to within fifteen yards of me, and might have gone right past the tent without seeing it at all, had I not banged my elbow against the teakettle, making a resounding clank. The wolf's head came up and his eyes opened wide, but he did not stop or falter in his pace. One brief, sidelong glance was all he vouchsafed to me as he continued on his way.

It was true that I wanted to be inconspicuous, but I felt uncomfortable at being so totally ignored. Nevertheless, during the two weeks which followed, one or more wolves used the track past my tent almost every night — and never, except on one memorable occasion, did they evince the slightest interest in me.

By the time this happened I had learned a good deal about my wolfish neighbors, and one of the facts which had emerged was that they were not nomadic roamers, as is almost universally believed, but were settled beasts and the possessors of a large permanent estate with very definite boundaries.

The territory owned by my wolf family comprised more than a hundred square miles, bounded on one side by a river but otherwise not delimited by geographical features. Nevertheless there *were* boundaries, clearly indicated in wolfish fashion.

Anyone who has observed a dog doing his neighborhood rounds and leaving his personal mark on each convenient post will have already guessed how the wolves marked out *their* property. Once a week, more or less, the clan made the rounds of the family lands and freshened up the boundary markers — a sort of lupine beating of the bounds. This careful attention to property rights was perhaps made necessary by the presence of two other wolf families whose lands abutted on ours, although I never discovered any evidence of bickering or disagreements between the owners of the various adjoining estates. I suspect, therefore, that it was more of a ritual activity.

In any event, once I had become aware of the strong feeling of property rights which existed amongst the wolves, I decided to use this knowledge to make them at least recognize my existence. One evening, after they had gone off for their regular nightly hunt, I staked out a property claim of my own, embracing perhaps three acres, with the tent at the middle, and *including a hundred-yard long section of the wolves' path.*

Staking the land turned out to be rather more difficult than I had anticipated. In order to ensure that my claim would not be overlooked, I felt obliged to make a property mark on stones, clumps of moss, and patches of vegetation at intervals of not more than fifteen feet around the circumference of my claim. This took most of the night and required frequent returns to the tent to consume copious quantities of tea; but before dawn brought the hunters home the task was done, and I retired, somewhat exhausted, to observe results.

I had not long to wait. At 0814 hours, according to my wolf log, the leading male of the clan appeared over the ridge behind me, padding homeward with his usual air of preoccupation. As usual he did not deign to glance at the tent; but when he reached the point where my property line intersected the trail, he stopped as abruptly as if he had run into an invisible wall. He was only fifty yards from me and with my binoculars I could see his expression very clearly.

His attitude of fatigue vanished and was replaced by a look of bewilderment. Cautiously he extended his nose and sniffed at one of my marked bushes. He did not seem to know what to make of it or what to do about it. After a minute of complete indecision he backed away a few yards and sat down. And then, finally, he looked directly at the tent and at me. It was a long, thoughtful, considering sort of look.

Having achieved my object — that of forcing at least one of the wolves to take cognizance of my existence — I now began to wonder if, in my ignorance, I had transgressed some unknown wolf law of major importance and would have to pay for my temerity. I found myself regretting the absence of a weapon as the look I was getting became longer, yet more thoughtful, and still more intent.

I began to grow decidedly fidgety, for I dislike staring matches, and in this particular case I was up against a master, whose yellow glare seemed to become more baleful as I attempted to stare him down.

The situation was becoming intolerable. In an effort to break the impasse I loudly cleared my throat and turned my back on the wolf (for a tenth of a second) to indicate as clearly as possible that I found his continued scrutiny impolite, if not actually offensive.

He appeared to take the hint. Getting to his feet he had another sniff at my marker, and then he seemed to make up his mind. Briskly, and with an air of decision, he turned his attention away from me and began a systematic tour of the area I had staked out as my own. As he came to each boundary marker he sniffed it once or twice, then carefully placed *his* mark on the outside of each clump of grass or stone. As I watched I saw where I, in my ignorance, had erred. He made his mark with such economy that he was able to complete the entire circuit without having to reload once, or, to change the simile slightly, he did it all on one tank of fuel.

The task completed — and it had taken him no longer than fifteen minutes — he rejoined the path at the point where it left my property and trotted off towards his home — leaving me with a good deal to occupy my thoughts.

The realization that the wolves' summer diet consisted chiefly of mice did not conclude my work in the field of dietetics. I knew that the mouse–wolf relationship was a revolutionary one to science and would be treated with suspicion, and possibly with ridicule, unless it could be so thoroughly substantiated that there would be no room to doubt its validity.

I had already established two major points:

1. That wolves caught and ate mice.
2. That the small rodents were sufficiently numerous to support the wolf population.

There remained, however, a third point vital to the proof of my contention. This concerned the nutritional value of mice. It was imperative for me to prove that a diet of small rodents would suffice to maintain a large carnivore in good condition.

I recognized that this was not going to be an easy task. Only a controlled experiment would do, and since I could not exert the necessary control over the wolves, I was at a loss how to proceed. Had Mike still been in the vicinity I might have borrowed two of his Huskies and, by feeding one of them on mice alone and the other on caribou meat (if and when this became obtainable), and then subjecting both dogs to similar tests, I would have been able to adduce the proof for or against the validity of the mouse–wolf concept. But Mike was gone, and I had no idea when he might return.

For some days I pondered the problem, and then one morning, while I was preparing some lemmings and meadow mice as specimens, inspiration struck me. Despite the fact that man is not wholly carnivorous, I could see no valid reason why I should not use myself as a test subject. It was true that there was only one of me; but the difficulty this posed could be met by setting up two timed intervals, during one of which I would confine myself to a mouse diet while during a second period of equal length I would eat canned meat and fresh fish. At the end of each period I would run a series of physiological tests upon myself and finally compare the two sets of results. While not absolutely conclusive as far as wolves were concerned, evidence that *my* metabolic functions remained unimpaired under a mouse regimen would strongly indicate that wolves, too, could survive and function normally on the same diet.

There being no time like the present, I resolved to begin the experiment at once. Having cleaned the basinful of small corpses which remained from my morning session of mouse skinning, I placed them in a pot and hung it over my primus stove. The pot gave off a most delicate and delicious odor as the water boiled, and I was in excellent appetite by the time the stew was done.

Eating these small mammals presented something of a problem at first because of the numerous minute bones; however, I found that the bones could be chewed and swallowed without much difficulty. The taste of the mice — a purely subjective factor and not in the least relevant to the experiment — was pleasing, if rather bland. As the experiment progressed, this blandness led to a degree of boredom and a consequent loss of appetite and I was forced to seek variety in my methods of preparation.

Of the several recipes which I developed, the finest by far was Creamed Mouse, and in the event that any of my readers may be interested in personally exploiting this hitherto overlooked source of excellent animal protein, I give the recipe in full.

SOURIS À LA CRÈME

INGREDIENTS:

One dozen fat mice	Salt and pepper
One cup white flour	Cloves
One piece sowbelly	Ethyl alcohol

[I should perhaps note that sowbelly is normally only available in the Arctic, but ordinary salt pork can be substituted.]

Skin and gut the mice, but do not remove the heads; wash, then place in a pot with enough alcohol to cover the carcasses. Allow to marinate for about two hours. Cut sowbelly into small cubes and fry slowly until most of the fat has been rendered. Now remove the carcasses from the alcohol and roll them in a mixture of salt, pepper, and flour; then place in frying pan and sauté for about five minutes (being careful not to allow the pan to get too hot, or the delicate meat will dry out and become tough and stringy). Now add a cup of alcohol and six or eight cloves. Cover the pan and allow to simmer slowly for fifteen minutes. The cream sauce can be made according to any standard recipe. When the sauce is ready, drench the carcasses with it, cover, and allow to rest in a warm place for ten minutes before serving.

During the first week of the mouse diet I found that my vigor remained unimpaired, and that I suffered no apparent ill effects. However, I did begin to develop a craving for fats. It was this which made me realize that my experiment, up to this point, had been rendered partly invalid by an oversight — and one, moreover, which did my scientific training no credit. The wolves, as I should have remembered, *ate the whole mouse*; and my dissections had shown that these small rodents stored most of their fat in the abdominal cavity, adhering to the intestinal mesenteries, rather than subcutaneously or in the muscular tissue. It was an inexcusable error I had made, and I hastened to rectify it. From this time to the end of the experimental period I too ate the whole mouse, without the skin of course, and I found that my fat craving was considerably eased.

It was during the final stages of my mouse diet that Mike returned to his cabin. He brought with him a cousin of his, the young Eskimo, Ootek, who was to become my boon companion and who was to prove invaluable to me in my wolf researches. However, on my first encounter with Ootek I found him almost as reserved and difficult of approach as Mike had been, and in fact still remained.

I had made a trip back to the cabin to fetch some additional supplies and the sight of smoke rising from the chimney cheered me greatly, for, to tell the truth, there had been times when I would have enjoyed a little human companionship. When I entered the cabin Mike was frying a panful of venison steak, while Ootek looked on. They had been lucky enough to kill a stray animal some sixty miles to the north. After a somewhat awkward few minutes, during which Mike seemed to be hopefully trying to ignore my existence, I managed to break the ice and achieve an introduction to Ootek, who responded by sidling around to the other side of the table and putting as much distance between us as possible. These two then sat down to their dinner, and Mike eventually offered me a plate of fried steak too.

I would have enjoyed eating it, but I was still conducting my experiment, and so I had to refuse, after having first explained my reasons to Mike. He accepted my excuses with the inscrutable silence of his Eskimo ancestors, but he evidently passed on my explanation to Ootek, who, whatever he may have thought about it and me, reacted in a typical Eskimoan way. Late that evening when I was about to return to my observation tent, Ootek waylaid me outside the cabin. With a shy but charming smile he held out a small parcel wrapped in deerskin. Graciously I undid the sinew binding and examined the present; for such it was. It consisted of a clutch of five small blue eggs, undoubtedly belonging to one of the thrush species, though I could not be certain of the identification.

Grateful, but at a loss to understand the implications of the gift, I returned to the cabin and asked Mike.

"Eskimo thinks if man eat mice his parts get small like mice," he explained reluctantly. "But if man eat eggs everything comes out all right. Ootek scared for you."

Ootek's acceptance of me had an ameliorating effect upon Mike's attitude. Although Mike continued to harbor a deep-rooted suspicion that I was not quite right in the head and might yet prove dangerous unless closely watched, he loosened up as much as his taciturn nature would permit and tried to be cooperative. This was a great boon to me, for I was able to enlist his aid as an interpreter between Ootek and myself.

Ootek had a great deal to add to my knowledge of wolves' food habits. Having confirmed what I had already discovered about the role mice played in their diet, he told me that wolves also ate great numbers of ground squirrels and at times even seemed to prefer them to caribou.

These ground squirrels are abundant throughout most of the Arctic, although Wolf House Bay lies just south of their range. They are close relatives of the common gopher of the western plains, but unlike the gopher they have a very poor sense of self-preservation. Consequently they fall easy prey to wolves and foxes. In summer, when they are well fed and fat, they may weigh as much as two pounds, so that a wolf can often kill enough of them to make a good meal with only a fraction of the energy expenditure involved in hunting caribou.

I had assumed that fishes could hardly enter largely into the wolves' diet, but Ootek assured me I was wrong. He told me he had several times watched wolves fishing for jackfish or Northern pike. At spawning time in the spring these big fish, which sometimes weigh as much as forty pounds, invade the intricate network of narrow channels in boggy marshes along the lake shores.

When a wolf decides to go after them he jumps into one of the larger channels and wades upstream, splashing mightily as he goes, and driving the pike ahead of him into progressively narrower and shallower channels. Eventually the fish realizes its danger and turns to make a dash for open water; but the wolf stands in its way and one quick chop of those great jaws is enough to break the back of even the largest pike. Ootek told me he once watched a wolf catch seven large pike in less than an hour.

Wolves also caught suckers when these sluggish fish were making their spawning runs up the tundra streams, he said; but the wolf's technique in this case was to crouch on a rock in a shallow section of the stream and snatch up the suckers as they passed — a method rather similar to that employed by bears when they are catching salmon.

Another although minor source of food consisted of Arctic sculpins: small fishes which lurk under rocks in shoal water. The wolves caught these by wading along the shore and turning over the rocks with paws or nose, snapping up the exposed sculpins before they could escape.

Later in the summer I was able to confirm Ootek's account of the sculpin fishery when I watched Uncle Albert spend part of the afternoon engaged in it. Unfortunately, I never did see wolves catch pike; but, having heard how they did it from Ootek, I tried it myself with considerable success, imitating the reported actions of the wolves in all respects, except that I used a short spear, instead of my teeth, with which to administer the *coup de grâce*.

These sidelights on the lupine character were fascinating, but it was when we came to a discussion of the role played by caribou in the life of the wolf that Ootek really opened my eyes.

The wolf and the caribou were so closely linked, he told me, that they were almost a single entity. He explained what he meant by telling me a story which sounded a little like something out of the Old Testament; but which, so Mike assured me, was a part of the semi-religious folklore of the inland Eskimos, who, alas for their immortal souls, were still happily heathen.

Here, paraphrased, is Ootek's tale.

"In the beginning there was a Woman and a Man, and nothing else walked or swam or flew in the world until one day the Woman dug a great hole in the ground and began fishing in it. One by one she pulled out all the animals, and the last one she pulled out of the hole was the caribou. Then Kaila, who is the God of the Sky, told the Woman the caribou was the greatest gift of all, for the caribou would be the sustenance of man.

"The Woman set the caribou free and ordered it to go out over the land and multiply, and the caribou did as the Woman said; and in time the land was filled with caribou, so the sons of the Woman hunted well, and they were fed and clothed and had good skin tents to live in, all from the caribou.

"The sons of the Woman hunted only the big, fat caribou, for they had no wish to kill the weak and the small and the sick, since these were no good to eat, nor were their skins much good. And, after a time, it happened that the sick and the weak came to outnumber the fat and the strong, and when the sons saw this they were dismayed and they complained to the Woman.

"Then the Woman made magic and spoke to Kaila and said: 'Your work is no good, for the caribou grow weak and sick, and if we eat them we must grow weak and sick also.'

"Kaila heard, and he said 'My work is good. I shall tell Amorak [the spirit of the Wolf], and he shall tell his children, and they will eat the sick and the weak and the small caribou, so that the land will be left for the fat and the good ones.'

"And this is what happened, and this is why the caribou and the wolf are one; for the caribou feeds the wolf, but it is the wolf who keeps the caribou strong."

I was slightly stunned by this story, for I was not prepared to have an unlettered and untutored Eskimo give me a lecture, even in parable form, illustrating the theory of survival of the fittest through the agency of natural selection. In any event, I was skeptical about the happy relationship which Ootek postulated as existing between caribou and wolf. Although I had already been disabused of the truth of a good many scientifically established beliefs about wolves by my own recent experiences, I could hardly believe that the all-powerful and intelligent wolf would limit his predation on the caribou herds to culling the sick and the infirm when he could, presumably, take his choice of the fattest and most succulent individuals. Furthermore, I had what I thought was excellent ammunition with which to demolish Ootek's thesis.

"Ask him then," I told Mike, "how come there are so many skeletons of big and evidently healthy caribou scattered around the cabin and all over the tundra for miles to the north of here."

"Don't need to ask him that," Mike replied with unabashed candor. "It was me killed those deer. I got fourteen dogs to feed and it takes maybe two, three caribou a week for that. I got to feed myself too. And then, I got to kill lots of deer everywhere all over the trapping country. I set four, five traps around each deer like that and get plenty foxes when they come to feed. It is no use for me to shoot skinny caribou. What I got to have is the big fat ones."

I was staggered. "How many do you think you kill in a year?" I asked.

Mike grinned proudly. "I'm pretty damn good shot. Kill maybe two, three hundred, maybe more."

When I had partially recovered from that one, I asked him if this was the usual thing for trappers.

"Every trapper got to do the same," he said. "Indians, white men, all the way down south far as caribou go in the wintertime, they got to kill lots of them or they can't trap no good. Of course they not all the time lucky to get *enough* caribou; then they got to feed the dogs on fish. But dogs can't work good on fish — get weak and sick and can't haul no loads. Caribou is better."

I knew from having studied the files at Ottawa that there were eighteen hundred trappers in those portions of Saskatchewan, Manitoba, and southern Keewatin which composed the winter range of the Keewatin caribou herd. I also knew that many of these trappers had been polled by Ottawa, through the agency of the fur trading companies, for information which might help explain the rapid decline in the size of the Keewatin caribou herd. I had read the results of this poll. To a man, the trappers and traders denied that they killed more than one or two caribou a year; and to a man they had insisted that wolves slaughtered the deer in untold thousands.

Although mathematics have never been my strong point, I tried to work out some totals from the information at hand. Being a naturally conservative fellow, I cut the number of trappers in half, and then cut Mike's annual caribou kill in half, before multiplying the two. No matter how many times I multiplied, I kept coming up with the fantastic figure of 112,000 animals killed by trappers in this area every year.

I realized it was not a figure I could use in my reports — not unless I wished to be posted to the Galapagos Islands to conduct a ten-year study on tortoise ticks.

In any event, what Mike and Ootek had told me was largely hearsay evidence, and this was not what I was employed to gather. Resolutely I put these disturbing revelations out of mind, and went back to learning the truth the hard way.

FROM
People of the Deer

THE LIFE BLOOD
OF THE LAND

On the day following the arrival of Hans and the children, I was awakened by the sound of heavy firing. The crash of gunshots intruded itself into my dreams until I thought I was again back in the Italian hills, listening to an exchange of rifle fire between the German outposts and our own. When I came to full consciousness the firing remained, so I hurriedly pulled on my clothes and went out into the June morning.

Franz, Anoteelik, and Hans were sitting on the ridge above the cabin and they were steadily firing their rifles across the river. On the sloping southern bank nearly a hundred deer, all does, were milling in stupid anxiety. I could see the grey bursts of dust as bullets sang off the rocks, and I could hear the flat thud of bullets going home in living flesh.

The nearest animals were waist-deep in the fast brown water and could not return to shore, for the press of deer behind cut off retreat. The does that were still on land were running in short, futile starts, first east then west again, and it was some time before they began to gallop with long awkward strides, along the riverbank. Their ponderous bellies big with fawn swung rhythmically as they fled upstream, for their time was nearly on them.

When the last of the straggling herd had passed out of range beyond the first bend of the river, the firing stopped and the three hunters ran down the bank and hurriedly began to clear the snow away from the green back of a canoe, which lay beside the cabin. I helped them and in a few moments the canoe was free and ready for the water. Franz and I pushed off into the still-flooded river, and we worked with all our power to gain the other bank before the current could sweep us out into the opening bay. It was hard and exciting work, but even in the fury of that struggle I had time to notice that the water was not all brown. Long, tenuous, crimson streamers were flowing down the river, fading and disappearing as they joined the full flow of the current. We grounded on the opposite shore and leaped into the water to beach the canoe, out of the river's grasp.

The excitement of the shooting, and of the river crossing, ebbed as suddenly as it had risen and I stood on the rough rocks along the slope and looked down on the dead and dying deer. There were a dozen of them lying in my sight along the shore. Their blood was still pumping thickly into the foam-flecked eddies at the river's edge, for only two of them were dead. The rest lay quivering on the rocks and lifted heavy heads to watch us blankly or, struggling to their feet, plunged forward only to fall again.

It was a sight of slaughter and of horror, and the knowledge that each of these dying beasts was swollen with young did not make the bloody spectacle easier to bear. I was seeing the blood of the land flow for the first time, but though my eyes were still those of a stranger and I was sickened by the sight, Franz was quite unperturbed. Rapidly, and with the agility of a deer himself, he leapt among the rocks to reach the cripples. He carried a short-bladed knife and as he reached each wounded doe he made one dexterous thrust into the back of her neck and neatly severed the spinal cord running inside the vertebrae. It was efficient and it was mercifully quick. Within ten minutes all the wounded animals lay still and Franz began the task of cutting up the meat.

One long stroke sufficed to open up the bellies. The sharp blade was used with such control that while it split the skin, it did not even mark the soft tissues of the swollen stomachs, distended with the fermenting leaves and lichens that the deer had fed upon. Then, reaching a bare arm into the hot cavities,

Franz disemboweled each beast with one strong pull. Carefully
he removed the livers and the kidneys and, using his knife as a
chopper, he severed the hindquarters from the trunks. Leaving
the forelimbs untouched, he sliced through the skin under the
chins and cut out the heavy tongues.

I watched with fascination and repulsion, but so sure were all
Franz's movements and so deft his touch, that the horror of the
scene began to dull. I was filled with admiration for the man's
skill. Though I did not know it then, I was watching a man of
Tyrrell's deer people do his work, for Franz had learned his
knacker's art at the hands of the Ihalmiut, who are, in truth, a
People of the Deer.

In less than twenty minutes all the carcasses were drawn and
we were carrying the hindquarters to the shore. Where half an
hour ago a herd of living deer had stood, now there were only
shapeless, bloody heaps of meat that steamed gently upon the
melting snow. The transition was too quick to have its full effect
upon me then, and by the time I had lived in the land long
enough to understand the truth behind a killing such as this, I
too came to view it through Northern eyes, and to recognize the
stark utility of death. But now it was my first spring in the
Barrens, and the deer had returned. With their coming the long
hiatus that life suffers during the interminable winter months
was over. Outside the cabin the meat-hungry dogs raised their
gaunt faces and howled exuberantly as each new change of
breeze brought the strong smell of deer.

Kunee and Anoteelik were in an ecstasy. Anoteelik rushed
knee-deep into the swollen river to help us land and eagerly
snatched up a piece of still-warm meat and wolfed it down with
feverish excitement. I remembered that this was the first fresh
meat he had tasted in long months, and Anoteelik had not yet
forgotten those starvation days by Ootek's Lake. Kunee was not
far behind him, and I cannot describe the emotions that filled
me as I watched this girl-child with a knife in one hand and a
great chunk of dripping back meat in the other, stuffing her little
face and burping like an old clubman after a Gargantuan meal.

For the first time Hans showed some animation. He smiled. I
do not know whether it was from pleasure in the killing or from
anticipation of fresh food. His smile was — well, expressionless.

Franz too was smiling as we unloaded the heavy cargo and he shouted at Kunee to get a fire going. A new spirit of enthusiasm and fresh life was in the place, as if new blood flowed through the veins of those about me. Even I was stung by an emotion I could not analyze, and I felt alive as I had never felt before.

The fire had just been lit and a pot of deer tongues just set to boil when a wild babble from the dogs brought me outside again. This time I looked directly to the crossing, and where the butchery had taken place there was a great new herd of does milling as it came up against the stream.

This time there was no shooting, though Hans could hardly restrain his urge to take up a rifle and empty it again. The deer seemed to ignore the cabin that stood in full view and in a minute they had all taken to the stream. Heavy as they were, they swam buoyantly and powerfully so that they made the crossing without losing ground and landed literally in our own front yard.

The dogs became insane and threatened to tear their tethering posts out of the frozen ground. The deer paid them, and us, but little heed. Splitting into two groups, they flowed past the cabin, enveloping it for a brief instant in their midst. The stink of barnyard was strong in our nostrils as they passed, then they were gone beyond the ridge.

In less than an hour I had seen so many deer that it seemed as if the world was full of them, but I had seen nothing yet. That afternoon Franz took me on his sled and we drove warily along the rotten shore ice of the bay, to the Ghost Hills. The heat was remarkably intense; at noon the thermometer had reached 100; and so we wore nothing but thin trousers and cotton shirts. Water lay deep upon the ice and the sled was really more of a boat than a land conveyance. An hour's travel took us to the north shore of the bay, and here we tied the dogs and climbed a long gentle ridge that faced the south. Below us lay Windy Bay, and beyond it the shattered slopes of the Ghost Hills. It was a scene to be recorded on grey paper, for the growing things had not been able to keep pace with the precipitate transition of the seasons, and the subtle overlay of color that would suffuse the summer plains had not yet begun to flow. The rotting surface of the ice was dark, but framed in ivory drifts, still lingering on the shores and in a thousand gullies and ravines. The hills were dun-colored heights sheathed in rock and long-dead lichens, with startlingly black patches of dwarf spruce spotted along their lower slopes. To the north, the plains sank into white and snow-filled hollows, hiding the muskegs and ponds; then lifted to reveal a hueless and leaden waste that stretched to the horizon.

From this vantage point all of this achromatic world lay somberly below us as we waited for the coming of the deer. We had not long to wait. Franz caught my arm and pointed to the convoluted slopes of the distant southern hills, and I could just discern a line of motion. It seemed to me that the slopes were sliding gently downward to the bay, as if the innumerable boulders that protruded from the hills had suddenly been set adrift to roll, in slow motion, down upon the ice. I watched intently, not certain whether the sun's glare had begun to affect my eyes so that they played fool tricks on me. Then the slow avalanches reached the far shore and debouched over the bay. I tried to count the little dots. Ten, fifty, a hundred, three hundred — and I gave up. In broken twisted lines, in bunched and beaded ropes, the deer streamed out onto the ice until they were moving north across a front of several miles.

From that distance they barely seemed to move, and yet in a few minutes they had reached the center of the bay and had begun to take on shape. I had binoculars, but in my preoccupation with the spectacle below I had not thought to use them. Now I lifted the glasses to my eyes. The long skeins dissolved at once into endless rows of deer, each following upon the footsteps of the animals ahead. Here and there along the lines a yearling kept its place beside a mother who was swollen with the new fawn she carried. There were no bucks. All these animals were does, all pregnant, all driving inexorably towards the north and the flat plains where they would soon give birth.

The leaders reached our shore and began the ascent, but across the bay the avalanche continued and grew heavier. The surface of the bay, for six miles east and west, had become one undulating mass of animals, and still they came.

Without hurry, but without pause, unthinking, but directly driven, they filed down to the ice and, following the tracks of those who had crossed first, made for our shore. Highways began to grow. The black ice was pounded and shattered until it again became white with broken crystals. The broad roads stretched across the bay, multiplied, grew into one another until at length they disappeared and the whole sweep of ice was one great road.

The herds were swelling past our lookout now. Ten paces from us, five, then we were forced to stand and wave our arms to avoid being trampled on. The does gazed briefly and incuriously at us, swung a few feet away, and passed on to the north without altering their gait.

Hours passed like minutes. The flow continued at an unbroken level until the sun stood poised on the horizon's rim. And I became slowly conscious of a great apathy. Life, my life and that of Franz, of all living things I knew, seemed to have become meaningless. For here was life on such a scale that it was beyond all comprehension. It numbed my mind and left me feeling as if the inanimate world had been saturated with a reckless prodigality in that sacred and precious thing called life. I thought of the twelve deer slaughtered on the banks of Windy River and I no longer felt horror or disgust. I felt nothing for the dead who were drowned beyond memory in this living flow of blood that swept across the plains.

It was nearly dusk when we roused ourselves. We walked silently to the sled and I felt a little sick. I began to doubt the reality of the vision I had seen. The ice had begun to freeze as the sun went down and the sled bumped so wickedly over the endless hoofprints that I was forced to run along behind it. A dozen times we passed close to a late herd of deer and each time the dogs, in defiance of Franz, lunged in pursuit and could be halted only when we overturned the sled to hold them back. There was no doubt about it — the vision had been real.

That night I sat for a long time on the ridge behind the cabin, smoking and thinking of that vision. I knew little of the People of the Deer as yet and now that I had seen the herds, I was aware that I knew nothing of the deer themselves. The People and the deer fused in my mind, an entity. I found I could not think of one without the other, and so by accident I stumbled on the secret of the Ihalmiut before I had even met them. I believe it was this vague awareness of the indivisibility of the Barrens People and the caribou that made my later attempts to understand the Eskimos yield fruit.

UNDER THE
LITTLE HILLS

Summer, which follows spring so closely that the two are almost one, was upon us before it was possible to travel to the shores of Ootek's Lake and meet the People. I had arranged with Franz to take me there while Hans and the children were to remain at Windy Bay to feed the dogs we left behind, and to care for the camp.

As Franz and I prepared for the journey north, I was excited and at the same time depressed. Much as I wished to meet the Ihalmiut in their own land, the fragmentary glimpses of their lives that I had from Franz had left me with a strong feeling of unease at the prospect of meeting them face to face. I wondered if they would have any conception as to how much of their tragedy they owed to men of my color, and I wondered if, like the northern Indians, they would be a morose and sullen lot, resentful of my presence, suspicious and uncommunicative.

Even if they welcomed me into their homes, I was still afraid of my own reactions. The prospect of seeing and living with a people who knew starvation as intimately as I knew plenty, the idea of seeing with my own eyes this disintegrating remnant of a dying race, left me with a sensation closely akin to fear.

We could not make the journey northward by canoe, for the raging streams which had cut across the Barrens only a few weeks before were now reduced to tiny creeks whose courses were interrupted by jumbled barriers of rock. No major rivers flowed the way we wished to go, and so the water routes were useless to us. Since the only alternative was a trek overland, we prepared to go on foot, as the Ihalmiut do.

But there was a difference. The Ihalmiut travel light, and a man of the People crossing the open plains in summer carries little more than his knife, a pipe, and perhaps a spare pair of skin boots called *kamik*. He eats when he finds something to eat. There are usually suckers in the shrunken streams, and these can sometimes be caught with the hands. Or if the suckers are too hard to find, the traveller can take a length of rawhide line and snare the orange-colored ground squirrels on the sandy esker slopes. In early summer there are always eggs, or flightless birds, and if the eggs are nearly at the hatching point, so much the better.

Franz and I, on the other hand, travelled in white man's style. We were accompanied by five dogs and to each dog we fastened a miniature Indian travois — two long thin poles that stretched behind to support a foot-square platform on which we could load nearly thirty pounds of gear that included bedrolls, ammunition, cooking tools, and presents of flour and tobacco for the Eskimos. With this equipment we were also able to carry a little tent, and food for the dogs and ourselves: deer meat for them, and flour, tea, and baking powder for us. We had more than the bare essentials, but we had to pay a stiff price for them.

Equipped with pack dogs, it took us better than a week to cover the same sixty miles that the Ihalmiut cross in two days and a night. I shall not soon forget the tortures of that march. While the sun shone, the heat was as intense as it is in the tropics, for the clarity of the Arctic air does nothing to soften the sun's rays. Yet we were forced to wear sweaters and even caribou skin jackets. The flies did that to us. They rose from the lichens at our feet until they hung like a malevolent mist about us and took on the appearance of a low-lying cloud. *Milugia* (black flies) and *kiktoriak* (mosquitoes) came in such numbers that their presence actually gave me a feeling of physical terror. There was simply no evading them. The bleak Barrens stretched into emptiness on every side, and offered no escape and no surcease. To stop for food was torture and to continue the march in the overwhelming summer heat was worse. At times a kind of insanity would seize us and we would drop everything and run wildly in any direction until we were exhausted. But the pursuing hordes stayed with us and we got nothing from our frantic efforts except a wave of sweat that seemed to attract even more mosquitoes.

From behind our ears, from beneath our chins, a steady dribble of blood matted into our clothing and trapped the insatiable flies until we both wore black collars composed of their struggling bodies. The flies worked down under our shirts until our belts stopped them. Then they fed about our waists until the clothing stuck to us with drying blood.

The land we were passing over offered no easy routes to compensate for the agonies the flies inflicted upon us. It was rolling country, and across our path ran a succession of mounding hills whose sides and crests were strewn with angular rocks and with broken fragments filling the interstices between the bigger boulders. On these our boots were cut and split and our feet bruised until it was agony to walk at all. But at that the hills were better walking than the broad wet valleys which lay in between.

Each valley had its own stream flowing down its center. Though those streams were often less than five feet in width, they seemed to be never less than five feet in depth. The valley floors were one continuous mattress of wet moss into which we sank up to our knees until our feet found the perpetual ice that lay underneath. Wading and stumbling through the icy waters of the muskegs, floundering across streams or around the countless ponds (all of whose banks were undercut and offered no gradual descent), we would become numbed from the waist down, while our upper bodies were bathed in sweat. If, as happened for three solid days, it rained, then we lived a sodden nightmare as we crossed those endless bogs.

I am not detailing the conditions of summer travel in order to emphasize my own discomforts but to illustrate the perfectly amazing capacity of the Ihalmiut as travellers. Over sixty miles of such country, the People could move with ease, yes, and with comfort, bridging the distance in less than two days of actual walking. And they, mind you, wore only paper-thin boots of caribou skin on their feet. It is not that they are naturally impervious to discomfort, but simply that they have adjusted their physical reactions to meet the conditions they must face. They have bridged the barriers of their land not by levelling them, as we would try to do, but by conforming to them. It is like the difference between a sailing vessel and one under power, when you compare an Ihalmio and a white traveller, in the Barrens. The white man, driven by his machine instincts, always lives at odds with his environment; like a motor vessel he bucks the winds and the seas and he is successful only while the intricate apparatus built about him functions perfectly. But the Barrens People are an integral part of *their* environment. Like sailing ships, they learn to move with wind and water; to mold themselves to the rhythm of the elements and so accomplish gently and without strain the things that must be done.

By the time we were in sight of the Little Lakes I was aware of a desperation not too far from madness. I cursed the land and the ephemeral dreams which had brought me to it. I cursed Franz and the poor dogs whose eyes were swollen almost shut by the constant assault of the insatiable flies. I was so tired that I did not greatly care whether or not I survived — if only those bloodthirsty legions of winged horrors would let me die in peace.

On the last day Franz was in the lead, followed by three dogs, while I trailed a half-mile behind trying to force my dogs to efforts beyond their powers. I heard Franz call and when I looked ahead I saw three human figures where before there had been only one. Franz stood on the crest of a ridge and beside him there were two other men, all three gesticulating and shouting at me down the slope.

The sight of strangers seemed to offer some kind of hope and I abandoned the plodding dogs and ran heavily up the hill, slipping and falling among the boulders. When I reached the crest, Franz and the other two men were sitting cross-legged on the rocks and a little breeze was playing along the ridge to cool them off, and to hold back the flies.

One of the strangers was manipulating a little drill which looked rather like a bow and arrow, with the arrow pointed down into a piece of wood upon the ground, while the bow, with its string wound twice around the arrow's shank, was being pushed back and forth parallel to the ground. From the spinning tip of the drill rose a little curl of yellow smoke and I realized that the fur-clad man was making fire.

Our matches had long since been ruined when the top of the can in which they were carried came off during a river crossing. For three days we had had neither a smoke nor a mug of tea — two things that just barely make life endurable for white men in the Barrens. Now I stood panting on the hill and watched an Eskimo casually producing fire as our distant ancestors had produced it in their time. The man looked up at me and smiled, a transfiguring smile which spread like the light of fire itself over his face.

Franz motioned me to sit down while he got out the pail and

the packet of sodden tea. Now the second Eskimo, a short and solid figure of a man, stepped forward, took the pail, and with a broad grin ran down the slope to fetch us water from a tundra pool. Franz nodded his head after the water-getter.

"Ohoto," he said. "One of the best of them. And this one over here is Hekwaw, the biggest hunter of the bunch."

It was again a succinct introduction, typical of Franz. It was so brief because from his long contact with the People he had come to see them with straight eyes and could not understand how weird and curious they would appear to me, who saw them with the oblique gaze of a man of civilized experience.

However, if Franz would tell me no more than their names, I could at least appraise them for myself. Both were dressed in *holiktuk* — parkas — of autumn deerskin with the fur side turned out. The parka of Hekwaw, the firemaker, was decorated with insets of pure white fur about the shoulders and by a fringe of thin strips of hide around the bottom edge. Ohoto's was even more dressy, for it had a bead-embroidered neck and cuffs. But despite the beads and insets, the general appearance of both men was positively scruffy. Great patches of hair were worn off the garments and rents and tears had been imperfectly mended, evidently by an unpracticed hand. Food juices and fat drippings had matted the thick hair that remained, and dirt from unidentifiable sources had caked broad patches of the fur.

Below these heavy parkas, which the two men were wearing next their skins, were short fur trousers called *kaillik,* and these were met, above the knee, by the yellow translucent tops of the skin boots.

My first reaction as I saw and smelled these men was one of revulsion. They seemed foul to me and I felt the instinctive surge of white man's ego as I wondered why the devil they couldn't find clean clothes to wear. That was, of course, the superficial thought of one who had no knowledge, but it typifies the conclusions drawn by most white men, particularly missionaries, when they view the "savage in his abhorrent state of nature."

But on that summer day in the Barrens I wasn't so interested in dress as it may seem. My curious glance at the clothing of the two men was quite perfunctory, for I was fascinated by the men themselves.

Hekwaw — the Bear, the others called him — was a mountain of a man, but a scaled-down mountain. His muscles bulged and flowed under the loose sleeves of his old parka and the rhythm of the spinning fire drill was reflected in the pulse of tendons in his short and massive neck. Sweat beaded up steadily under his lank black hair, then growing into drops it rolled down the oblique slant of his low forehead, ran along the deep seams of his skin until it found an outlet and, by-passing the broad planes about his half-hidden eyes, fell clear from the sprawling nostrils of his flattened nose. His broad and sensuous mouth with its wide, swollen lips worked in the same rhythm as the drill, and the half-dozen grizzled hairs that were his beard wagged to the same quick tempo.

It was a parody of a face, a contorted parody which was meant for comedy but which had a wild essential quality that restrained my desire to laugh. There was a deep intelligence where one might expect to see only brute instinct, and there was humor and good nature that belied the weathered hide crinkling, ape-like, on the brow and on the flat-planed cheeks.

Hekwaw removed the drill and shook a little pinch of smoldering ash from the fire board onto a pile of dry and brittle moss. Then he knelt before it and his cheeks swelled while his eyes disappeared altogether under their taut folds of skin. He blew, and the fire caught, giving birth to a minute greenish flame.

Ohoto returned with the water and with a great armful of green willow twigs, none bigger in circumference than a lead pencil. Franz took our precious "tea-stick" from one of the dogs' packs and jammed it into the moss so that the pail hung suspended from it over the tiny fire. And the day was so brilliant that the sun obscured the flames and only a twist of smoke from the green wood showed that the water was slowly being brought to the boil.

Now I had opportunity to see Ohoto. His was a young face, still rounded and without the crevassed wrinkling of old Hekwaw's. His hair had been roughly cut so that it hung like the uncouth tonsure of some pagan priest, and it was as coarse as the hair of the deer. The cut hair disclosed a high, broad forehead and the eyes below it had not yet retreated into caves to escape the glare of winter snows. They were black and very bright, with the alert curiosity of a muskrat. Ohoto had an empty stone pipe clenched between his immense and regular white teeth, and I was not too slow to take the hint. I pulled out a bit of plug, damp and covered with debris, and when Ohoto saw it, he beamed broadly.

Now I forgot the discomforts and despair of the long trek. At last I was amongst the People, in the heart of their own land. And it was evident that at least some of my forebodings had been groundless.

The tea pail boiled over and the tiny fire hissed feebly and died. Franz flung a handful of leaves into the pot and while they steeped I relaxed on the fragile sphagnum mosses below the crest of the high ridge. For the moment I was free of the blindness which had been mine while we had been forced to struggle so hard against the unmerciful antagonism of the land. I was free to look out over the summer plains and for the first time to feel something of their beauty, and begin to understand the libel that is perpetrated by that name — the Barrenlands.

In winter perhaps the name has validity, and at all times of the year it has validity for those whose minds have hardened over visions of great forests or neatly cultivated fields. Even after two years in the land, I too have often found myself using the word, and meaning it.

Staring out over the limitless expanse I at first saw only a rolling world of faded brown, shot through with streaks and whorls of yellow greens, for when I tried to see it all, the individual colors merged into anonymity. It *was* a barren sight, and yet that desert face concealed a beauty that rose from a thousand sources, under the white sun. The deep chocolate bogs, laden with rich sepia dyes that stain the streams and pools, were bounded by wide swales of emerald sedges and tall grass. On the sweeping slopes that rose above these verdant meadows, the dark and glossy greens of dwarf birch scrub formed amorphous patches of somber vitality that were illuminated by broad spaces where the brilliance of ten million minute flowers drew to themselves small butterflies as gorgeous as any in the world. Even on the shattered ridges that are given over to the rocks, the creeping lichens suffused the grey stone with a wash of pastel tints ranging from scarlet through the spectrum into velvet rosettes of perfect black. There was no lack of color rising from living things — but it is only that the eye beholds too much in this land that has no roof and no containing walls. The colors flow together and are lost in distance that the eye cannot embrace. And so we only see the barrenness that follows when beauty flows too thinly into the sponge of an illimitable space.

These were the living colors that I saw upon the land, but there was much else to see as well. The lakes beneath us were quite uncountable, a meaningless jumble, looking like the shattered fragments of a great mirror. Between the shining shards of water were the Little Hills, low formless ridges whose slopes seen from the distance were grey-green with lichens, and whose crests were mottled with black rock. To the horizon on the north, the fading glint of lakelets caught the sun and glittered like dew upon brown grass. I knew that somewhere in that maze must lie the twisted course of Innuit Ku, River of Men, but for the life of me I could not distinguish it in the aquatic puzzle spread out below.

While I stared, Ohoto came over and squatted on his hams beside me, also looking out over the land — his land. I lowered the glasses. He grinned again, and, in the grand manner of a small townsman showing his city friend the sights, he began to point out the things of interest.

It did not matter that he could not speak my language, nor I his. Ohoto had the power of expression without words. There was a directness that made his gesticulations seem as clear as printed English. Now he stretched his arm toward a rather large lake that lay only a few miles to the north, and said, "*Ootek Kumanik!*"

Looking with my glasses, I could see three little greyish pimples by the shores of Ootek's Lake and as I strained my eyes I could also see a fine thread of smoke. The tents of the People!

Rapidly Ohoto swung his arm to the north and pointed out the other lakes: Halo Kumanik, Kakumee Kumanik, and, lastly, Tingmea Ku, the little Goose River that leads the lakes into the great current of Innuit Ku itself. But I could still make nothing of Innuit Ku. It seemed to be only a string of lakes, set amongst countless other lakes, and lacking all the continuity of a great river. Later, when I travelled on it, I was to marvel at its clear-cut shape and its directness; but seen from the distance it simply blended into the watery chaos and disappeared. It became part of the chameleon shape the Barrens show to all outsiders.

We drank our tea on the crest of the hill, then packed up and started down into the Ihalmiut land. The two Eskimos led the way, and their bounding agility over the rough rocks would have put a caribou to shame. We followed painfully a long way behind, and at last came to the low shores of Ootek's Lake.

Across the water we could clearly see the three tents, blending so well with the weathered gravel ridge behind that they might have grown from the hills. People and dogs were running aimlessly about amongst the tents and two new fires had been lighted, for the distant vision of the People had shown them that strangers were approaching, and it is mandatory that all strangers must be fed as soon as they arrive.

I was to learn later that the camps of the People were arranged in little groups of two or three tents on the shores of several lakes, for there is not enough willow scrub in the land to support the cooking fires of more than three families at any single spot. Here at Ootek Kumanik were the tents of Hekwaw, Ootek, and Ohoto, and a few miles eastward on Halo Kumanik were the three tents of Halo, Yaha, and Miki. On Kakumee Kumanik there were three separate camps, Katelo and Alekahaw having their tents at one spot, Owliktuk and Onekwaw at a second, while the two tents of old Kakumee stood alone on the far side of the lake.

Thus, within a radius of three miles of each other, dwelt all the living People in a land which stretches for five hundred miles from south to north, and three hundred miles from east to west. It was the most ancient camp of the Ihalmiut, and it was also the last. And I was the first outlander to come upon it in all the centuries that tents had stood beside the Little Lakes. Yet if that thought filled me with excitement, the prospect of meeting a white man for the first time in their lives was filling the women and children from the tents ahead with equal excitement.

We rounded the lake and came up toward the camp. Here the foreshore sloping to the lake was not composed of rocks, but almost exclusively of bones. This was an ancient site and the piles of whitened caribou bones had mounted with the years until they had reached staggering proportions, for in the Barrens neither wood nor bone ever seems to rot or pass away. Dogs and the weather had broken up the larger pieces of bone and spread them evenly around until they formed a pavement all about the camp. But neither dogs nor weather had greatly affected the skulls, and these, with their huge antlers, formed a dead forest of white snags. Later on I counted over two hundred skulls within a hundred yards of an Ihalmiut tent, and these represented only a fraction of the total number of beasts whose remains lay in that place, for only the heads of kills made close at hand are ever brought to camp.

The three tents stood on a sloping ledge where they would catch whatever breeze might blow, for the breeze serves as the sole protection from the flies. Near each tent was a rough stone hearth and beside each fire a tremendous mound of willow twigs. These were, of course, quite green and the little fires were giving out great rolling coils of smoke. On the nearest fireplace was a huge iron pot looking ridiculously like the pots that cannibals seem to favor in our magazine cartoons.

As for the tents themselves, each was a cone about fifteen feet in diameter at its base and perhaps ten feet high. They were patchwork affairs composed of roughly scraped deer hides hung on a wooden frame. The hides had been stitched together while they were still green and, as they dried, the seams had pulled apart so that broad cracks outlined the position of each hide. Around the bottom of the tent a ring of boulders acted as an anchor. In that land you do not drive wooden pegs, even if you have them, for if the rocks did not prevent you, then the perpetual frost which often lies only a few inches below the surface of the ground would shatter the peg before it got a grip. The doorways faced the north, the direction from which the returning deer would come. The doors themselves were made of single hides, untanned, and dried to the hardness of wood.

In a way the Ihalmiut camp seemed only to accentuate the apparent desolation and emptiness of the Arctic plains, and yet in the immediate vicinity of the tents was this little pocket of life in the center of the human vacuum that otherwise possessed the Barrens. We felt that we could breathe easily here, for we were no longer entirely alone, though I was still a little afraid of our reception.

It was a foolish fear. Hekwaw and Ohoto had run on ahead, shouting loudly as they went, but their warning was superfluous, for every man, woman, and child was out about the fires, driven to a kind of ecstatic fury by the approach of strangers. One old woman, bent and beaten as if by the rocks of the land, frenziedly blew at the coals of a fire and heaped fresh twigs upon it until she smothered it completely. Ootek's wife, Howmik, was wrestling with the hindquarters of a deer, still dripping wet, which she had hauled out of the cold storage of the frigid lake for supper. Between snatching furtive glances at us and trying to cut off chunks of meat with her curved *ulu*, or woman's knife, she was in imminent danger of slicing off her fingers too. Her wooden hair ornaments swung and jumped like live things as she hurried, and her child, Inoti, who lived in the back of her parka, screamed with pleasure as he batted at her flying braids.

Even the dogs caught the excitement. Three pups simultaneously began to chase their tails while a pair of older dogs joined noisy battle. Children hustled among the dogs, kicking them lightly in their exposed bellies either to drive them off, or just to have something to do as we approached.

Franz and I stopped about a hundred yards short of the nearest tent and the three men, Ootek, Hekwaw, and Ohoto, came out to welcome us formally into their homes. Ohoto and Hekwaw acted as if they were meeting us for the first time. They were very correct and very solemn as they gravely touched our finger tips. Then, with the formal greeting over, Ootek produced a stone pipe, loaded with *atamojak* — the dried leaves of a low, bushy plant which make an inadequate substitute for tobacco — and offered me a smoke. Together we walked to Ootek's tent while the women and children ceased their frenetic labors and watched us with unconcealed anticipation. We had been welcomed formally, so that it was now good manners to give way to curiosity, a thing one must not do until a visitor is settled, lest you embarrass him thereby.

All the children, women, and old people from the entire camp crowded closely into Ootek's tent behind us, and collectively they produced an overpowering odor — which, however, was cancelled out by the obvious good nature and good feeling which also emanated from these People.

Ootek bade us sit down on the sleeping platform, and while his wife was organizing the other women in preparation for a feast, I had a good look at this home of the Ihalmiut. The tent was not even vaguely weather tight. Great streaks of sky showed along the joints between the skins. Under those portions of the tent which were more or less whole, were the belongings of the family, and these possessions were simple almost to the point of nonexistence.

Along one half of the enclosed circle was the low sleeping bench of willow twigs and lichens, covered with a haphazard mattress of tanned deer hides. This was the communal bed where the entire family slept together under a robe or two of softened skins. The rest of the floor space was given over to an amazing litter of half-eaten, ready-to-be-eaten and never-to-be-eaten bits of caribou. I saw an entire boiled head that had been pretty well chewed over, and a pile of leg bones which had been cracked for marrow and then boiled to extract the last precious drop of oil. On one side of the tent was a more or less complete brisket, with skin attached, of a deer that obviously should have been eaten long ago. Later I discovered this was a sort of snack bar where hungry visitors could slice off a bit of raw, but well tenderized, meat while waiting for mealtime.

Around the inner surface of the tent, suspended from the dozen precious poles, were the odd bits of clothing not required for the moment. A few pairs of *kamik*, stiff and dry and half transparent, waited for their owners' feet. Nearby lay a couple of inner parkas, called *ateegie*, and some children's overalls that are one-piece garments of fawn hide. Pushed under one pole was a huge wad of dried sphagnum moss waiting the needs of the young child Inoti, for diapers are not used in the Barrens, where nature has provided a more efficient sponge.

And that about completed the furnishings of Ootek's tent, except for an ancient wooden chest which held the treasures of the family: the amulet belt of Ootek, the sewing kit of Howmik with its bone needles and hank of caribou sinew thread, half a dozen empty .44-40 brass cartridge cases which someday might ornament the bowls of stone pipes, a bow drill, a musk-ox horn comb, and some children's toys.

While I was getting my bearing, Franz produced a plug of trade tobacco, which is nearly as vile as the Ihalmiut product, and it went the rounds. I noticed with great interest that Ootek, after filling his pipe with the precious stuff, passed it to his wife so that she might have the first smoke. In fact, she smoked most of it before returning it to Ootek. A small gesture this, but one that I was to find was typical of the consideration and affection with which the Ihalmiut men treated their wives.

There was a tremendous amount of talk while we sat about the tent waiting for supper, most of it between Franz and the three Eskimo men, while the rest listened avidly and interjected comments and bursts of laughter. Franz translated a little of what was being said and the conversation was, as always, mostly about the deer. Where were they? Had we seen any fresh tracks? How long did we think it would be before *Tuktu* — the deer — came from the north? It was an engrossing subject and I wanted to be in on it, but only by begging Franz to tell me what was going on could I get the gist at all. I began to get bored after a while, feeling left out, for Franz was soon too interested to waste time translating for me. To occupy myself I got out my notebook and began idly to sketch a caribou. The talk rose and fell about me and with no conscious thought I sketched a pipe in my caribou's mouth and gave the beast a self-satisfied and human leer.

I had not realized that I was being closely watched. Hekwaw, who sat a little behind me, had been peering intently over my shoulder. At first he was baffled, but suddenly the full humor of a caribou that smoked a pipe struck him with the force of a physical blow, and before I knew what was happening, he had rolled off the bench, quite literally, and was in the grip of a first-class attack of hysterics.

Startled, I thought he had gone mad or had had a seizure. Both Franz and I jumped to our feet in real consternation. The little notebook fell face upward on the floor where it was pounced on by Ohoto who took one quick look and burst into wild guffaws. The book was snatched from his hand and passed around the circle of eager faces, and with the rapidity of chain lightning the laughter spread and grew wilder until it engulfed the tent in one insane pandemonium.

Very slowly it dawned on me that this was neither a war dance nor a mass attack of zaniness, but a tribute to my wit. I grinned self-consciously at those about me who were shrieking and weeping with completely uninhibited mirth. Then I rescued my book which was about to disappear out the door in the hands of a howling small child. I looked at my drawing. Oddly enough it struck me, too, as being hilariously funny, and with no regard for propriety I began to bellow with laughter at my own feeble joke. The thing was now quite out of control. Hekwaw had a choking fit and someone hauled him outside for treatment. One old crone lost her balance and fell against the tent. The taut skin burst with a great boom and she sprawled, still shrieking like a demented thing, on the sharp rocks outside.

I began to worry. Really, I knew I couldn't have been as funny as all that. But mass hysteria had seized the People, and nothing seemed capable of stopping it. Nothing, that is, except food.

Howmik appeared in the doorway, looking properly curious and bearing a big wooden tray heaped high with steaming chunks of deer meat. The steam struck the roisterers and as if by magic the rich aroma quelled their mirth. Hekwaw, still a little shaky, came back into the tent, followed by the old woman, and everyone sat down and stared expectantly at the meat tray.

FEAST
AND FAMINE

I sat down, or rather squatted down, to eat my first meal with the People. Howmik placed the great tray on the floor of the tent and we five men grouped ourselves around it. That tray was a magnificent piece of work, nearly four feet long by two feet wide with upcurved ends and sides. It had been constructed, with what must have been heartbreaking labor, from little planks hand-hewn from the tiny dwarf spruce of the southern Barrens. At least thirty small sections of wood had been meticulously fitted together and bound in place with mortised joints and pegs of deer horn. The seams had then been tightly sewn with sinew so that the whole tray was waterproof.

The tray was magnificent, but its contents were even more impressive. Half a dozen parboiled legs of deer were spread out in a thick gravy which seemed to be composed of equal parts of fat and deer hairs. Bobbing about in the debris were a dozen tongues and, like a cage holding the lesser cuts of meat, there was an entire boiled rib basket of a deer.

There were side dishes too, for Howmik made a trip to a cache outside and returned with a skin sack, full of flakes of dry meat, which she unceremoniously dumped on the cluttered floor beside me. Nor was that all, for Hekwaw's wife fetched a smoking bundle of marrowbones as her contribution to the feast. These had been neatly cracked so that we would have no trouble extracting the succulent marrow.

I was very hungry, yet the sight of this vast array of meat left me a trifle weak. But it was evident that I was the only one to suffer any qualms of stomach. The others were waiting impatiently for me, as the major guest, to make the first move. The etiquette of the situation eluded me. I took my sheath knife and cautiously sawed off a good-sized chunk of leg meat, scraped the encrustation of hairs from it, and cuddled it in my lap since there was nothing else that could serve as a plate.

Now Franz and the three Ihalmiut men tusked in — I use that word advisedly — and Ohoto seized an entire leg. Sucking the gravy from it with appreciative lips, he sank his teeth into the tough muscle while with his left hand he held the joint away from his face, and with his right hand made a quick slash at the meat with his knife. I watched in horrified fascination. The sharp blade no more than cleared the tip of his broad nose, and he made his cut without even bothering to look where it was going. But the nose survived; the mouthful of meat was severed at the joint and was chewed a time or two and quickly swallowed.

Hekwaw seemed to prefer the soup. He dipped his cupped hands in it and then sucked up the greasy fluid with gusty relish, taking time out now and again to chew at a deer's tongue which he dropped back into the soup to keep warm between bites.

It struck me that I was being a little prissy. So I put my knife back in its sheath, took a deep breath and, seizing my meat in both hands, began to gnaw away on it. It was delicious.

Then Ootek, beaming with the pride of a good host, pressed me to try a marrowbone and showed me how to tap it with a little rock so that the long, jelly-like piece of marrow dropped out intact. I know I was in no position to be an epicurean judge, and you can doubt me if you wish when I tell you that I have never tasted anything quite as good as that hot marrow. Fat, but not oily, it did not compare at all with the insipid beef marrow we know. In fact it beggars all description, and it was wonderful!

By this time I had begun to understand why the Ihalmiut parkas were so badly matted, for they were pressed into service as table napkins and as bibs. A steady stream of juice and gravy trickled from Hekwaw's massive chin and was absorbed by the fur of his *holiktuk*. Try as I might, I couldn't entirely restrain a minor stream that was quickly saturating my flannel shirt. After a while I thought, "The devil with it!" and gave up any efforts to divert the flood.

Howmik, who seemed to be constantly on the run, now reappeared lugging the great iron cooking pot I had seen outside. Only it was no longer filled with meat. The dinner having been cooked, the pot was now doing duty as a tea "billy," without benefit of an intervening washing. We supplied the tea, of course, and the canny Ihalmiut had sought out the biggest vessel they owned to brew it in. Had there been a bathtub handy the tea would have been brewed in it, for if the People have one uncontrollable vice, it is tea drinking.

That tea was blacker and solider than any I have ever seen and it was also fortified with the inevitable scum of deer hair and with odd bits of meat. But it was popular enough. Ootek, who is a rather little man, filled and drank three pint mugs of it, stopping only for a burp or two between mugfuls. Then he ate a tongue and drank three more pint mugs of tea.

Everyone else was just as thirsty and the big pot only lasted about twenty minutes before it was sent back for a refill, with the old tea leaves left in it to help strengthen the new brew.

Naturally such a tremendous fluid intake had its inevitable results and the dinner guests were constantly leaping to their feet and dashing out behind the tent — all save Hekwaw, who was too old and dignified a man to dash out on such a trivial errand. He solved the problem by making use of a large can standing near the bed. He simply reached for it when it was needed. As it grew full — and it did frequently — his elderly wife removed and emptied it.

It wasn't long before I was too full to tackle even one more marrowbone. Franz felt the same, but the other men continued their attack on the heaping mound of meat until it was all gone, to the last drop of gravy. Then while they sat back and burped with prolonged fervor, Howmik took the tray away, refilled it, and the women had their meal.

That was my first dinner with the Eskimos but not, as may have seemed inevitable, my last. Five times each day we sat down to a new meal, and in between we had light lunches. While there is food in the Ihalmiut camps, five meals a day is considered barely adequate, though on the trail a man must manage to subsist on three.

The cooking varied somewhat, but the food did not. The rule was meat at every meal, and nothing else but meat, unless you could count a few well-rotted duck eggs which served as appetizers. To satisfy my curiosity I tried to estimate the quantity of meat Hekwaw put away each day. I discovered he could handle ten to fifteen pounds when he was really hungry — though otherwise he probably subsisted on somewhat less.

This tremendous intake of protein probably explains the Eskimo thirst for tea or, if no tea is available, for water. The toxic wastes from such quantities of meat would strain the best of human kidneys, and only by drinking several gallons of fluid every day can the Ihalmiut manage to adjust to their amazing diet. Their bodies seem to have undergone some physical modifications as well, for when you see an Ihalmio naked — as a visitor sees them every night — you notice that their body thickness, back to front, looks as great as their body width, both measurements taken at the waist. This typical shape presumably results from the enlarged liver needed both to store glycogen against lean periods and to deal with the completely protein diet. It most certainly is not a sedentary "pot."

The words "food" and "deer" are practically synonymous throughout the Barrenlands, but though there is a certain monotony in the choice of food, there are many ways of preparing it. First there is the natural style, and I have eaten my meat this way and found no complaint with it, except perhaps that raw meat is singularly tasteless. If the Ihalmiut hunter shoots a deer for food when he is on a trip far from the camps, he seldom bothers to go to the trouble of building a fire. Usually his first act is to cut off the lower legs of the deer, strip away the meat, and crack the bones for marrow. Marrow is fat, and an eternal craving for fat is part of the price of living on an all-meat diet.

With the marrow disposed of, the hunter may slit the animal's throat and catch a cup of blood, for while the People do not know the use of salt, they do seem to crave it and to satisfy their craving with blood, where the saline concentration is very high.

Now having satisfied some of his specific cravings, the hungry hunter slices through the flank of the beast and carefully picks off the bits of suet clinging to the entrails. If he is still hungry — and he usually is — the hunter may also cut off part of the brisket if the animal is fat. Before leaving the carcass he takes out the tongue and sometimes the kidneys, and these he carries with him until he can find time and fuel to light a fire.

All the parts that I have so far mentioned can be eaten cooked, of course, and when it is possible they *will* be cooked, for the Ihalmiut do not eat raw meat from choice. When only an open fire is available, cooking methods are delightfully simple. The roast is simply shoved into the coals and left there until it is well charred on the outside. Pulled out and scraped, the inner core is found to be well cooked to a depth of an inch or so, and this part is eaten, then the roast is again pushed into the fire and the process repeated until the bone itself is reached and the hot marrow is ready for extraction.

When meat is cooked at camp it is usually boiled, if fuel permits, for the soup is greatly loved by everyone. Originally, and not so many years ago, the Ihalmiut used great square-cut stone pots made of a kind of soapstone. These were filled with water and chunks of meat, then hot pebbles were added to the water to bring it to a boil. It was a slow chore, and parboiling was usually chore enough, but now iron pots have been obtained in trade from the coastal Eskimos, and boiling meat is easier than it once was.

Amongst the special boiled delicacies I must mention fawn's head. Any deer head is good when boiled, but the heads of fawns are best of all. They are sometimes skinned before cooking, more often not, but the meat from them is the most delicious from the animal and the fat behind the eye is the best part of the head. Incidentally, when occasional fish are speared in summer, the boiled heads are again considered to be the choicest part.

Nearly all of the caribou is eaten, one way or another. But as you may have noticed, the steaks and roasts that we prefer don't often appear on the Ihalmiut menu. Usually the dogs get the rumps and thighs, for these parts of the caribou seem to be lacking in the specific nutriments that a meat-eating man requires. The Ihalmiut believe that only by eating all parts of the deer can they achieve a satisfactory diet. So the heart, kidneys, intestines, liver, and other organs are greatly esteemed and often eaten.

There is a third way of using deer meat, and that is by preparing *nipku*, or dried meat. The Ihalmiut make this dish because it is a variation of an otherwise monotonous diet and because it can be easily stored to tide them over times when the deer are not about. *Nipku* is made by slicing muscle tissue paper-thin, then spreading it to dry on willow bushes near the camps. It looks, and tastes, like cardboard sparsely sprinkled with icing sugar, and it is as tough as blazes, but an excellent trail food since it equals five times its weight in fresh meat. I liked *nipku*, finding it as good as most Ihalmiut dishes, though I must admit to a certain indignation when Ohoto gave me a bag of it that was already in the possession of a lively collection of fly maggots.

Undoubtedly the most important item of Ihalmiut food is fat. Amongst the coastal Eskimos the supply of fat is limited only by the number of sea mammals that are killed, and blubber, that grossly overworked Arctic word, is obtained in immense quantities from seals, walrus, narwhals, and other aquatic mammals who build thick blankets of fat as an insulation against the cold of the Arctic seas. The coastal people have so much fat and oil available that they can meet all their dietary needs and have enough left over to heat and light their igloos, and to cook upon. Well, they are lucky. The inland people of the plains must depend for fats on what they can obtain from the deer, and the caribou is no substitute for a seal as a source of oil.

In the fall of the year, just before the rutting season for the bucks and just after for the does, the deer are in their best physical condition and this is the only time of the entire year that fat can be obtained from them in any quantity. Buck deer, killed in the autumn, may carry thirty pounds of pure white suet under their hides, and though this sounds like a lot, when it is rendered down it gives a much smaller quantity. It takes a great many fat buck deer to equal one seal in the production of oils.

During the fall hunt the Ihalmiut must collect sufficient fat to meet the year's needs, but there is never enough to provide fuel, food, and heat together. As a result the winter igloos generally remain entirely unheated, and almost without artificial light during the interminable winter darkness. Yet the People manage to survive temperatures of fifty degrees below zero in their winter homes because fat *is* being burned — within their bodies. Each man is his own furnace, and as long as there are enough blocks of deer fat to last until spring, the People manage to stay alive under conditions which seem completely inimical to the maintenance of human life. Enough fat is the answer, and the sole answer, to winter survival in the Barrens.

The importance of fat as a fuel is, however, only part of the story. Even in summer, when the problem is to stay cool, fat remains absolutely essential to the well-being of the People. I had its importance demonstrated to me during one long canoe trip Franz and I took. We were short of supplies — in fact we were completely out of them except for a pound of tea, half a pound of lard, and some ammunition. So we lived by the rifle, and we lived on deer.

It was late summer then and the deer were extraordinarily thin as a result of long months of persecution by the flies, and so our diet consisted almost entirely of lean meat. For the first few days I made out very well on three meals of lean meat a day, but before the end of the week I was smitten with an illness which for want of a better name I called *mal de caribou*. It was an unpleasant illness to have during a canoe voyage. The river was fast and filled with rapids, but nevertheless I had to go ashore at frequent intervals, whether we were in "white water" or not. And I had to expose myself so often to the insatiable flies that it became painful for me to sit down.

But persistent diarrhea was only a part of the effect of *mal de caribou*. I was filled with a sick lassitude, an increasing loss of will to work that made me quite useless in the canoe. I began to get really worried. Memories of dysentery in Sicily came uneasily to mind and the thought that the nearest medical aid was three hundred miles away did not bring me much comfort.

Then Franz turned physician. One evening he took our half-pound of precious lard, melted it in a frying pan, and, when it was lukewarm and not yet congealed, he ordered me to drink it.

Strangely, I was greedy for it, though the thought of tepid lard nauseates me now. I drank a lot of it, then went to bed; and by morning I was completely recovered. This sounds like a shock cure, but in fact I was suffering from a deficiency of fat and did not realize it.

OF HOUSES
AND TONGUES

◆

After his first Arctic summer, Mowat returned to the Barrenlands in 1948 for a second visit, this time accompanied by a friend from the pre-war years.

◆

We arrived much earlier in the season than on my first visit, and winter had not yet begun to show signs of releasing the land to spring. After the plane had left us, Andy and I began to make our way over the ice to the shanty, and it was so cold the frost from my breath prevented me from seeing that this time we were to be met and welcomed at Windy Cabin. Andy caught my arm suddenly and pointed to the snow-shrouded shore, and I saw the dark shape of a man running swiftly toward us.

We waited, and on the glare ice of the bay, with the wind moaning its dirge from the Ghost Hills, we were confronted by the man Ootek. He stood before us and on his gaunt face a smile spread and grew until it could not contain the wild laughter, born of relief, that sprang from his throat. It was indeed a most happy meeting for Ootek. When the three of us had reached the cabin and burrowed through the drifts to its dubious shelter, Ootek explained with signs and gestures that he had come from the Little Hills in the forlorn belief that white men might have returned to Windy Bay. Starvation had driven him to this place, though he knew it was deserted and had been so for much of the winter. A hope, kept alive by old memories, brought him south, and it did not die even when he saw the unmarked snow in front of the cabin. Stubbornly he stayed on for two days without food, and with only the blind hope that help might come from the skies to sustain him. On the third day he had begun his dark journey homeward when he heard the miraculous roar of *Konetaiv* — the wings of the white men.

Ootek remained with us only long enough for a meal and to receive some ammunition for his rifle. The forerunners of the deer herds were already in the plains and so, now with shells for his gun, the spring famine was at an end for Ootek. Yet had we not come, or had we come a month later, the evil spring when Kunee and Anoteelik were orphaned would have been repeated. It appeared that the recognition so tardily extended to the Ihalmiut by the government had been only temporary, and had been withdrawn again.

During the next month Andy and I spent most of our time near Windy Bay studying the returning herds of the deer. We were not lonely, since only four days after Ootek left us he returned accompanied by all the men of the Ihalmiut. Those were cheerful and pleasant days, for the Innuit were as delighted to welcome us as if we had been benevolent Gods. Ootek and his fellows could not do enough to show their joy at our arrival. When there was wood or water to get, the Ihalmiut jumped at the opportunity to serve us. They made special hunting trips over the hills to find for us the few rare deer that were fat, and to bring us deer tongues. At night they crowded into the cabin and stayed until we were so exhausted we had politely to pack them off to bed. Hekwaw and Owliktuk had arrived with white fox pelts, and these they gave to us as tokens of friendship, accepting our return gifts with deep gratitude.

Unfortunately all this popularity had its drawbacks. Andy and I were not traders and we had brought with us only sufficient supplies for our own needs. By the time we had also met the urgent needs of the Ihalmiut we were running short of many things including the most precious item of all, ammunition for our .30-30 rifles. We had to become parsimonious with our gifts, and this seemed inexplicable to the Ihalmiut, who were willing and anxious to give us anything and everything they possessed. They believed, not without reason, that white men could call on unlimited sources of supply. I made strenuous efforts to explain that we were not traders and were in effect only poor men endowed with nothing of greater value than big curiosities. But it didn't go over.

The barrier of language which had bothered me the preceding year now seemed even more formidable and frustrating, for it was impossible to convey our explanations in sign language alone. I missed Franz, though his interpreting had always been sketchy and he had never been very willing to act as my tongue with the People. Yet without him I found myself in a growing web of confusion, and it was clear that, as things stood, I could never hope to delve into the memories and minds of the Ihalmiut. Unless I could learn the Ihalmiut tongue I would leave the Barrens in as great ignorance of its People as when I came. But I had been led to believe by "old Northern hands" that learning an Eskimo language entailed many years of hard labor, and I was loath to begin a task that could not come to anything in time to be of service to me. So for a month Andy and I blundered about like deaf men whose eyes could not tell us the things our ears needed to know. Then one day, in complete exasperation at some impasse that had arisen between Ootek and myself, I took the bull by the horns and made it clear to the man that I was damn well going to learn the language of his People.

I don't know quite what I expected his reaction to be. Disinterest, perhaps, or reluctance. Or even worse, the attitude of one who is presented with an infantile demand and who treats it carelessly and without thought.

But I got none of these responses from the Ihalmiut. The unadorned fact that I, a white man and a stranger, should voluntarily wish to step across the barriers of blood that lay between us, and ask the People to teach me their tongue, instead of expecting them to learn mine — this was the key to their hearts. When they saw that I was anxious to exert myself in trying to understand their way of life, their response was instant, enthusiastic, and almost overwhelming. Both Ootek and Ohoto, who was called in to assist in the task, abruptly ceased to treat me with the usual deference they extend to white strangers. They devoted themselves to the problem I had set them with the strength of fanatics. To begin with, Ootek taught me the meaning of the word *Ihalmiut*. When I had mastered its meaning by the aid of devious drawings executed in sand, Ootek stood Ohoto in one place, then placed me a few feet away to the south. Now he pointed to Ohoto, and repeated "Ihalmiut" over and over again with a remarkable excess of emotion in his voice as he spoke. At last he came over, took me by the arm, and led me to the side of Ohoto. Both men now beamed at me with the anxious expressions of people who hope their acts have been understood, and fortunately I did not disappoint them. I understood. I was no longer a stranger; I was now a man of the Ihalmiut, of the People who dwell under the slopes of the Little Hills.

It was an initiation so informal, so lacking in the dramatic gestures, that for a little while its deep significance was not clear to me. It was some time before I discovered that this simple ceremony of Ootek and Ohoto had not only made me an adopted man of the land, but had also given me a relationship with both men. I became their song-cousin, a difficult relationship to define, but one that is only extended on the most complete and comprehensive basis of friendship. If I wished, I might have shared all things that Ootek and Ohoto possessed, even to their wives, though this honor was not thrust upon me. As a song-cousin I was a counterpart of each man who had adopted me. I was his reflected image, yet cloaked in the full flesh of reality.

Of course, under the law, it was assumed that I would reciprocate to the fullest, and had I been born an Ihalmio I would have given that reciprocity without any thought. Yet as a white man I unconsciously refused it to both Ohoto and Ootek times without number, but never did they feel the need to retaliate by withdrawing any of the privileges of the relationship they had so freely extended to me.

As a man of the People it now became a matter of urgent need that I should learn the language. Ootek and Ohoto put their heads together and for the space of two days they discussed the problem from all angles. At last I grew impatient and seized the initiative by asking the names of objects about me, and by acting out verbs. This, though I did not know it, was what they had planned, though they preferred to let me believe I was setting the pace. One or the other and usually both of my two mentors would attend my efforts with such serious concentration that sometimes we all tried too hard, and finished up the pursuit of a simple word by becoming so completely confused that nothing short of an outburst of laughter could destroy the impasse. Nevertheless I learned quickly, so quickly that I thought the tales I had heard of the difficulties of the Eskimo language were, like so many popular misconceptions about the Innuit, absolute nonsense.

In a month's time I was able to make myself understood and I could understand most of what was said to me. I became pretty cocky, and started to consider myself something of a linguist. It was not until nearly a year had gone by that I discovered the true reason for my quick progress.

The secret lay, of course, with Ootek and Ohoto, who, with the cooperation of the rest of the People, had devised a special method of teaching me a language that is, in reality, a most difficult one. They had approached the problem with great acumen, first reasoning that a white man probably possesses a rather inferior brain which cannot be expected to cope with the full-blown intricacies of the language. They made a plan and, apparently letting me lead the way, they actually led me by a shortcut invented solely for my personal use.

When I asked the name of an object, they would give me a straightforward answer not burdened with detailed explanations. Deer, for instance, was simply *Tuktu*, an easy word to remember and one I could include in fairly complex sentences without much trouble. But I did not know that, properly, it has an exceedingly limited usage. It means only deer as an entity, in the largest sense. For specific reference to a deer, as to a two-year-old buck, there is one special word which accurately defines it. Thus it happens that there are dozens of words in the tongue of the Ihalmiut which mean "deer" in some specialized sense. Ootek wisely refrained from overloading my inadequate memory with such a superabundance of shades of one meaning, and he not only allowed me to use the one generic term in all possible cases where I needed to speak of the deer, but the People, in their turn, refrained from using any of the other specific words in their conversations with me.

It was the same with most nouns. The People taught me a root word, shorn of the multitudinous suffixes and prefixes which give their language a flexibility and a delicate shading of meaning that is probably unsurpassed by any tongue spoken today. In effect, they developed a specialized "basic" Eskimo entirely for my use, and they themselves learned to use it, not only when talking to me, but when talking to each other within my hearing. The development of a pidgin tongue is not new, of course. But with most races these bastard languages come into being over many decades of gradual growth, and no conscious effort is involved. But the Ihalmiut deliberately set out to develop such a tongue. It was planned, carefully taught, and spoken solely for the benefit of one man, and he a stranger to the land.

So I learned an Innuit vocabulary, and I was tirelessly drilled by Ohoto and Ootek until I mastered all the subtle sounds of their words. I found I was able to speak about quite abstract subjects, and incidentally give the lie to those who say that these "natives" are unable to think, or express themselves, in abstract terms. I was pretty proud of my prowess, until the truth came out.

A year after I became an Ihalmio, I had an opportunity to talk with a coastal Eskimo near Churchill. Nonchalantly and with perfect confidence I addressed a long-winded remark to him for the primary purpose of impressing some white friends who were present. And the blank stupefaction that swirled over the Eskimo's face was reflected in mine as it dawned on me that he hadn't the faintest idea of what I was saying. It was not just that the words were strange (many of the Ihalmiut words are not known at the coast) but simply that the construction and idiom

119

I used with such perfect assurance were incomprehensible to him.

It was a sad disillusionment, but it shed a revealing light on the character of the Ihalmiut. I wonder what other men in this world would have gone to the trouble of devising what amounted to a new language, simply for the convenience of a stranger who happened into their midst. I know of none.

In time I was gradually weaned away from the special jargon to a more exact knowledge of the language. But I must frankly admit that I never came to speak the real tongue of the People. Despite this, I did come to know the Ihalmiut, their life, some of their folk tales, and some of their history, and I believe I came to know these things with truth. That was my gift from the Ihalmiut — the most precious thing they could have given, for it was made under no compulsion other than the sympathy of men for another.

OHOTO

During our days at Angkuni Lake, and while we were travelling north and west on the Kuwee, Ohoto had been an incomplete man. He had been under the shadow of a great apprehension, greater than the depression we two white men felt at the sight of the empty tent circles and the scattered rock graves. That we had seen no deer and had found only their old tracks meant more to Ohoto than a temporary absence of the beasts from this land. He felt that he had been transported into a sort of Ihalmiut hell, a hell of the worst possible kind where there were no deer and never would be any deer.

The hell and the heaven of the Ihalmiut are real places that co-exist in this world. Thus "heaven" might be likened to the land where the deer may always be found whenever man has need of them. An actual glimpse of this paradise is vouchsafed to the People in the days when the great herds pass through their country. So "hell" is the place that knows nothing of the deer, and it too is present in reality during those times when there are no deer on the plains.

Inevitably Ohoto confused the nebulous concept of the Ihalmiut hell with the unreality of the Angkuni country. The impact of this lifeless land was therefore much greater on him than it was on us — and *we* felt it strongly enough. We shared his sensation of existing as disembodied nonentities. We felt, at times, as if all reality were escaping from us. We two white men were irritatingly aware of moving through an imponderable void which became more and more oppressive.

All this, I think, helps to explain two shocking things which happened to Ohoto during our voyage of exploration into the north and the west.

During our trip up the Kuwee, Ohoto developed an abscess on his cheek. With each passing day it grew deeper and angrier, but he was so engrossed in the gloom of his own thoughts that he seldom complained about it. I dressed it a few times, and after the fourth day it had become so ugly that we took a chance and lanced it. But still it persisted. At first I thought the presence of the sore was probably due to a nutritional upset, since Ohoto had never before gone without meat or existed on the devitalized foods of white men for so long a time.

By the time we reached the headwaters of Kuwee, the abscess had grown so deep and so large that Andy and I became seriously disturbed about it, and even the stoical Eskimo began to show signs of physical reaction to it. His appetite began to fail, and this is the most serious symptom an Innuit can betray, for food means more to him than almost anything else.

We made a good camp not far from the place where Kuwee left the unknown lake, and here we decided to stay until the sore began to show some signs of healing. Ohoto accepted our gesture with evident disinterest. He set up his little travel shelter, crawled into it, and showed no further signs of life until darkness had come. We were all tired with the long fatigue which comes from hard travel on empty stomachs, and I fell asleep as soon as I had crawled under my fly net.

About midnight I was awakened by blood-chilling screams. They were inhuman sounds, far beyond the power of mere pain to induce, for they carried an overtone of such abject terror that

I broke into a sweat without any knowledge of what had induced those fearful cries.

I lay there for a moment, but the shrieks were so penetrating they could not be ignored. Andy was sitting up in his bedroll, and he called out to me.

"Good God! What the hell is that?"

"Ohoto, I think," I replied. Then, without bothering to put on any clothes, I crawled stark-naked from under my net, grabbed a rifle, and ran out over the broken rocks toward the tiny shelter where Ohoto lay.

The screams ceased before I got there. Instead my ears were assailed by a gurgling whimper, as if the man's voice had been overcome by sheer terror, leaving him with only an animal echo of sounds. I flung open the door flap of his tent with such vehemence that I ripped it and part of the wall clean off the poles. Ohoto was crouched inside, his body nearly filling the tiny space of the shelter, and he was staring at one of the slim poles with eyes as empty of all expression as those of a dead ox. His lips hung slack and his great white teeth shone eerily in the light of the stars.

I shouted his name, but the cringing thing on the rug paid no heed to me. Whimpers of fear still bubbled out of his throat. I became conscious of a feeling of panic, for *I* could see no sign of a danger capable of instilling such a fear in a man. For a moment I thought Ohoto had gone mad, and was perhaps in the grip of the dread Arctic hysteria which makes insane murderers out of sane men. The potentialities of being stranded in this empty wilderness with a mad Eskimo came unpleasantly to my mind.

I acted by instinct. Dropping the rifle, I grabbed Ohoto by the hair and shook him so violently that he fell over and crashed into the frail wall of his tent. Then to my relief he made a tremendous effort, straightened up so that he was resting on his knees, and pointed a shaking hand at the blank stretch of canvas behind one of the poles of his shelter.

The gesture was a mute appeal to me, and his eyes were fixed on my face. But where he pointed I could see nothing at all except the discolored canvas and the smooth peeled surface of the sapling pole.

I still had no idea what was causing his terror. Finally, and with no coherent reason, I picked up the rifle and swung the butt as hard as I could against the slender tent pole. It was, for me, only a release of tension, but by the luck of fools and of white men I unwittingly had done the right thing.

Ohoto relaxed with the abruptness of a deflating balloon. His eyes closed and his erratic breathing sank to a long, deep rustle. He curled up like a dog, and in a moment the anticlimax of the night's work was on me. Ohoto began to snore loudly!

He snored and snored. I became aware of the multitudes of mosquitoes clinging to my naked flesh and went hurriedly back to my bed and gave a garbled account of what I had seen to my anxious companion. Then for hours I lay, and could not sleep, while the echo of Ohoto's snores sounded like a mocking denial of what had happened.

But it *had* happened, and it was no nightmare of the sleep-drugged mind but a nightmare in reality. When dawn came we got dressed and went to see Ohoto. He was sleeping gently and I nudged him with my foot until he woke, dazed by the depths of his slumber. This was itself odd, for during the previous week he had not slept except in brief naps, for the pain in his face had banished sleep.

He lay still for a moment, then his eyes widened again and stared as they had stared at me during the night. His mouth drew back in a grimace and I thought, "Oh, Lord! Here we go again!" But he only rolled over so that he could see the tent pole against which I had driven my rifle butt. Then he spoke.

"The Ino!" he cried. "Now it is gone!"

He got up then, scrambling out of the wreck of his tent, and as he turned sideways to us, we both saw with a distinct shock that his abscess was almost healed! What had been a draining wound the night before was now dry and scabbed with the healthy look of growing skin. Ohoto carefully touched the hole in his cheek and, for the first time in many days, he smiled.

"Look!" he said, turning to us. "Now that the Ino is gone the pain has left this thing in my face! Soon this will heal and I will forget it as I have already forgotten the pain!"

It seemed to be a time for explanations. I asked my questions and Ohoto readily answered them, for it appeared that he owed

me a debt of gratitude. I listened to what he told us and I was
in two minds about it. Under the bright morning sun, it sounded
like so much supernatural gibberish, yet I could not deny the
evidence of my eyes as they dwelt on that inexplicably dried up
sore. I listened and could not tell what was real and what was
sheer fantasy.

The abscess had been the work of a devil — that was the first
thing. This visit of a malignant Ino — and Ohoto was specific
about him, telling us that it was the spirit of a man who had not
been buried, and whose body had been eaten by wolves — had
brought on the running sore as the first step in the destruction of
Ohoto. But the devil chose to dally, and it was not until the
night before that it decided to finish its job. It came with darkness. When Ohoto looked up from his pain-ridden sleep, he saw
it clinging to the pole of the tent, grinning evilly down upon
him.

Ohoto thanked me profusely for my intervention. According
to him, it was my haphazard swing of the rifle, coupled with
some blasphemy I had not realized I was uttering, that convinced
the Ino I was more than a match for it. It fled. The pain in
Ohoto's face vanished on the instant, and by morning the abscess
was well on the way to being cured.

In the time when the deer were hurrying south to the forests
to evade the impending onslaught of winter, we too made our
farewells to the Barrens. The nights had already grown long,
the days had grown brief, and the season of *Kaila*'s wrath was
upon us. We saw little of sunlight or starlight. The grey cloud
scud raced in from the east and the roof of the world was so
close above us that we could stand on the full moss of the ridges
and feel the chill wraiths of the driven mists in our faces. The
land was dying, and it was time for us to return to our own
world.

Our canoe, old now with the weight of her journey, lay with
her scrofulous sides on the shore. Beside her was the meager pile
of supplies which must see us out of the land. It was raining. A
fine penetrating haze as cold and dismal as the grey sweat on
the face of a corpse hung over us.

Ohoto and Ootek came to help us stow our sparse dunnage against the rough, splintered ribs of the canoe.

Ohoto was smoking his little stone pipe, a tiny and shapely object of semi-translucent stone, neatly and artistically bound with the brass from an old cartridge case. I said good-by to him in the white man's way, and after we had shaken hands he took the pipe from his mouth and, without speaking, handed it to me. It was a trivial gift in farewell. And yet — how trivial was it? I knew how that pipe had come down from a century that is gone, for it was the pipe of Elaitutna, Ohoto's father. It had seen more of the land and more of the things in the land than any man living had seen or would see. It was to have gone with Ohoto into his grave, to remain with him as a familiar thing in the eternity he sought at the end of his days. Now it would go with me, instead, out of the land, to lie warm and smoldering in the palm of my hand as I remembered the things I needed to say if the voices of the Ihalmiut were to be heard in the world of the Kablunait.

I think Ootek, my song-cousin, was crying a little, but perhaps it was only the film of moisture which lay over all our faces as the cold east wind drove the spume low over the hills. Why, after all, should he cry? The white men were leaving the land, leaving it to the People. And we would not return, for in the time that can be measured in a handful of years nothing would remain to draw us back to the great plains.

The current gripped our canoe and as we passed down to the mouth of the river, I looked back. But I saw nothing worth remembering in that last glance. Thick mists obscured the Ghost Hills and the dark crest of the cabin by the shore. So I turned and looked forward as the old canoe made her way down the long arm of the bay and to the open waters of mighty Nueltin.

For nearly a week we coasted the shores of Nueltin, until we came to a maze of bleak little islands crowding the northernmost bay of the lake. Here, after much searching, we found the contorted passage which leads to the bay of Thlewiaza — the Great Fish River — which flows to the sea. Once on that river we were too busy to think again of the land of the Little Hills. The canoe leapt, shied, and started like a frightened beast as she took the first rapid. We shot out at its foot and then paused to still our frightened hearts before we went on down this river that has been run by no more than three or four white men in all time. After the briefest of respites, the rapids roared at us again.

Thlewiaza is the only river running from the land of the People to the seacoast in the East. It barely tolerates men who try to descend it, and any man who tried to ascend it into the heart of the land would be brutally rebuffed. The river does not flow, but debouches insanely over a landscape which resembles a titanic slag heap spewed out by some tremendous subterranean smelter. It is a world which looks as hell might, if hell's fires were quenched. The river roars angrily over this chaos and spills its fury almost at will over the land, spreading out to envelop as much of the broken debris as it can reach.

In five days we covered a hundred miles. We had soon given up any attempt to count the rapids. They were often continuous for many miles at a stretch, and the interludes of calm water were so rare, and therefore so startling, that they impressed us more than the rapids would have done on any other river.

Although the season was too advanced for men in a canoe, we had no choice but to travel, whether through rain or into the hatred of sleet. At first we feared our slim load of food would not be enough, but soon we were thankful that we carried no more weight with us. Many times we were saved from destruction in the shallow violence of the rapids only because the canoe was so light that she could meet the hungry caress of the rocks without feeling their teeth.

I remember only two things out of that ordeal not connected with the hazardous confusion of rocks and boiling masses of water. The first of these is the memory of two great caribou bucks standing on the summit of a hill and facing each other defiantly with the silent challenge of the rut in their tense attitude. I saw them for only an instant before the ever-present storm scud whipped over our heads and blotted out the images of the two magnificent beasts.

The second thing I remember was a cairn of rocks on the shore which we mistook for a stone man. During our first five days on the river we had seen no sign that men had ever come down this torrent. When we saw the Inukok we fought our way free of the current and landed to inspect it more closely. It was no stone man, but only a little heap of flat stones piled over the grave of a child. Wolves or foxes had nosed aside some of the rocks and the white bones were scattered about in the gravel.

Only those two memories remain. The rest is a nightmare confusion of black, curling waves; of white, driven spray, and the half-seen glimpses of evil, dark rocks under the keel of the canoe.

Thlewiaza brought us out of the Barrens, but it did so with savagery and with the clear warning that it would tolerate no attempt at a return.

Late in September the canoe, shrunken now by the ponderous swells of Hudson Bay, began feeling the sting of salt spray in her wounds. It was almost the end. There remained a day and a night when we fought with an offshore gale and a blinding snow blizzard and, for a while, held on to the canoe, and to our lives, only because we found a reef and were able to stand waist-deep in the frigid green waters for the long hours until the tide changed and the wind dropped.

We turned north and at last found refuge behind the long yellow dunes of Eskimo Point. Our night on the reef had made it obvious that we could not hope to navigate a hundred-odd miles south to Churchill in our crippled canoe. After a week at Eskimo Point we were picked up by a wandering Royal Canadian Air Force plane, and then for the last time I looked down on the immutable face of the Barrens and watched it recede from me, carrying with it the People I had known in its depths.

FROM
The Desperate People

THE ORDEALS
OF KIKIK

◆

A decade after his first visits to the people of the deer, Mowat returned to learn what had happened to his Eskimo friends. "The Ordeals of Kikik" tells of the fate of Halo, Ootek, Owliktuk, Howmik, and others.

◆

On the morning of April 19, 1958, the Territorial Court of the Northwest Territories convened in the beer-parlor-cum-recreation-hall of the North Rankin Nickel Mine which squats upon the western shore of Hudson Bay a hundred and fifty miles north of Eskimo Point. Ceremoniously the judge took his place behind a deal table while on his right six jurors shifted their bottoms uncomfortably upon a wooden bench. In front of the judge (and awkwardly aware of the needs of propriety), an audience consisting mainly of off-shift miners' wives tried not to drown out the proceedings in the clatter of folding chairs. Outside the doubly insulated building a Husky nuzzled at a garbage can as the sun beat down upon the white immobility of a frozen world.

The prisoner sat at the right hand of the judge. She smiled steadily at the assembled court, but in her eyes there was the blankness of total bewilderment, of such an absence of comprehension that she might have been no more than a wax mannequin. Yet perhaps, since there was the flush of life under the brown shadows of her skin, she more nearly resembled a denizen of some other world who had become inexplicably trapped in ours. It is not too far-fetched a simile, for this woman had indeed been plucked out of another time and space in order that she might be brought to this alien place to answer to the charges laid against her.

Those to whom she would have to answer had also come great distances in space. The judge and the crown attorney had flown eastward from Yellowknife, some 700 miles away. Another plane had brought a learned doctor, together with the young attorney for the defense, from Winnipeg, which lay 900 miles to the southward. From Ottawa, more than 1400 miles distant, representatives of the Department of Northern Affairs had come to serve as friends to the accused. Through many days, aircraft had been converging from across half a continent upon the transient cluster of drab buildings which huddled under the gaunt headframe of this Arctic mine. Between them they had spanned vast distances; yet none had come a fraction of the distance that this woman had traversed in order that she might stand before this court and listen while a white man spoke incomprehensible words to her.

"You, Kikik, of Henik Lake, stand charged before his Lordship in that you, Kikik, No. E 1-472, did murder Ootek. . . . How say you to this charge?"

During the long night of February 7, the great wind from off the congealed white desert of the Arctic sea came seeking south across five hundred miles of tundra plains, to strip the unresisting snows from the black cliffs at Henik Lake and to send the snowdevils dancing like dervishes across the ice. The driven snow scoured the darkness like a blast of sand until no living thing could face it. Nothing ran, nor crawled, nor flew over the broken ridges, the frozen muskegs, and the faceless, hidden lakes.

Yet there was life unseen beneath the wind. On the shores of a narrow bay in North Henik Lake two snow houses crouched against the implacable violence of the gale and, within their dark confines, people listened to the wind's voice. Its muted roar changed pitch as the night hours advanced, until before the dawn it had become a high-throated wail that sank into the mind like needles into naked flesh.

In the smaller of the two houses — it was in reality no more than a snow-block barricade roofed with a piece of canvas — there were four people. One of these, the year-old boy Igyaka, lay rigidly inert, and did not hear the wind. His small body was shrunken into a macabre travesty of human form by the long hunger which, two days earlier, had given him over to the frost to kill.

Beside him on the sleeping ledge of hard-packed snow his two sisters lay. There was Kalak who had been born deaf and dumb out of a starvation winter ten years earlier, and there was little Kooyak who was seven years of age. They lay in each other's arms under the single remaining deerskin robe — and they were naked except for cotton shifts grown black and ragged through the months. There were no more robes to lay across their bloated bellies and their pipestem limbs, and none to hide the frozen horror of the boy who lay beside them — for the other robes which the family had possessed when winter came had long ago been eaten, as had the children's clothes; for all of these had of necessity been sacrificed to hunger.

Oddly contorted from the paralysis which had stricken her in 1949, the mother of the children crouched over a handful of white ashes by the sleeping ledge. These ashes had been cold through the three days of the blizzard, for the willow twigs which were the only fuel available had long since passed in evanescent flame. Howmik crouched motionless; and in that meager shelter the darkness was so absolute that she could not see her husband, Ootek, who lay against the farther wall and stared with wide open eyes that saw through darkness, and which could see death as vividly before him as other men might see the sun.

In the second of the two shelters, a hundred yards away, were Kikik, her husband Halo, and their five children. Hunger had laid its mark upon all of these, but death had as yet been unable to take any of them; its long assault upon this family had not yet overmastered the indomitable resistance of a man who could not comprehend defeat. Through all his years Halo had never known defeat, nor had he even recognized its shadow, for always he had looked no farther than the hour in which he lived. He had not looked back into the dark days of the past, nor yet had he stared forward into the obscurity of the future which awaited him and all his race. He had been free to live within the confines of the moment — to live with a kind of frenzied vigor which made each day give life to him and his. And he owed this special freedom to his song-cousin and lifelong companion Ootek, who had been the visionary and the unraveller of timeless questions for the two of them.

They complemented each other so completely, these two, that they were almost a single man. Slightly built, and with no great reserves of physical stamina, Ootek had never been more than a mediocre hunter, relying often enough on Halo's help to keep his family fed. Yet Halo had always relied upon Ootek to shoulder and resolve those nebulous problems of the mind and spirit which have confronted man since he *was* man. In a true sense they were the two archetypes of Man: the one, who sought to limit and assuage the hostility of fate with his mind's weapons — the other, with the weapons of his hands.

These two families were the people whom the wind had found, and they were almost alone in the wind's world on that February day; alone in a particular hell that had not been of their contriving, but which had been contrived for them by men of good intentions. They were almost alone, because eight of the nine other Ihalmiut families had seen their doom approaching and had made desperate efforts to escape it by attempting to trek, on foot, to Padlei Post.

Owliktuk, he who had tried to stand against acceptance of the soul-destroying dependence on the whites for so many years, had been amongst the first to flee the Henik country and to beg for food at Padlei. With his defection, there was no strength left in the People, and the rest began to follow after. Not all of them survived that savage journey to the sanctuary which they sought.

Onekwaw and his wife Tabluk, with the orphaned boy Angataiuk, made their attempt to escape inevitable death during the last week in January. As with the rest of the Ihalmiut, they had almost no caribou skin clothes, and were dressed largely in castoff cloth garments given them by the white men. They might almost as well have gone naked into the white winds. The boy survived five foodless, fireless days and nights; but on the last day of the passage of the ice of Henik Lake, he died.

Onekwaw only lived a few days longer. He died a mile or two

beyond the lake, and many measureless miles from Padlei Post. Thus, of that little group of doomed and driven people, only Tabluk survived; and she did so only because she was discovered by a Padliermio hunter with a dog team, who brought her safely to the post.

Ootnuyuk and her two children had left Henik early in December, for she knew the land, and knew what winter portended there. When she reached Padlei she reported that the young man Kaiyai lay helpless in his snow house. He had frozen his leg, she said, and it had thawed and then been frozen a second time, and thawed again so that now it had swelled like a great dead fish in summertime, and stank like one.

The post manager radioed Eskimo Point and asked that the police plane fly a rescue mission to Henik Lake at once to bring Kaiyai to hospital — for he had recognized the description of gangrene. But the short days and the long nights passed, and the plane did not come, and Kaiyai could wait no longer. His wife Alekashaw placed him on a small hand-sled, and with her two baby sons upon her back, she set out to haul her husband to the post. She had fifty miles to go. She hauled that sled for eight days — and then there was no need to haul it any farther, for Kaiyai was dead. Alekashaw with her two children eventually reached Padlei — but her feet were frozen marble white and hard, and she spent many months in hospital.

This was the pattern of that winter flight. By the time the belated dawn was staining the storm with the opaqueness of a blind man's eye on February 8, the flight was almost over. Yaha's family was still en route, and only Halo and Ootek and their families remained in the promised land to which they had been led by the white men.

For these families, too, the time had come when they must flee, or meet a certain death within their wind-swept camps.

Ootek was aware of this, but he was also aware of a harder truth — it was too late for him to go. He and his family had stayed too long. Having now eaten most of the skin clothing and robes with which they had begun the winter, they could no longer escape from the snow-shelter which had become Igyaka's coffin. Ootek knew this beyond any doubt, and yet in the morning he spoke to Howmik saying:

"I shall go to the trading place; and in a little time I will return with food for all."*

Howmik looked slowly up into her husband's face but she made no reply. She knew that he could not reach the post alive. But Kooyak, who knew only that she was bitter cold and that her bowels were twisted in agony by the glut of caribou hair and crushed bones which filled them, moaned — and cried aloud.

That cry must have been an intolerable reproach, and Ootek, who had never before raised his hand against any man, least of all against a child, stumbled toward the sleeping ledge, his smooth and gentle face contorted into a sudden savagery. He raised his hand so that it hung trembling over the girl. "I *shall* bring food!" he cried — and struck his daughter on her shrunken lips. . . .

Indeed it was too late for Ootek, but it was not yet too late for Halo and his family to flee, for they still had the means. As Halo took his ice-chisel and fought his way against the gale toward the lake, there to chip laboriously through two feet of new-made ice which covered his fishing hole, he knew that the time had come when he must try to reach Padlei. He thought about the implications of his decision as he squatted, back to the whining wind, keeping his jigging line in motion. Two hours later he caught a small fish. He took it back to the snow house and the family shared it — and when they had finished they were starving still.

Meanwhile, Ootek had crept out of his own place and had turned to face the north. His eyes were blind as he took half a dozen faltering steps toward the goal that he would never reach. The gale scourged him until he staggered and fell to his knees — and he sobbed deep within his emaciated chest, and turned away defeated and went stumbling across that lesser distance to the house of his companion and his friend. He came into Halo's house and crouched exhausted and blank-eyed against the inner wall.

So they sat, these two who had been closer than brothers. Halo

*The events and conversations in this chapter are taken from the detailed police interrogations, the transcripts of the trial, and from independent interrogations of survivors.

offered Ootek the tail of the fish, and Ootek wolfed it. When it was gone he asked for the few remaining bones of the fish to take home to his family, and these were given to him; but still he sat against the wall and waited. Perhaps he sensed what Halo would say even before the words were framed. Yet it was a long time before Halo could bring himself to speak.

"There is nothing left in this place," Halo said at last. "And so, when the storm weakens, I must take my family and go somewhere. There are few fish in this lake. If we stay we will all be as Igyaka is."

Thus it was done. With those few words Halo dissolved the bonds which had held these two men through the many years. He cut them ruthlessly, for he had no other choice. But he did not look again at Ootek as he picked up his line and went out once again to take up his vigil at the fishing hole.

Ootek made no protest even though sentence of death had been passed on him and on his family. He knew that he no longer had the strength to travel, nor to endure at the fishing hole, nor even to scrabble under the snows for willow twigs. He knew all this, yet he did not protest. He sat silently for a long time watching Kikik, who was his half-sister for, though these two had been born of different fathers, their common mother had been Epeetna who had starved to death in the spring of 1947.

At last Ootek rose, smiled strangely at his sister, and said quietly, "Now I will go to Padlei. Only first I will shoot some ptarmigan with Halo's rifle so my children can eat when I am gone." So saying he picked up Halo's .30-30 and left the igloo.

He had not far to go — and he had sufficient strength to carry him on that final journey. Perhaps he no longer even felt the cold, or knew the agony within him. He went before the storm, directly driven toward the one thing in all the world which could sustain him.

Unseen, unheard, shrouded by the snow and wind, he did not pause until he stood a single pace behind the crouching figure of his other self. Perhaps he stood there for an eternity, knowing what he would do, yet hesitating until the wind, blowing through the torn cloth parka, warned him that he must finish quickly. For indeed this *was* the finish — not only of the broken life that Ootek had led through the long years but, so he believed, the finish of the interminable struggles of the people who called themselves Ihalmiut.

When such an ending comes, it is not good to go alone. Ootek intended that the few survivors by the shores of Henik Lake should be together at the end — and so he raised the rifle and, without passion, blew in the back of Halo's head.

The wind swallowed the thunder of the shot as the sea swallows a stone. Soundless still, Ootek climbed the slope to Halo's house. He leaned the rifle in the snow outside the tunnel and crawled inside.

He came as nemesis — but he was a weak and tragic emissary of the fates for he was so chilled that he could not even raise his arms until Kikik used some of her few remaining twigs to brew him a cup of tepid water. The warmth revived a little of the purpose in his sad design and he attempted to persuade the children to leave the igloo on some absurd pretext. When they would not go, and when he began to be aware that his sister was disturbed by his strange behavior, he could think of nothing else to do but turn and leave the place himself. He was so easily defeated; as he had been defeated all his life by the necessity of doing. He was the dreamer, and the doer no longer lived; and Ootek was no longer whole.

Standing irresolute, and hopelessly confused, in the arms of the storm again, he picked up the rifle and aimlessly began to brush the snow away from the metal parts. He was still there a quarter of an hour later when Kikik emerged from the igloo tunnel.

Kikik had become seriously uneasy. Not only was she surprised that Ootek had borrowed Halo's rifle and had not brought it back, but she was perturbed by his odd actions. Yet when she scrambled to her feet and looked into Ootek's eyes, she lost all other emotions in a surge of fear.

"Give me the rifle," she said quickly.

Ootek made no answer, and his hand continued to stray over the steel, brushing away the snow. Kikik stepped forward sharply and grasped the gun, but Ootek would not release it and so brother and sister began to struggle with one another in the whirling center of the storm. Kikik slipped and stumbled and when she recovered herself it was to see Ootek slowly bringing the rifle to his shoulder. But his movements were painfully slow and she had time to step in and push the muzzle to one side so that the bullet rushed harmlessly away into the wind.

Now the woman, better fed and stronger, and driven by a fierce anxiety for her five children, easily overpowered the man. He fell, exhausted, and she fell on him and her slight weight was sufficient to pin him, helpless, in the snow. Ootek struggled faintly as Kikik shouted to her eldest daughter, Ailouak, telling the child to fetch Halo from the jigging hole.

Ailouak came from the igloo, glanced in terror at the struggling pair, and then went racing toward the lake. She was not gone long. Sobbing wildly she emerged from the enveloping ground drift. "My father cannot come, for he is dead!" she cried.

What followed has the quality of nightmare. Sprawling astride the feebly resisting body of her husband's killer, who was her own half-brother, Kikik began to question him with the quiet and detached voice of someone speaking in an empty room. There was no rancor and no passion in her voice, nor in the steadfast, half-whispered replies of the man. There was only a terrible remoteness as these two emaciated travesties of human beings, whose hold on life was almost equally tenuous, engaged each other in dead words while the wind roared darkly over them and the quick snow drifted up against their bodies.

They talked so — but even as they talked Kikik was coming to the realization of what she must do next. In Ootek's mind the certainty of their common fate might be inevitable; but Kikik would not accept this truth. She was well fitted to be Halo's wife for she too was of adamantine stuff. Therefore she did not think, she *knew*, her children would survive — and of the many obstacles which lay between her and their survival, the first was Ootek.

She called Ailouak again who, horrified and frightened, had retreated to the igloo.

"Daughter! Bring me a knife!" Kikik demanded.

Ailouak crawled out, closely followed by her younger brother Karlak — and both children had knives clutched in their hands. . . .

"I took the larger knife from Ailouak and I stabbed once near Ootek's right breast but the knife was dull and would not go in.

Then Ootek grasped the knife and took it from me, but as we struggled for it it struck his forehead and the blood began to flow. Karlak was standing near and so I took the small knife which he handed me and stabbed in the same place near the right breast. This time the knife went in and I held it there until Ootek was dead. . . ."

The killing might have been easier for Kikik had there been passion in it — but there was none. She acted out of intellect, not out of emotion, and she knew exactly what she did. She knew too what lay ahead of her. She had no illusions. She was fully aware of the almost insupportable burden which Halo's death had laid upon her. There would be no more food of any kind. There would be no man's strength to haul the sled if she moved camp. The inevitable doom which Ootek had envisaged was in reality only a step away. Yet stubbornly, and with a singleness of purpose which will be her epitaph when she is gone, Kikik engaged her fate in battle. As Ootek died she ceased to be a woman and became instead an unfaltering machine. The humane passions left her. Love, pity, sorrow, and regret were past. With terrible efficiency she stripped away these things so that nothing might weaken her indomitable resolve.

After Ootek was dead she placed the two knives upright in the snow beside his head and went at once into her snow house. She found the children hunched together under the skins upon the sleeping ledge, staring at her out of black, depthless eyes. Brusquely she ordered Ailouak to follow after, and together they went out into the unabated storm, dragging Halo's heavy sled down to the jigging hole. Together they raised the already frozen body of the husband and the father, laid him on the sled, and brought him home to lie beneath the snow beside the door. The effort exhausted both of them and they crawled back into the igloo to lie panting on the ledge.

"We will sleep now," Kikik told her children, and there was a quality in her voice that belonged to the north wind itself. "And in the morning we will go to Padlei where we will find food."

That night, in Ootek's snow house, his children and the crippled woman huddled close to one another so that no part of their ephemeral body warmth would be wasted. Kooyak still whimpered in her agony, and Howmik gave her water, for there was no food. Even water was only obtainable at a fearful cost, for there was no fire, and Howmik was forced to melt handfuls of snow in a skin bag warmed by her slim reserves of body heat.

Howmik herself slept little that night, for with Ootek's failure to return to the igloo she could only assume he had meant what he had said, in which case death would have soon overtaken him amongst the drifts along the route to Padlei. She believed that she was now alone except for Halo and his family, and she knew that they could give her no assistance.

Before dawn on February 9, the wind fell light; the sky broke clear and the temperature plummeted to forty-five degrees below zero. Kikik, who had also slept little enough that night, roused her children, gave them each a cup of warm water in which some scraps of deerskin had been softened, and bade them prepare to travel. They went about their tasks readily, for there was no gainsaying the inexorable resolution in their mother's face. Within an hour the few possessions which were essential for the journey had been placed aboard the long sled; then Kikik tore down the canvas ceiling of the igloo and cut it into halves. One piece she placed over her husband's grave. With the other she made a bed for her younger daughters, Nesha and Annacatha, upon the sled. These children were too young to stagger through the snow and, in any case, they had no skin clothing left. Their clothes had long ago been sacrificed as food for Halo and the elder children so that they could hunt, and gather fuel.

It was at this juncture that Howmik emerged from her snow-shelter and came hobbling across toward the others. She stopped beside the sled, shivering uncontrollably, for her own clothing had been reduced to tattered remnants. She did not need to ask what was afoot, for she could see and understand the implications of the loaded sled. She knew too, as Ootek had known, that there was no point in protesting; and so she contented herself with asking Kikik if she knew where Ootek had gone.

Kikik was evasive. She denied any knowledge of her brother, except to intimate that he had probably gone towards Padlei in which direction, so she said, Halo had already gone to break a trail for Kikik and the children. This was a very thin explanation for Halo's absence from the scene, but Howmik did not question it. Her mind was filled with thoughts of Ootek, and with the certainty of his fate.

"If he has gone for Padlei, he is dead by now," she said, half to herself.

Kikik made no comment. Imperturbably she continued with her preparations. She had been Howmik's best friend, and had helped the other woman with domestic tasks for fifteen years; but as of this moment that was past and dead. She could do nothing more for Howmik, nor for Howmik's children and, since this was so, she dared not even allow herself the luxury of pity.

And this was the second of the bitter things that Kikik was forced to steel herself to do — to deny her friend, and to leave her by the shores of Henik Lake to die.

Howmik understood. As unemotionally as if she had just concluded a casual morning visit, she said "Well, I am pretty chilly now. Perhaps I will go home till Ootek comes."

And Kikik, straightening from her task, watched as the cripple limped away across the snows.

So Kikik left the camp by Henik Lake. With the hauling straps biting into her shoulders she dragged the awkward sled upon which Nesha and Annacatha crouched beneath two deerskin robes. Her youngest child, the eighteen-month-old boy, Noahak, rode upon her back in the capacious pocket of her parka. Karlak and Ailouak trudged stolidly along behind.

For a time the going was good. The gale had packed the snow, and the route lay over the level surface of the lake. Seldom pausing to rest, Kikik forced the pace to the limit of the children's endurance. When the pace began to tell upon Karlak, she ordered him to climb upon the sled, and she toiled on. By late afternoon she had gone ten miles; and then something occurred which must have made Kikik believe she had outdistanced the hounds of fate.

A mile ahead, near the tip of a great rock point, she saw a centipede of human movement on the ice. She came erect, stared for a long moment, and then her voice rang out through the crystal air — and the distant movement slowed and ceased.

In a little while Kikik was talking to four of her own people.

The four were Yaha (who was Howmik's brother), his wife Ateshu and their six-year-old son Atkla, together with the last survivor of Pommela's adopted children, the young man Alektaiuwa. They too were making for Padlei, but Ateshu's lung sickness (it was tuberculosis), and the fact that both of Alektaiuwa's feet were frozen, had slowed their progress to a fatal crawl. They were in desperate straits, and they could offer no island of hope and strength to which Kikik could drag herself and her own children.

Kikik's sick disappointment when she discovered that Yaha's family had barely enough resources to enable them to survive for a day or two longer, let alone a surplus to share with others, must have been a crushing blow. Yet she could bear that too. She told her tale and Yaha heard that his own sister and her children lay abandoned only ten miles distant — and he knew he could do absolutely nothing for them. He was carrying on his back the last food that his family owned — two or three pounds of caribou entrails dug from underneath the snows where it had been discarded in the fall. Yaha had no sled, and his pace was therefore that of the sick woman and the injured boy. He was by no means hopeful that his family would ever get to Padlei alive, and he knew that to turn back for Howmik would only mean certain death for all. He made his inevitable decision, as he listened to Kikik's story, and when she was done he said no word, but turned again toward the northeast. Into the darkness of that frigid evening the little group crawled slowly forward. When they could no longer see their way, they made camp in a tiny travel igloo which Yaha built, and here exhaustion held them till the dawn.

That night *Kaila*, the unpredictable and heartless goddess of the weather, struck again. Before dawn the wind was back in all its frenetic fury; but the ten people who fled could not hide from it. They dared not stay in their minute igloo and hide. So they went on.

The agonies of that day, facing a growing blizzard, freezing, and pitifully weakened by the long starvation, were such that the younger children who took part in it have lost its memory — to them it is now no more than a blank white space in time. But the older ones, and the adults, remember. . . .

As the long hours passed and the straggling column slowed even more (for Kikik, with her load, could not keep up), Yaha knew that they would find no sanctuary except beneath the snows. When dusk came he and his family, with Karlak and Ailouak, had left Kikik a mile behind. Such was the exhaustion of these people that Kikik could not close the gap to the travel igloo Yaha built, nor did any of those at the igloo have the strength to go back for her. Kikik crouched in the snow all that roaring night with her three youngest children huddled underneath her body.

In the morning Kikik threw off the snows that all but covered her and faced north. She saw the little igloo and struggled to it. Yaha's wife gave her warm water and a fragment of caribou gut, and when she had drunk and eaten, Yaha spoke to her. His speech was gentle, for he was a gentle and a childlike man.

"You must stay in the snowhouse," he told Kikik. "If I take your sled to pull my wife, we may go fast enough to reach Padlei before we starve. Then we will send help. Perhaps the airplane will come. If it does not, then the trader will send his dog team. But you and your children must remain here and wait."

Kikik, recognizing the truth of this, made no demur. Yaha and his family left soon afterward and she remained with her five children inside the frail snow shelter, and strained her hearing to catch the rustle of receding footsteps against the whine of the wind.

Kikik and her children remained in that travel igloo through five full days.

During that timeless interval they ate nothing — for there was nothing to eat; but Kikik gathered some dead spruce branches and she made a tiny fire so that they at least had water. More than that, she was even able to squeeze a few drops of bluish liquid from her shrunken breasts for the child Noahak.

For five interminable days the children and their mother huddled together under their two robes and the fragment of canvas, and simply waited — with no certainty. They did not talk much, for even words require strength to utter them. They waited while the storm waxed and waned, and waxed again; and while the keening of the wind heralded the sure approach of the malevolent pursuit.

But Yaha's promise had not been made in vain. On February 13, three days after leaving Kikik, he and his family reached the shelter of Padlei Post, where the trader fed them first, then listened to their tale. With Yaha's arrival all but two of the Ihalmiut families had been accounted for, and now the trader knew what had happened to the rest.

He was appalled. He had earlier radioed his concern about the people to the police at Eskimo Point and now he sent a message which brooked of no delay. In the outer world the slow and almost toothless gears of bureaucracy meshed suddenly. The R.C.M.P. patrol plane which had been so fatally delayed in Kaiyai's case came thundering out from Churchill and on February 14 it reached Padlei. With the trader aboard as a guide, it took off again for Henik Lake, landing on the wind-swept ice of that place shortly before noon.

The policemen went ashore toward the two almost buried igloos and at Howmik's house they found the crippled woman and two children miraculously still alive. They, and the body of Igyaka, were carried to the plane — light burdens all, for the living too had been reduced to skeletal caricatures of human beings. Then the police found Halo's grave, and after a little time they stumbled on the snow-covered body of Ootek. These two were also taken to the plane, and so Halo and Ootek, those enduring friends, came together for the last time, lying stiffly contorted at the feet of Howmik and of her two surviving children.

What followed must constitute the most inexplicable aspect of this whole dark tale. The police aircraft left Henik Lake for Padlei and though it flew directly over the area where Kikik and her children were known to be waiting in the travel igloo, no real attempt was made to find them. Nor can the entire weight and majesty of the police prevail against this truth. The events which followed provide corroboration which cannot be assailed.

The patrol aircraft returned to Padlei. But despite the suggestion of the trader that it remain overnight in order to have the advantage of the precious extra hours of daylight to search for Kikik the next day, the police decided to fly on to Eskimo Point, bearing three dead bodies out of the land, and leaving six who might be alive to wait a little longer. In making this decision the police sacrificed the advantages of having two more hours of daylight for a search on February 14 — assuming that they had indeed intended to make such a search.

In the event, however, the patrol aircraft did not return to the interior at all the following day.

It was not prevented from doing so by bad weather, or by any other physical cause. It was not sent back simply because it was considered to be more important to send the aircraft north to Rankin Inlet in order to fly the coroner down to Eskimo Point to conduct an inquest into the cause of death of the three bodies which were already on hand.

Had the trader at Padlei known that the police had no intention of returning, he would undoubtedly have sent his post servant Karyook by dog team to search for Kikik; and Karyook would easily have been able to reach her on that day. But in the belief that the police plane would arrive at any minute, the trader did not send Karyook out.

Thus for two additional days and nights, Kikik and her children remained abandoned.

Sitting in Yaha's travel igloo Kikik heard the double passage of the plane on February 14, and when that day drew to a close and no help had come, she was convinced that none would ever come.

This should have been her moment of ultimate despair — but no fiber of her being would acknowledge it. There was no more hope — but what of that? On the morning of February 15, while the police plane was winging its way north to Rankin Inlet on official business, Kikik wrapped Annacatha and Nesha in the skin robes and used the piece of canvas to make a crude toboggan on which to haul them. Then these six, who had eaten no food for seven days, and little enough in the preceding months, set out for Padlei.

It was a blind, almost insensate, effort. Staggering like demented things, they moved a yard or two, then paused as Karlak or Ailouak collapsed on the hard snow. Blackened by frost, and as gaunt as any starving dog, Kikik would rest beside them for a moment and then remorselessly would goad them to their feet — and they went on another yard or two.

Kikik drove the children with a savage, almost lunatic obsession. She drove herself, hauling what had become a gargantuan weight behind her, and bowed beneath the incubus of the child Noahak upon her back. She had become a vessel filled with a kind of stark brutality — filled with it to the point where there was room for nothing else.

In six hours they moved two miles closer to their goal — which still lay twenty-seven miles ahead.

It was dark by then, but Kikik had no strength to build a shelter. The best that she could manage was to scoop a shallow hole in the snow using a frying pan as a shovel. Into this depression the six of them huddled for the night — the long and bitter night, while the ice on nearby Ameto Lake cracked and boomed in the destroying frost.

That shallow hollow should have become a common grave for all of them. They had no right to live to see the slow dawn's coming. Yet when the grey light broke in the east, Kikik lifted her head and looked toward the unseen Padlei Post. Still she would not give her hand to death.

And now she came to the most frightful moment of her years; for Kikik knew that they could not all go on. She could no longer think to save them all; and so in the dark half-light of morning she came to the most terrible of all decisions.

Quietly she roused Karlak and Ailouak from their mindless sleep, and firmly forced them to their feet. Then she drew a caribou hide softly across the faces of the two little girls who still slept on. While the elder children watched, wordless and mercifully uncomprehending, she laid sticks across the hole and piled snow blocks on top.

Early on the morning of February 16, three figures moved like drunken automata on the white face of a dead land . . . and behind them, two children slept.

In the morning of February 16, the R.C.M.P. plane came back. It did not reach Padlei until the day was well advanced and then it landed to pick up the trader once again. It was noon before the search began.

On his arrival at Padlei, Yaha had given the trader explicit instructions as to how to find the travel igloo, and this time the aircraft went directly to it, experiencing no difficulty in locating it — as there would have been no difficulty two days earlier. But by now the igloo was empty.

Airborne again, the plane lumbered uneasily through the frigid edge of dusk while the men aboard strained their vision for a sight of motion on the snows below. They saw nothing. Dusk was rushing into the land as they turned back for Padlei — but then, on a last suggestion from the trader, the plane deviated slightly to pass over an abandoned trapper's cabin. There, by the door, the searchers saw a human figure, its arms upraised in the immemorial and universal gesture of a supplicant.

As for Kikik — as she watched the plane circle for a landing — that indomitable structure which she had created so ruthlessly out of her own flesh and spirit began to crumble into senseless ruin. She could sustain it no longer, for there was no longer need of it. As the plane came to a halt and policemen began to run toward her, she faced them with nothing left in her but dust, and the apathy of nothingness.

They asked many, and urgent, questions, for it was almost dark, and they were very anxious to get away. Where were her children? Three of them were in the shack. Where were the other two? What had she done with them? Coherence left her and she could explain nothing, for out of the emptiness an old emotion had quickened into life within her. She who had known no fear through the aeons of her travels now remembered fear. She answered out of fear of those who were her rescuers. She lied. Believing that Nesha and Annacatha must now be dead, she told the police that they had died and she had buried them.

The police were not so anxious this time to recover bodies, and so they flew Kikik and her remaining children out of the land to Eskimo Point, after leaving a constable behind at Padlei with orders to collect the dead children by dog team the next day.

The constable followed his instructions and late on February 17 he reached the unobtrusive hummock in the snow where Nesha and Annacatha lay. The Eskimo guide who had accompanied him stopped in terror as they approached the grave, for he had heard a voice — a muffled, childlike voice. The constable tore away the snow blocks and the twigs, and there he found the children. Insulated from the killing cold by the snow crypt, Annacatha was alive — but Nesha had not lived.

So the ordeal of the winter ended for all of the Ihalmiut — except for Kikik, and her ordeal had only just begun.

The flight to Eskimo Point bridged the final chasm between her time and ours in one gigantic and immutable step. Within the day she ceased to be the woman she had been, for now she sat under arrest in a small igloo beside the police barracks, a woman of *our* times destined to live or die according to our laws. The transcendent fortitude she had displayed; the agony that she had voluntarily embraced when she left Nesha and Annacatha to their long sleep; the magnificence of her denial of death itself — all come to this: Kikik had killed a man — Kikik had willfully abandoned two children in the snow — Kikik must answer for her crimes.

Through interminable weeks she remained at Eskimo Point, her children taken from her and she herself subjected to endless interrogations. She was not even told that Annacatha had survived until it suited the needs of the police to confront her with this information in a successful attempt to force her into the admission that she had lied. She endured two preliminary hearings before a justice of the peace at Eskimo Point and she was searchingly examined by a very competent crown attorney who was flown from Yellowknife for the occasion. There was no defense attorney present at either hearing. The verdict of the justice was that she must stand trial on both charges.

She knew nothing of the shape of what awaited her; she only knew that her life remained in jeopardy. She endured. She who had already endured so much could still endure.

In the middle of April they flew her to Rankin Inlet and there the whole mighty paraphernalia of our justice closed about her, and she was tried.

But here, if anywhere in this chronicle, there emerges some denial of the apparent fact that man's inhumanity to man is second nature to him. Kikik was tried before a judge who understood something of the nature of the abyss which separated Kikik from us, and who was aware that justice can sometimes be savagely unjust. In his charges to the jury, Judge Sissons virtually instructed them to bring in a verdict of acquittal. And be it to the everlasting credit of the handful of miners who held the woman's life in their hard hands, they did acquit her, not only of the murder of Ootek, but also of the crime of "unlawfully, by criminal negligence, causing the death of her daughter Nesha."

Thus, on the sixteenth day of April in the year of our civilization 1958, Kikik's ordeal ended. At 9 P.M. under the glaring lights of the improvised courtroom the judge looked at the woman who sat, still smiling blankly, still uncomprehending, and he spoke gently:

"You are not guilty, Kikik. Do you understand?"

But Kikik did not understand, as she had understood so little through the days since she had come to Eskimo Point, except that a threat she could not comprehend, and one more fearful, therefore, than any she had met and mastered in the months and years behind, lay over her.

At length a white man who is almost an Eskimo in his feeling for the people came forward and led her, unresisting, from the room. He took her into the adjoining camp kitchen, sat her down, and gave her a mug of tea. Then, standing over her and looking down into her eyes, he spoke in her own tongue.

"Kikik," he said softly. "Listen. It is all finished now — it is all done."

And then at last that fixed smile faltered — and the black eyes looked away from him toward the darkened window, and past it, and into the void beyond.

IV.

THE
WESTERN
OCEAN

FROM

THE GREY SEAS UNDER, 1958
THE SERPENT'S COIL, 1961

FROM
The Grey Seas Under

The number of ships that get into difficulties in the North Atlantic — difficulties from which they can be extricated only by highly trained and competent salvage teams — is staggeringly large.

When Richard Chadwick entered the salvage business in 1930 with his new company, Foundation Maritime Limited, he found that the variety of troubles which beset ships is almost legion. A random list of the commonest causes of disablement includes the loss of a propeller while at sea; the breakdown of the propelling machinery; damaged or lost rudders; fires and explosions; leaking; structural failure; shortages of fuel, of supplies, of water and — at least in one well-authenticated case — of rum; strandings (on dry land as opposed to) groundings (on underwater shoals and reefs); collisions with other ships, drifting wrecks, whales, icebergs, buoys, and anything else afloat; being caught in ice-packs; enemy action in times of war, and afterwards through loose mines drifting about the seas; the effects of winds and storms in general; and failure of the crews due to illness, inexperience, exhaustion, injury, and mutiny.

Chadwick also discovered that a salvage company must be able to give assistance by conducting sea searches; by escorting partially disabled vessels safely into port; by steering rudderless ships by means of lines taken from their sterns; by towing every type of disabled vessel, ranging from ships broken in half, through the smallest trawlers, up to the largest liners; by fighting fire; by saving life under a formidable variety of circumstances; by supplying materials to stricken ships (such things as food, water, fuel, and repair materials); by supplying special services, including transportation, man power, electric and steam power; by keeping sinking ships afloat with pumps and other gear; by raising and emptying ships that have already sunk; by releasing vessels trapped in ice; by releasing grounded and stranded ships, using ground tackle, pumping, pulling, dredging, jettisoning, and a score of other methods; by repairing damaged ships and making them temporarily seaworthy; by cargo salvage from wrecked or sunken ships; and by breaking up vessels that have become total losses, but whose bones form an obstacle to the safe navigation of other ships.

As if all this was not enough to occupy his mind, Chadwick was also made aware of the peculiar and singular difficulties of salvage work in the area where his company would have to operate.

The North Atlantic is a hungry ocean, hungry for men and ships, and it knows how to satisfy its appetites. From September through to June a sequence of almost perpetual gales march eastward down the great ditch of the St. Lawrence valley and out to the waiting sea. They are abetted by the hurricanes which spawn in the Caribbean and which drive northeastward up the coasts as far as Labrador. Only in summer are there periods of relative calm on the eastern approaches to the continent, and even in summer, fierce storms are common.

Gales, and the high seas that accompany them, are, of course, the weapons of all oceans; but this unquiet seaboard has two special weapons of its own.

First of all it has the ice — continental masses of it that come sweeping down with the Greenland current to form a great, amoebalike bulge extending from the coasts of Nova Scotia eastward as much as a thousand miles, and southward five hundred miles from Flemish Cap. The bulge swells and shrinks and throws out new pseudopods from month to month, but there is no season of the year when it or its accompanying icebergs withdraw completely from the shipping lanes.

The second weapon is in many ways the most formidable of all. It is the fog. There is no fog anywhere to compare with the palpable grey shroud which lies almost perpetually across the northern sea approaches, and which often flows far over the land itself. There are not a score of days during any given year when between Labrador and the Gulf of Maine the fog vanishes completely. Even in the rare fine days of summer it remains in wait, a dozen or so miles offshore, ready at any moment to roll in and obliterate the world. It has presence, continuity, and a vitality that verges on the animate. In conjunction with its ready ally, the rock-girt coasts, it is a great killer of men and ships.

The coasts themselves are brutally hard. Newfoundland, Labrador, Nova Scotia, and the Gulf shores appear to have been created for the special purpose of destroying vessels. They are of malignant grey rock that has flung its fragments into the sea with an insane abandon until, in many places, these form impenetrable *chevaux-de-frise* to which the Newfoundland seamen, out of a perilous familiarity, have given the prophetic name of "sunkers."

The coasts are of tremendous length. Newfoundland alone exposes nearly six thousand miles of rock to the breaking seas. Everywhere the shores are indented with false harbors that offer hope to storm-driven ships and which then repulse them with a multitude of reefs. The names upon those coasts betray their nature. Cape aux Morts, Cape Diable, Rocks of Massacre, Dead Sailor's Rock, Bay of Despair, Malignant Cove, Baie Mauvais, Misery Point, Mistaken Point, False Hope, Confusion Bay, Salvage Point, and a plethora of Wreck Bays, Points, and Islands.

Yet by the very nature of their animosity towards seafaring men these coasts have brought out of themselves the matter of their own defeat. Men in these parts have always had to take their living from the sea, or starve; and those who survived the merciless winnowing became a race apart. There are no finer seamen in the world. The best of them come from the outports of Newfoundland and Nova Scotia, and from the islands of Cape Breton and the Magdalens. The best of them are men to ponder over, for they can hold their own no matter how the seas and the fog and ice and rocks may strive against them.

DEAD MAN'S
ROCK

Although the depression was still being keenly felt in Canada's Maritime Provinces in 1935, at least one major company was still doing a good business. This was Dominion Steel and Coal Company — the colossus which overstrode much of Nova Scotia and which, to all intents and purposes, was the financial master of Cape Breton Island.

Dosco owned or controlled most of the coal mines in the province, and to get its coal to the buyers it was Dosco's policy to charter a fleet of ships each spring. Most of these vessels were from England, where there were far more bottoms than there was cargo to be carried in them and where vessels could consequently be chartered for a pittance.

Kafiristan was one of Dosco's chartered fleet, and another of these hard-driven ships was the *Berwindlea*, fifty-two hundred tons, out of Aberdeen. *Berwindlea* had crossed the Atlantic in the early spring of 1935, and through the summer and autumn she had been almost constantly at work hauling slack coal through the Gulf and up the St. Lawrence River. In mid-October she was free at last, for her charter had expired. She and her weary crew were ready to sail for home; but first she had a cargo of pulp to load at Dalhousie for delivery in England.

It was a clean cargo, and *Berwindlea*'s people were in a good mood as she put out from Dalhousie on October 22. The lateness of the season and the prevalence of autumnal gales and heavy fog did not dismay them. They were homeward bound.

Berwindlea's master was in a hurry. His ship would only log seven or eight knots, and Aberdeen was a long way off. He wished to make the best time possible while he remained in the relatively sheltered waters of the Gulf, for he knew that the winter storms on the open sea would strive against his vessel for every mile she made.

As darkness fell on October 22 it brought with it a black, impenetrable pall of fog. *Berwindlea* drove into it and disappeared. Her navigation lights glowed feebly, each contained in a hemisphere of fog not ten feet in diameter. The mate upon the bridge could not see the foredeck of the ship, and members of the crew vanished from each other's ken before five paces intervened between them.

The night was calm, but cold. There was no sound except the rusty *blat* of *Berwindlea*'s whistle as it tried to pierce the fog, but which was blanketed and absorbed almost as it left the whistle's throat.

The course line laid out on the chart in the wheelhouse began to waver. The little penciled crosses which represented *Berwindlea*'s position became fewer and less firmly placed. Dead-reckoning alone was an uncertain pilot on such a night.

At 3:50 A.M. the master, Captain Williams, stood at the chart table with the officer of the watch beside him. They stared intently at the last dead-reckoning position. It showed *Berwindlea* on course and ten miles south of the dangerous nest of islands called the Magdalens. Williams was uneasy. It was not much of an offing on such a night, and he was contemplating ordering the vessel's head to be brought a little more toward the south when, without any warning, *Berwindlea* went on.

Men who have spent their lives sailing the Gulf make no pretense of familiarity with the strange currents which flow through it. *Berwindlea*'s people — strangers all — had no way of knowing in advance what the current had been doing to their ship that night. But now they knew what it had done.

Berwindlea took the ground with a great shudder and the sound of crumpling steel.

In the engine room the chief was already starting up the bilge pumps even before the frightful shuddering of the initial shock was over. The bosun, thrown to the deck by the impact, had already regained his feet and had begun to turn forward to sound the wells, even before the order to do so reached him from the bridge. The moment of confusion which is close to panic and which always seizes on a ship at such a time was short-lived. It was succeeded by a questioning silence broken only by occasional hails from the officers to the men who had gone forward. It was a period of fantastic tension, of hope struggling with the fear of what must soon be known.

The destruction of the ship began within ten minutes of the

time she struck. The bosun's measurements showed water rising fast in number one and number two holds, and when the pumps not only failed to reduce the flooding but were powerless even to slow its rapid rise, it was obvious that not only the vessel's bottom but her inner bottom too was ruptured.

Captain Williams listened grimly to the reports of his officers, then, at 4:15 A.M., he ordered Sparks to make his call. At 4:20 the international distress frequency woke to life.

At 9 A.M. Salvage Superintendent Reginald Featherstone at Foundation Maritime's Halifax headquarters received a telegram from one of his "intelligence sources":

> SS BERWINDLEA REPORTED ASHORE DEAD MANS ROCK
> MAGDALEN ISLANDS STOP BELIEVED FLOODED FORWARD
> BUT NO IMMEDIATE DANGER PRESENT WEATHER STOP
> FULLY LADEN PULP

Featherstone considered the information for fifteen minutes. He knew that this late in the season good weather in the Gulf could not be expected to last for more than two or three days. He was familiar with Dead Man's Rock and he knew that a ship on that exposed pinnacle would be doomed by any gale which blew. There was no time for him to try to make arrangements with the ship's agents. There was, perhaps, just enough time to save the ship if the Company's salvage tug, *Foundation Franklin*, sailed at once.

So *Franklin* sailed "under forced draft," as the papers would have it. Once more Captain Power was on her bridge; but Featherstone himself intended to proceed by train to Canso Gut and meet the *Franklin* there, for he wanted to collect Drake, the local Salvage Association man, en route.

Franklin had thick fog and heavy weather all the way north, but she picked up Featherstone and Drake at Mulgrave at 3 A.M. on October 24 and by 4 P.M. of that day she had reached Dead Man's Rock.

The islet is a forbidding sight at the best of times. The craggy peak of a submerged mountain rising abruptly out of the waters, its area is only a few acres. Its shores are so precipitous that there is only one spot where boats may safely land; and this lies on the opposite side to the cliff where *Berwindlea* had driven ashore. Men seldom visit Dead Man's Rock, but on the north shore there is a tiny turf and stone shack where fishermen, or shipwrecked sailors, may find some meager shelter.

The place has a hard reputation — as hard as its name; but neither its reputation nor its name meant much to Featherstone. What counted in his mind was the terribly hazardous position of any vessel ashore upon it.

As *Franklin* came in Featherstone saw that the light north wind which had been blowing all that morning had kicked up such a sea that, even on the lee side of the rock where *Berwindlea* lay, a boat could not safely be launched. What must inevitably happen in the event of a real gale rising from the south, the east or west was brutally apparent.

As things stood Featherstone considered it too dangerous to attempt a landing, so *Franklin* withdrew into the lee of Amherst Island for the night. During those hours Featherstone was in radio contact with Williams, and he learned some of the details of the problem which he faced.

Berwindlea was flooded and tidal in number one and number two tanks (open to the sea in these), while her forepeak tanks and most of the remaining double bottom tanks were also flooded. Mercifully the engine room was still dry, but there was every prospect that it too would flood unless the weather moderated soon. On this score Featherstone and Power were not immediately worried. Knowing the signs by instinct they expected the northerly to fall light with darkness, and they hoped they would then have a period of a day, or perhaps two, before the wind came around through east to south and began to blow.

Featherstone and Power made their plan. Williams was ordered to flood his deep tanks in order to hold *Berwindlea* firmly on the rocks and prevent her from working. At dawn *Franklin* would come in, lay two sets of ground tackle off *Berwindlea*'s stern, land an air compressor on her and, after blowing the forward tanks and pumping the after ones, would try to take her off with her own winches.

Impelled by the knowledge that time was against them, the salvors went to work at dawn with demoniac energy. Within five hours both sets of ground tackle had been laid out. Featherstone, Tom Nolan, and Drake went aboard *Berwindlea* and supervised the reeving and setting-up of the purchases. Nolan's helper, Alan Macdonald, brought *Franklin*'s little motorboat in through the surf with a two-ton air compressor balanced across the gunwales and safely delivered it aboard the wreck. Nolan went over the side to make an underwater examination and to begin patching, if this proved feasible. Having fully assessed the situation, Featherstone radioed an urgent request to Sydney for a small coastal vessel which could bring out stevedores and coal, and which could take off bulk pulp if jettisoning proved necessary. The coal was particularly needed since *Berwindlea*'s bunkers were low — her master having intended to bunker at Sydney before setting out across the North Atlantic.

Everything was in readiness for the first attempt to refloat the big ship at evening high tide, when Featherstone made a shocking discovery.

During her summer season *Berwindlea* had been unloaded, not with her own deck gear, but with shore equipment. Consequently her engineers had removed certain vital valves from the deck winches in order to prevent corrosion — and these valves had never been replaced. No one had thought about the matter until late afternoon on October 25, when Featherstone called for steam on the winches in order to take the preliminary strain on the ground tackle.

When the discovery was made that the winches were useless, it was too late to search out the missing valves and install them in time to make use of that evening's tide. Nothing more could be done until the following day.

Meanwhile Power, aboard *Franklin* lying at anchor half a mile off shore, had heard some disquieting news on the standard broadcast radio. A violent hurricane had cut a swath of destruction across Haiti on October 23, killing more than two thousand people. The track the hurricane was following had not yet been plotted with any certainty, but Power knew that it might well run northeast over the Maritimes — as Caribbean hurricanes so often do.

With this possibility in mind, Power watched with increasing apprehension as the afternoon waned and as the wind came out of the east, then switched freakishly to the southwest and began to rise. Power kept his fears to himself until 4:45 P.M., when he radioed Featherstone:

> WIND AND SEA RISING FAST SUSPECT HURRICANE TRACK WILL COME THIS WAY SUGGEST YOU ABANDON BERWINDLEA AT ONCE

Featherstone was not infallible. He could make mistakes; and when he did they were monumental. He made one now.

Irritated by the affair of the winches and by the fact that he had been robbed of a quick success by such a trivial matter, he made up his mind to stay aboard *Berwindlea* and have another try at dawn. He did not think much of the hurricane scare. In his experience a southwest gale was not likely to last more than a few hours.

Whether or not they were influenced by Featherstone's example, the officers and crew of *Berwindlea* also elected to remain aboard their ship. Drake too decided to stay, while Nolan had no thought of leaving if Featherstone remained.

At 5:30 P.M. Alan Macdonald was told to return to *Franklin* with the motorboat. It was none too soon. While rounding *Berwindlea*'s stern Macdonald was caught in the surf and his boat was nearly swamped. Damaged and leaking badly it barely managed to get him back to *Foundation Franklin*'s side.

Contrary to Featherstone's expectations the gale did not slack off. Instead it mounted with a ferocity that was terrifying. At 9 P.M. *Franklin* began dragging both her anchors and was forced to heave them in and stand offshore into the teeth of a Force 8 gale and a wild and savage sea. She rose to most of the big ones, but she took it green across her decks many times that night.

Clamped in the vise of the rocks, *Berwindlea* could do nothing but accept her punishment. By midnight she was being swept from end to end and spray was breaking high above her mastheads against the glistening rocks of the cliff face.

Berwindlea had her crew accommodations aft, while her bridge and officers' quarters were well forward of amidships. Her boats were aft as well and the only communication between the poop and the bridge was over the open decks.

By midnight this route had been closed. Black water was

falling on the decks to a depth of six feet. The stanchions of her rails were smashed, and the rails themselves carried away. Her starboard boat was shattered in its chocks. Her hatches began to break under the ponderous impact of the seas and she began to flood in number three and number four holds.

Her crew were now besieged in their quarters aft and dared not open a door or port. Forward, in the bridge structure, the officers with Featherstone, Nolan, and Drake were marooned in a more ugly position — close to the destroying rocks.

By midnight the ship had begun to work so much that the sound of her plates grinding and gnashing on the rocks rose clearly above the high-pitched scream of wind and the sonorous thunder of the breaking seas.

Franklin was now hove-to some miles off shore and barely able to hold her own. Emergency weather reports were coming in steadily from the government stations, and these were increasingly ominous. The hurricane had indeed tracked up the American seaboard, and the center of that whirlpool of tortured air was rapidly approaching the Maritimes. Already the distress frequency was crackling with calls and McManus was logging them between his attempts to keep in touch with *Berwindlea's* young operator.

At 3:30 A.M. on October 26 there was no answer to McManus's signals. He fought his way to the bridge to tell Power, and found the skipper peering shoreward through the driving murk with his night glasses. There was no need for Sparks's message. Power had seen the dim glow of *Berwindlea's* lights suddenly go out.

Aboard *Berwindlea* both the ground-tackle wires had parted under the strain imposed by that irresistible sea, and the ship had swung broadside, tearing her belly out as she was flung across the reefs. She heeled over and the seas flooded into her engine room; the lights flickered once and then went out. Within half an hour she was flooded in every compartment and her doom was sealed.

That she did not break up immediately was tribute to her Scottish builders. Any lesser ship must have quickly gone to pieces under the merciless assault of the mounting seas; yet *Berwindlea* hung on, a shell of a thing, her bottom gone and her side plates buckling until her deck was hogged like a boar's back. She was dead, but not yet destroyed.

The storm-wracked daylight hours of October 26 were an ordeal that drove one officer mad, and that led the crew to the panic act of attempting to launch the remaining boat. It was swept from them like a chip and only a miracle spared the men who launched it. They crawled back into their prison and hung on.

At dawn the radio operator managed to get his emergency power working, and communications with *Franklin* were restored. It was a desperately anxious Power who talked to Featherstone, but though he was immeasurably relieved to hear that the men aboard the wreck were still alive, Power was driven half-distracted by the fact that he could do nothing for them. Until the hurricane had passed it was all that he could do to keep *Franklin* afloat; any attempt to venture close to Dead Man's Rock would have been suicidal. Standing three miles off shore he could not see *Berwindlea* at all. He could only see a succession of gargantuan columns of white spray such as might mark the seas which break across a submerged reef in a great gale.

The news upon the distress frequency was as chilling as the spectacle before Power's eyes. The steamer *Vardulia*, the same ship which had rescued the crew of the *Aggersund* off Newfoundland in that memorable spring of 1932, had called for help from several hundred miles east of Halifax, and then had not been heard again. She had gone down and taken her crew of thirty-seven with her. Nor was she alone. The Nova Scotian three-masted schooner *Esthonia*, from Barbados to Shelburne, also died that day, although her crew of ten were saved.

As the number of distress calls mounted, Power's frustration increased. Several times he sailed *Franklin* dangerously close to the foam-sheathed rock, but each time he was forced away before he had come close enough even to see *Berwindlea* through the driven spume.

Aboard the doomed vessel there were two kinds of men. There were those who saw death at arm's length, and who were afraid of him. And there were those who could not see him, either because they lacked understanding of their plight, or because they were too preoccupied to notice. Featherstone and Nolan belonged to this latter group. With a cigar thrusting aggressively out of his heavy jaw, Featherstone still would not admit defeat. Plan after plan to save not just the men but the ship as well went through his mind, and the notes in his little pocket notebook grew numerous as plan after plan had to be abandoned.

Not until noon of October 26 would he accept the fact of *Berwindlea*'s loss; and then he concentrated his efforts on how to save her people. He knew that no boat could live in the hell's brew about *Berwindlea*, and that it would be death to try to leave her until there was a lull. He made plans for the moment when she would go under. He began a long and reasoned discussion with the ship's officers as to the relative merits of rafts and boats versus ladders, as life-saving gear; and he was irritated when the distracted officers refused to listen with the proper degree of attention to the niceties of his arguments. Somewhat grumpily he left them to their fears and turned to the phlegmatic Nolan.

"Best way in the world to leave a wreck on a lee shore — a ladder. Hold you up fine as you go through the surf, then with any kind of luck you can use it to bridge the breakers so you don't get bashed to bits. After that you can use it to climb up the cliffs. You get a ladder ready, Tom."

Tom routed out a ladder, but not because he thought it would be needed. He was not much worried by their plight, for as a Newfoundlander born and bred he had long since learned never to worry in advance about what the sea might do to him. What bothered him at the moment was the problem of finding grub; and he was considerably disgruntled by the steward's failure to provide an adequate grub locker in the officers' saloon.

The day passed in different ways for different men. Some were silent and withdrawn as soldiers are before the battle which they suspect will be their last. Some were violent in their futile rage. Some concentrated all their effort in the attempt to achieve sufficient self-control to fool their fellows. The madman screamed insensate things at sea and wind.

The hurricane continued unabated all that day and into the next night. At 1:30 A.M. on October 27 *Berwindlea* began to go. She split amidships, separating the two little groups of men one from the other, and the bow section began to settle steadily as she broke up below the waterline.

The salvage men and the ship's officers were soon driven out of the saloon by the invading waters. They made their way to the bridge — and the waters followed until they were knee deep.

For a time the thundering breakers drove over the bridge structure as if it were no more than a piece of flotsam, and then, temporarily content with the destruction they had wrought, they slowly began to lose their fury. At long last the gale began to ease.

It was now or never for the men aboard the wreck and at 2 A.M. *Franklin* radioed a general SOS on their behalf, which was picked up and immediately rebroadcast by the powerful government station on nearby Grindstone Island.

> SS BERWINDLEA ASHORE DEAD MANS ISLAND URGENTLY
> NEEDS ASSISTANCE SHIP WITH LARGE LIFEBOATS

There was no immediate reply, for there were few ships left at sea that night. A few minutes after sending the SOS Featherstone, his mind as agile as ever, radioed Power with a suggestion of his own.

> DO YOU THINK YOU COULD LAND SOME MEN AT THAT
> SHACK ON THE LEE SIDE OF THE ISLAND AND CROSS THIS
> SIDE AND RIG LINES FOR A BREECHES BUOY FROM THE CLIFF

To which Power replied:

> DONT THINK POSSIBLE LAND BOAT NOW BUT WILL DO SO
> AT DAYLIGHT IF HUMANLY POSSIBLE

This message was interrupted by a call from a strange voice. It belonged to a rare bird, the Japanese freighter *England Maru*, who reported herself as being abreast of East Point, Prince Edward Island, and able and willing to come to *Berwindlea*'s assistance.

Her message brought a surge of hope, for it was a voice from a world that the survivors on the wreck had all but despaired of knowing once again. With the Gulf swept almost clear of shipping by the hurricane they had come to think of themselves as utterly abandoned. So *England Maru*'s message brought hope, though of a tenuous kind, for they knew she could not reach them until late the following morning — and there was every likelihood that *Berwindlea* would have vanished before then.

Featherstone put the feelings of all of them into this brief message to Power:

> THANK JAP BUT WE ARE RELYING ON WHAT YOU CAN DO
> WITH SHORE PARTY

Nothing can better tell the story of the next few hours than the radio log kept by McManus. It is vivid, for it is truth.

England Maru to *Berwindlea*: WE ARE PROCEEDING YOU FULL SPEED BUT ONLY MAKE SIX KNOTS IN HEAVY SEA GOOD WISHES

Franklin to Grindstone Radio: DO YOU KNOW OR CAN YOU FIND OUT FROM FISHERMEN IF MEN CAN WALK AROUND BEACH OF DEAD MANS OR MUST THEY GO OVER TOP TO CROSS

Grindstone to *Franklin*: SORRY DONT KNOW AND CANT GET INFORMATION ALL PHONES DOWN

Berwindlea to *Franklin*: WHERE ARE YOU MAKE ALL POSSIBLE SPEED

Franklin to *Berwindlea*: AM NOW ABEAM ISLAND COMING AROUND AND UP LEE SIDE

Franklin to *Berwindlea*: GETTING BOAT READY UNDER COMMAND DOBSON WHO WILL HAVE SIGNAL FLAGS TO TALK FROM BEACH HOW ARE YOU AND HOW IS SHIP IS SHE BREAKING UP FAST

Berwindlea to *Franklin*: GLAD NEWS FROM YOU WE ARE WELL ALL HOPE IS IN YOUR EFFORTS THIS SHIP IN BAD WAY BREAKING BACK BUCKLING AND BATHED IN GREAT SEAS EVERY FEW MOMENTS

England Maru to *Berwindlea* via Grindstone: 28 MILES FROM YOU PROCEEDING BEST

Franklin to *Berwindlea*: BOAT OVER WITH MEN MAKING FOR ISLAND

Berwindlea to *Franklin*: ARE THEY MAKING GOOD PROGRESS

Franklin to *Berwindlea*: BOAT BEING SWEPT INTO BREAKERS THEY ARE ON EDGE OF BREAKERS WILL BE SWAMPED THEY ARE MAKING BIG EFFORT TO PULL CLEAR [And five minutes later] BOAT ESCAPED BREAKERS IMPOSSIBLE FOR THEM TO LAND AND LIVE SEAS SWEEPING BROADSIDE ON BEACH

Berwindlea to *Franklin*: FEATHERSTONE SAYS COME BACK
STAND BY TO WINDWARD OF US AND COOPERATE WITH JAP
STEAMER THERE MAY BE SLIM CHANCE FOR BOAT TO ROUND
OUR STERN AND LEE SIDE STOP THERE IS A ROCK ON SHIPS
PORT SIDE AMIDSHIPS RIGHT AGAINST HER

Franklin to *Berwindlea*: HAVE YOU ANY BOATS LEFT AND
CAN YOU LAUNCH THEM AND COME OUT

Berwindlea to *Franklin*: BOAT SMASHED BUT WILL TRY IT
IF ALL ELSE FAILS

These messages cover only three hours in time; but that was
a decade in the lives of those concerned.

Power's attempt to land a boat upon the north side of the
island had been nobly prosecuted. Second Officer Dobson (who
was to die a few years later as a destroyer commander in the
war), with three deck-hands and two firemen — all volunteers
— had put off from *Franklin* in a twelve-foot boat. During the
launching a sea had swept the little craft so hard against
Franklin's bulwarks that it was half stove-in before it took the
water. Once afloat it was at the mercy of the great seas, for the
hope that Dead Man's Rock could provide a lee in the face of
the hurricane was a delusion. There were three miles to pull in
order to reach the roaring shingle beach. Dobson and his men
were exhausted before they reached the line of surf. Dobson
himself knew that there was little possibility of his crew's surviving an attempt to enter the surf, yet he decided they should
try. The lifeboat was immediately caught, spun end-for-end and
almost swamped. Half-full and leaking badly, it was still two
hundred yards from land. There remained only the hope that
the boat's crew could save themselves. With the strength of
desperation they pulled clear of the surf and then dropped over
their oars in a state of near collapse as the wind carried their
boat clear of the islet and out into the Gulf. *Franklin* bore down
upon them, and was able to retrieve them by a near-miracle of
seamanship on Power's part. The broken boat was left to drift
away.

All this took place between dawn and 6 A.M. *Franklin* then
fought her way back around the islet and stood by the *Berwindlea*;
but she was now completely helpless to assist the shipwrecked

men, for she had only the motorboat left and, apart from the hull damage it had sustained earlier, its engine would no longer run.

It was at this juncture that the distant smoke of the *England Maru* came into sight. Power and the Japanese master were in radio communication and by 9 A.M., when the freighter was close upon the scene, they had devised a plan. It was an incredibly risky one that could only succeed if *England Maru's* big boat could be so packed with oarsmen that they could defy the wind and surf.

With a quality of seamanship that could hardly be believed, the Japanese skipper, Captain Honja, maneuvered his big vessel (she was light and therefore doubly hard to handle) broadside to the islet and less than half a mile from *Berwindlea*.

Honja then launched his biggest boat, a thirty-footer, and manned it with twenty oarsmen. Despite the bitter cold of that October morning the Japanese sailors were naked to the waist. They took up the stroke and made for the waiting *Franklin*, who was hove-to in *England Maru's* lee, halfway between her and the wreck.

Chanting in unison and rowing like superhuman beings, the Japanese crew slipped under the shelter of *Franklin's* lee, while Power eased his tug inshore.

Two hundred yards off *Berwindlea*, *Franklin* stopped. Not even Power dared to take her farther in. Now the lifeboat was on its own. It did not hesitate but plunged straight into the breaking seas that rose as high as *Berwindlea's* foretop.

The boat shot under the wreck's stern, seeking her lee side, but found instead a pinnacle of rock thrust into *Berwindlea's* belly that made a cul-de-sac from which there could be no escape. Second Officer Anto cried one shrill order, and in the last instant the men reversed their stroke and the boat came out alive.

Anto now took the only alternative. He brought his fragile craft in against *Berwindlea's weather* side. Bosun Okabe leaped to the boat's gunwale to prevent her being crushed against the wreck and with his own body took the shock of impact. It smashed seven of his ribs and nearly killed him — but he saved the boat.

The people on *Berwindlea's* after-part swarmed over the rails as one man. They had not far to drop, for already the after deck of the dying ship was awash. The lifeboat leaped away on a receding sea and pulled for safety.

Leaving her cargo of half-frozen survivors on *Franklin*'s deck, the Japanese boat went back again — this time right into the surf in an attempt to reach the little group marooned on *Berwindlea*'s bridge. She reached them too, but just how she did it no man can tell. Featherstone, his cigar still in his mouth, was amongst the last to leave and he recalls that moment in strange fashion.

"It wasn't the sea and the gale that bothered me just then. It was the seals. There must have been a thousand of them hanging about the wreck, just waiting to see us drown. They kept popping their silly heads up and staring, as if we were some kind of circus for their special benefit."

He was most indignant about those seals.

He was indignant too about the loss of *Berwindlea*, but philosophical as well. The loss of the ship pointed his favorite moral.

"Salvage on these coasts is always a knife-edge proposition. One little thing goes wrong, and you've lost out. There are no second chances. The wind and water sees to that."

The wind and water saw to *Berwindlea*. Within three days nothing remained of her except a frieze of flotsam on the beach of Dead Man's Rock.

THE MAN
FROM BURIN

The outports of Newfoundland cling to the broken coasts of that rock island in much the same way that the ancient maritime cities of Greece clung to their own inhospitable mainland. There are more than a thousand outports, some of them consisting of only a handful of families; but they are old settlements, many of them dating from the seventeenth century. During all the time of their existence they have been walled-off from one another by the almost impenetrable rock barrens of the interior. They have only known one road to human intercourse — the sea.

They have lived by and from and on the sea. Nothing of them has permanence except that which pertains to the sea: neither their neat frame houses, their straggling wharves, their canted flakes — nor yet their men. Through a dozen generations these men have sailed out to the Grand Banks and hand-lined for cod out of their little dories, with two hundred miles of searoom between them and the nearest land. They have sailed to Labrador and up that Arctic coast as far as the cod would lead. And every summer their little ships put out, deep laden with salt fish, for Portugal and Spain and Italy.

The two- and three-masted schooners of Newfoundland (some of them not much larger than the Norse longboats) dared the Western Ocean in their hundreds for two centuries. They were good seaboats — it may be that there were none better — but they were built of poor timber and they were ill-found, for they were born of poverty. Many of them did not come back. Each year the flotsam on the coasts of Europe contained new fragments of Newfoundland jack pine and spruce.

The men of the island took to the sea young. There was no choice. At twelve some of them were hand-lining on the Banks, and by the time they had reached fourteen years only the sons of those feudal lords — the merchants — still remained ashore.

Mainlanders are sometimes heard to say — in envy and with discontent — that all Newfoundlanders are conceived in dories — standing up. If that were really so the people born on the Newfoundland coasts could not be better attuned to the environment in which they spend their lives than they are now. For they are truly of the sea.

It was these men, and there were scores of them across the years, who were the sinew and the marrow of *Franklin*'s crews. Not many of them remained with her over the years, for there was always the island calling them; but when one left the ship another came. It is not possible to speak of all of them by name or to tell their tales — but there was one amongst their numbers who is fit to represent them all.

In the town of Burin on Placentia Bay, a boy was born to the name of Harry Brushett in the year 1898. He grew to manhood; and at the age of twelve he went out to the Banks and learned to fish. He had five years of the dories before he became mate of one of the Burin schooners — a two-master called the *Vanessa*. At the age of eighteen Harry Brushett was master of the *Vanessa*, sailing to Alicante in Spain with cargoes of salt fish.

On his nineteenth birthday he was storm-taken in mid-Atlantic and, after thirty-six days of struggle, the *Vanessa* sank under the young skipper, leaving him and his crew of six adrift in a broken dory. Then days later they were picked up by a Norwegian tramp steamer and so they returned by stages to their own home port.

Two days after his homecoming Harry Brushett put to sea again, this time as master of the schooner *Mary II*. Her destination — Alicante.

He sailed her until 1920, when he became skipper of the new three-master *George A. Wood* and, at the same time, bosun to a slight and lively Burin girl called Eva. Burin girls do not stay at home when the captain goes to sea, and so for the next five years Eva sailed in the *George Wood* from Burin to Cadiz, Portugal, Jamaica, and Italy.

In 1925 the local company in Burin which owned the *Wood* went bankrupt and, with reluctance, Harry Brushett turned to steam. He spent the last years of the decade skippering coastal steamers running to every known port (and to some hardly known at all) along the Canadian and Newfoundland seaboards; and he grew intimate (but never foolishly familiar) with them.

The depression was the dark time. Newfoundland sank into an abyss of suffering that was medieval. Good skippers could be had for seaman's wages, and there were too few ships to go around. Harry, who had never bothered to take his examination for a foreign-going ticket, discovered that he was lucky to get a mate's berth in the ratty little steamers in the Newfoundland and Nova Scotian coastal trade.

He did not enjoy that life. It was a dull, bruising routine. Shipowners are seldom generous men and in those days they were particularly penurious and grasping. The coastal steamers worked twenty-four hours a day; they were undermanned and their people grossly underpaid. It was a living — just.

In 1938 Brushett was on the beach in Halifax when there came a chance to join *Foundation Franklin*, on one trip to sea. It was no permanent job, and the pay was not even as good as on the coastal steamers; but that single voyage left an indelible imprint on Brushett. What he saw of salvage work was enough to convince him that here was a life well suited to his independent character. He went back to the coast tramps after that single voyage, but he kept his eyes on the salvage tugs thereafter.

When Woollcombe met him on the street one day in early 1941 and casually inquired whether Harry would care to take command of *Franklin*, there was no hesitation. So it was that in April of that year a most remarkable vessel and a most remarkable man became an entity.

In 1941 Brushett was forty-three years of age, and in that particular prime which relative youth and thirty years at sea alone can give. His face betrayed few indications of his character and kind, for it might well have been the face of a scholarly pedagogue in some small outport village. He was long and thin, "a tall, lean drink of water," as one of his men called him, using the word "water" quite advisedly, for Brushett never drank hard liquor. This abstinence (which was not a matter of principle but simply of distaste) made him somewhat incomprehensible to the salvage crews, most of whom tended to the other extreme. And Brushett's untouchability, his incisive quality of command, and his aura of almost Victorian rectitude also tended to set him apart from the men who served under him. In outward appearance and in casual conversation he seemed the antithesis of the roaring, hell-for-leather tug-boat man. But in his actions he was — by the admission of everyone who served with him — beyond compare. And, as they would learn, he *could* be roused — if there was good reason — to the kind of fearsomeness for which Newfoundland skippers have a wide renown.

When he took command of *Franklin*, Brushett also took command of a fine crowd of officers. There was an unpredictable genius named Neil McLeod as chief engineer, with steady, indomitable Reginald Poirier as second. On deck there was Tom Paisley as first officer and Emile Forgeron, one of a huge family of boys, most of whom were in the tug-boat business, as second. Marryat occupied the radio shack. Tom Nolan had been transferred to the *Aranmore*, but *Franklin* now had Bill Henderson, a man who had spent most of the preceding thirty years beneath the surface, and who was Tom Nolan's peer. And the man who ran the pumps and who was in fact foreman of the salvage gang was Buck Dassylva, of whom it is said that — had it been necessary — he could have refloated the *Queen Mary* single-handed.

Apart from a hard core of Newfoundlanders, the stokers, oilers, and deck-hands who made up the balance of the twenty-four-man crew were a motley lot. The Navy and the Merchant Marine had taken the pick of those available, and the tugs were manned from what was left. Nevertheless the men who signed on for salvage work were often the most experienced seamen on the seaboard, even if they did have certain idiosyncrasies which made them appear undesirable aboard the merchant ships.

"The first day out," a chief engineer recalls, "my gang was useless. Then they'd begin to sober up. But before that awful moment of pure sobriety disabled them they would get into the vanilla extract. Then we'd have steam!"

Not all the hands were old shellbacks. A good many of them met the sea for the first time aboard the tugs. There was one poor Jewish lad, out of a clothing shop, who got into a small spot of trouble ashore and hurriedly shipped out on *Franklin*. He made a fine stoker once he had conquered his scruples against fat sowbelly. Then there was a six-foot Iroquois Indian, wanted by the police on a manslaughter charge, who turned to the seaman's life for reasons of health. There was also a poor fellow afflicted with hallucinations who had escaped a mental home. He would hold long conversations with *Franklin*'s boilers, or with her bilge pumps, but he became an excellent oiler nonetheless. And there was an educated and highly imaginative Frenchman, who tried to abandon *Franklin* in mid-Atlantic when he discovered a small leak in a pipe and assumed with direct French logic that the ship inevitably must fill and sink.

They were not a dull crowd. To the last man they were individualists, from unorthodox molds. And they were probably the only kind of men who could have survived the years which lay ahead and, more than that, who could have accomplished the impossible with such monotonous regularity.

When *Franklin* put to sea under her new master, the shape of the war had changed. The early months of confusion were largely past. The Canadian Navy had shown a heartening growth, and just in time, for the U-boats had crossed the Atlantic in numbers and were about to begin a sustained assault upon the western end of the great convoy bridge. For months to come the Navy was to be outmatched and even outnumbered by its adversaries, and during this period scores of ships were to go down off the Canadian seaboard, while others floated with their bellies ripped by torpedo blast, waiting in hopes of rescue.

Halifax itself had changed out of all recognition. All ships (with the exception of vessels of sixteen knots or better) bound for Allied ports in Europe came first to Halifax. Here they were either assigned to the fast HX convoys, or they were sent on to Sydney to become part of the slow SC convoys.

Bedford Basin a day or so before a major convoy sailed was wonderful. On occasions more than a hundred freighters of every size and nationality lay so thickly clustered that from the heights of the old citadel they appeared as an unbroken expanse of spars and superstructures. Halifax had become the most important port in the Western world, for through it passed more than three-quarters of the total tonnage which was sustaining Britain in her darkest hour.

This mighty concentration of ships, and the circumstances which surrounded them, continued to make for a steady increase in the number of maritime accidents. During 1941 Foundation's salvage vessels rescued twenty-seven ships, almost all of which would have been lost but for the efforts of the tugs.

Yet spectacular as this record is, it represented only a part of the salvage tugs' activities. When a ship was in distress a tug went out to her. When there were no SOS calls, the tugs worked even harder at a myriad other tasks.

LIBERTY SHIP

At this stage of the war the mass-produced United States Liberty ships were becoming numerous in the North Atlantic. Their contribution to the winning of the battle of supply was increasingly important, and it may well have been that without them the war might have dragged on for a longer period. However they were by no means perfect ships. They were the largest all-welded vessels ever built until that time, and their builders had not yet mastered the technique of plate welding for ocean-going vessels. As a result the early Libertys had a distressing tendency to break apart when they encountered heavy weather, and the number of them which were lost at sea due to this cause alone was staggering. Most, but not all, of those which broke went down. One of the few to survive was the *Joel E. Poinsett*.

The *Poinsett*, proud bearer of one of the triple-barrelled names which were in vogue in the American Merchant Marine during the war, was outbound for Europe in convoy in late February. At the turn of the month the convoy ran into a period of heavy weather and hard gales and, on the night of March 1 at a point four hundred miles southeast of St. John's, the *Poinsett* succumbed to the buffeting of the long seas and began to break. Her deck plates tore right across just forward of her bridge, and the jagged rent moved quickly down her flanks. Girders bent and snapped and stanchions bowed. The scream of breaking metal fought with the wind for precedence and in those terrible few minutes it won out.

There was very little time in which to abandon ship. The crew was mustered to boat stations and the boats went over into the darkness laden with half-clothed men who carried with them not much more than their lives. They were fortunate. A corvette was close at hand and she steamed down to give them a lee, while another merchant vessel rounded-to and picked the *Poinsett*'s crew out of the black waste of waters. Then the rescue ships rejoined the convoy and steamed on. The dismembered and abandoned *Poinsett* drifted into the gale spume and disappeared.

It was to be assumed that the two sections of the casualty would sink within a few hours; but due to a freakish bit of luck she had broken between the two cargo holds, and the bulkheads fore and aft had both held firm. With the next dawn a long-range Coastal Command aircraft making its lonely swing into the western sea spotted the stern half of the broken Liberty and radioed naval headquarters in Halifax.

Naval Operations called Foundation. It seemed a long-odds chance to send a tug four hundred miles into that gale-lashed sea to try and save the stern of the Liberty. But it was a chance worth taking, for once more the U-boats had come back to gain the upper hand, and once again Allied shipping losses were rising to appalling figures. Half a ship, with her engines undamaged, could sail again with a new forward section welded on.

Woollcombe agreed to take the gamble. He went down to the docks, where he found Brushett aboard *Franklin*, writing up the report of his last operation.

"We've got a tough one for you, Cap," he said. "The stern half of a Liberty, four hundred miles to the east. You know what the weather's like. The planes have spotted her twice now, but only through rifts in the overcast, and they never got a position you could use. You'll have to look for her blind."

Franklin put to sea within the hour and despite foul weather, driving snow squalls, and the usual heavy seas, by March 3 she had reached the approximate position where the *Poinsett* had last been seen. There was nothing to see now, and no way to see it in any case. The snow squalls had become so nearly continuous that a lookout was lucky to get one glimpse through a "hole" for each hour spent staring into the white nothingness.

The search seemed hopeless. It was doubtful if the hulk was still afloat, for the gales had gone northwest and the seas were big enough to belabor a whole ship into submission. It required little enough imagination to visualize what they would do to the thin bulkhead of a half-ship. Nevertheless, Brushett set up a search pattern and began steaming in twenty-mile legs from north to south along the *Poinsett*'s probable line of drift.

For *Franklin*'s people what followed was frigid monotony, combined with the usual fatigue of life at sea during a winter storm. Once a day, if they were lucky, they got a hot mug of tea from the galley. Usually they ate hardtack and canned stuff. The fug and stench continued to build up in the tightly closed accommodations until men who had been to sea for thirty years were sick unto exhaustion. The seas beat down upon the old iron decks with a steady, insistent clangor. In the stokeholds the black gang shovelled coal and hauled out ashes, and the engineers watched the steam gauges with bloodshot eyes.

They searched — and every time they thought that there was no more hope, an aircraft radioed a report that the *Poinsett* was still afloat. Seventeen times Brushett laid a course for the rough positions given by the planes. Seventeen times he found only snow-blurred, empty ocean.

The search continued for eight interminable days. When *Franklin*'s people wanted change and exercise they emerged from the alleyways, roped in pairs, and fought the accumulating ice with picks and axes until the cold penetrated their wet clothes and drove them in again.

On the evening of the eighth day, a Royal Navy armed trawler bore down upon them and flashed a signal:

HAVE FOUND YOUR GIRL JUST FOLLOW ME

Franklin swung up into the wind and followed avidly. But not quite believing. And then, very suddenly, the high grey hulk of half a ship loomed up ahead.

"She was a terror to behold," Brushett recalls. "Seeing her suddenly and close up like that, after days of staring at empty sea, she looked as big as the whole of Newfoundland. We had no time to stare at her, though. I figured we had to get a line on her that very hour or we would lose her in the night. Grandy and Bellfountain, my deck officers, came to the bridge and we planned the thing.

"Grandy and three men were to take a dory and board her somehow, while I brought *Franklin* in so the two ships were stern to stern and close enough so the boarding crew could hoist the pendant and shackles aboard by man power alone. There was no time for anything else that night. We knew it was pretty risky, but with the *Franklin* under us nobody worried very much."

Brushett's assessment of the situation varies in only one detail from that of his men. As Innes, the new chief engineer, put it, "With Brushett on the bridge, nobody worried very much."

Brushett was worried, all the same. He always hated to see

any of his men leave *Franklin* during bad weather, even in that paragon of virtues, a Newfoundland dory; and he sweated until they were safely back aboard again. This evening, in darkness that was already so heavy that the searchlight had to be switched on, he watched Grandy, Bo'sun Harry Strickland, and Able Seamen Stanley Young, Clifford Boudreau, and Angus Chiasson jump into the dory as it lay heaving wildly at *Franklin*'s rail. He watched as the four men took their stroke and the pumpkin seed flipped high on the crests of waves that were running twenty to thirty feet in height, and then slid away again toward the towering bulk of the *Poinsett*. He waited until he saw them against the side of that steel cliff; and then he began to handle his ship.

Words can tell little of what it means to back a vessel to within spitting distance of the stern of a derelict that is looming mountainous above your transom, and to do it in a full gale, at night, in the depths of the winter ocean. Words cannot say how it is done, either. Only the hands of men — of the helmsman at the wheel, of the skipper on the telegraph handle, of the engineer officer at the throttle — can *show* how it is done.

When the maneuvering was over, *Franklin*'s stern lay eight feet from the massive blades of *Poinsett*'s propeller as these rose clear of the water, hung ten feet in the air, and then crashed down to vanish in white foam again.

In order to con his ship, Brushett was forced to take a position on the tiller grating in the extreme after part of the tug. From this precarious vantage point he directed things by means of men posted at the head of the engine room companion and at the foot of the bridge, who relayed his shouted orders to the chief engineer and to the helmsman.

As the *Poinsett* began each ponderous lift, and her cruiser stern began to rise full fifty feet above the pygmies who would try to save her, Brushett edged *Franklin* in. Then as that four-thousand-ton pile-driver of grey steel began to fall, *Franklin* inched out to let it clear her by the span of a man's arms.

Meanwhile the boat's crew had gone aboard — but not as easily as that. Grandy and his gang had come alongside and had tried to seize the dangling boat falls and shinny up them, but the dory was lifting and falling so steeply that this proved impossible. Grandy had thought it might be so, and so he had come prepared with a coil of light line attached to a small grapnel. Waiting until a wave brought them up within twenty feet of the *Poinsett*'s rail, he threw his iron, and it caught. As the dory fell away he paid out line, but already Stanley Young was halfway up to the deck far above. Three of them went up that way, shinnying up a single thin rope that was already coated in freezing slush.

Their job then was to catch a heaving line from *Franklin*'s stern and, without bothering to use a messenger, to haul in the ends of two one-hundred-and-fifty-foot wire pendants and make them fast on the port and starboard after bollards.

Each pendant was a leg of the bridle which would take the towing wire. Each pendant, with its shackles, thimbles, and its share of the common swivel, weighed six hundred pounds. Three men had to take each pendant up by the strength of their arms alone.

They did it; but only because Brushett held *Franklin* in, through the thirty minutes of that struggle, with such unbelievable skill that she never once swung out to drag the shackles overboard and thereby tear the pendants from the hands of the three straining men above.

When they had one pendant fast to the *Poinsett*, things became even touchier aboard the tug. She could no longer get away even if she wanted to. Her movements became those of a terrier on a close tether. The *Poinsett* rose and fell, and just as the second pendant was made fast, she fell too soon.

Brushett describes that moment perfectly:

"I looked up at her," he said, "and I could see she was going to come down square in my lap. But she was one woman who wasn't welcome to sit there."

Brushett got clear, but the *Poinsett* came down on *Franklin* with such irresistible force that she squashed the bulwarks flat and drove *Franklin*'s stern three feet under water. That she did not smash the steering gear was one of those little miracles which sometimes occur so that seamen can live their lives to a full conclusion.

Franklin's propeller was already turning frenziedly as her stern came up again, and she scooted out from under like a puppy whose tail has just been stepped upon. The winch began to hiss and chatter as the towing wire paid out, and the men of little faith who had closed their eyes at the moment of impact opened them again with a memorable relief.

The dory crew came back in darkness, and although they were not completely exhausted, nevertheless it took strong hands to haul them over the rail to safety. Then, and then only, Brushett could relax and take the hard-bitten, empty pipe out of his teeth, and fill it with a steady hand.

"We thought, y'know," he remembers with a half smile, "that the worst was over. Sailors always think like that — perhaps they have to. But we might have known . . . she turned out to be the most terrible thing to tow that I have ever seen! She simply would not come. She would do everything but somersault on the end of the wire. Two or three times an hour she would turn right end for end, and we'd be staring back right into her open wound. She should have sunk herself, but it looked like she wanted to sink us first."

Grimly *Franklin* hung on to the incubus astern. Stubbornly her engines labored and at their best managed to turn up enough revolutions to give the tow three knots. At the worst *Franklin* stood still.

"The only hope we had of moving that abomination, and of keeping her under some kind of control, was to tow dead into wind," Innes remembers, "and by the grace of God we had a nor'east gale most of the way home. It didn't quite last out though, and on the last day we had to heave-to and wait forty-eight hours for the wind to veer back into the east."

It was probably the first and last time in *Franklin*'s history that any of her people looked with real affection on a nor'east gale.

The tow home took a week. While they were still four days out of port *Franklin* ran short of grub and the ubiquitous Grandy and his crew took to their dory and fetched a barrel of butter, a case of canned meat, and ten pounds of tea from the hulk. And for this act of piracy they were later severely castigated by the War Shipping Administration in Halifax. That castigation was the closest thing they ever got to recognition for the services they rendered to the bureaucrats who ran the war at sea.

They did not care. They got their recognition elsewhere, and it was of the kind that counts.

As they neared the coast the murk lifted a little and Brushett found to his horror that he and his recalcitrant floating anchor were heading fair and square into the middle of an outbound convoy of a hundred ships.

It was a dreadful moment. *Franklin* had not a hope of hauling clear and Brushett did not wish to break radio silence and thereby jeopardize the convoy by asking its commodore for instructions. He gripped his pipe a little more fiercely, and waited for events.

The armada bore down irresistibly. "A whole damned ocean full of ships," Innes recalls with awe. And at the moment when it seemed that *Franklin* must be overwhelmed, a signal string showed from the commodore's ship. It said:

> ALL VESSELS WILL ALTER PORT AND STARBOARD TO CLEAR THE TUG AND TOW.
> And to the *Franklin*: STEER YOUR COURSE AND BEST OF LUCK GOOD FRIEND.

And so they did as they were told and steered their course. Right down the middle of that phalanx *Franklin* steered, her funnels belching black and her crew all out upon the deck. And as they passed through the vast convoy, each merchant ship in turn saluted with her whistle; and the outbound crews lined the rails and cheered the little one who had saved one of their sisters from the northern seas.

That was the kind of recognition that had meaning for the salvage men. It was the only kind they ever cared about.

FROM
The Serpent's Coil

The Serpent's Coil *tells how a hurricane unexpectedly cut through the North Atlantic shipping lanes in September 1948, disabling or sinking any number of ships.* Leicester, *a Liberty ship in ballast, was one of those disabled. She was found and rescued by* Foundation Josephine, *successor to* Foundation Franklin, *after an ordeal lasting six weeks, part of which is recounted here. The story begins before* Leicester's *crippling disablement had been discovered.*

❖

While *Lillian* was streaking for Halifax — every man aboard her with his fingers crossed, and an eye cocked apprehensively on the door of Sparkie's shack — and while *Josephine* headed for North Sydney, another vessel was about to claim the attention of Foundation Maritime.

She was the 5000-ton Greek collier *Orion*, en route from Sydney to Botwood on the northeast coast of Newfoundland with a cargo of soft coal.

Orion was typical of a class — or family perhaps — of vessels notorious the world over. With their predilection for antiquities the Greeks had, over the years, collected under their flag some of the most ancient, worn-out, and misbegotten vessels of all time. When a ship flying some other flag finally grew so old and rickety that she was only fit for the shipbreaker's yard, chances were always good that some Greek skipper would come along and buy her for a song. Sometimes he would have financial help from his officers who were often his sons or sons-in-law. The old ship would then become very much a family affair. Her cabins would be filled to overflowing with buxom wives and numerous children. Any available clear space on her deck would sprout pens for sheep, goats, chickens, and even a cow or two. She would become, in the best usage of the word, a true ocean-going tramp beating her way around the world; going wherever she could get a cargo, and taking that cargo wherever its owner wanted it delivered.

Orion had not been home to Greece for two full years. To trace her course over those years would be to imitate the Odyssey; but on the next-to-final lap of her wanderings she had come to Sydney looking for a cargo, and she had found one there.

She was so old that no one admitted to a knowledge of her birth date. Rust had eaten her plates paper-thin, and her ancient Scotch boiler and triple-expansion engine really deserved a place in some museum on the Clyde. Still, the engine worked, and *Orion* plodded about the oceans at a laborious eight knots.

She was working up through the Straits of Belle Isle on the night of September 19th when the gale which had plagued the two salvage tugs overtook her. The waters she was sailing were narrow, and renowned for their inhospitality to vessels during heavy weather. *Orion* had no radar, of course, and her ancient radio transmitter was hardly of much more use than a crystal set. Her people presumably possessed a chart of Belle Isle Straits but, if they did, it did not prove of much service to them.

Wallowing and snorting through the storm like a water buffalo, the aged vessel was almost up to Flower Island in the Straits when she found herself attempting to take a short-cut through the land behind that island. She was not up to it. There was an ugly sound of crumpling iron plates, followed by an outraged uproar from the chickens, the sheep, and the vessel's cow.

But *Orion* was so low-powered, and had so little way on her, that even running into a cliff could not do her any mortal damage; and at dawn on the 20th she was able to back off the shore under her own steam.

She was afloat again, but her people were in something of a

quandary: her forward hold was taking water and the soft coal was turning to slush in the bilges and clogging the bilge pumps. Worse still, the coal was heating up by spontaneous combustion — and had probably been doing so ever since she sailed from Sydney. The influx of salt water after the collision with the shore simply hastened the process, and wisps of smoke together with a strong smell of coal gas were soon seeping out from under her forward hatches.

Some of the crew now began looking back wistfully at the land from which they had so recently parted company. When, shortly after 0900 hours, the forehatch blew off with a resounding WHUMPH and smoke began to pour from the opening, her Captain promptly headed *Orion* back for the familiar rocks.

That Captain was an unfortunate man. When he wanted to stay in deep water he ran into the land. Now that he wished to run his ship ashore and beach her, he ran her hard on an off-lying reef nearly a mile from shore.

Shortly after she hit the reef, *Orion*'s radio officer managed to transmit an SOS. At 1030 hours Foundation Maritime in Halifax received the following cable from their agents in St. John's, Newfoundland:

GREEK STEAMER ORION 5000 GROSS TONS CARGO COAL
SYDNEY BOTWOOD REPORTED AGROUND FLOWER ISLAND
SHIP ON FIRE CREW ABANDONING

Featherstone immediately checked *Orion*'s antecedents in the biblical-looking *Lloyd's Register of Shipping*. He was not impressed. Still, a ship in trouble is a ship in trouble, and Foundation boasted that it had never failed to do its best for any ship that needed help. A message went out to *Josephine* — then some hundred and fifty miles away from Sydney — telling Cowley to divert at once and proceed to *Orion*'s rescue. By noon *Josephine* had altered course to pass through the Cabot Straits, bound for Belle Isle.

The distance was about thirty-five hours' steaming at full speed for *Josephine*. By late evening of the 21st she raised Flower Island Light and her people could dimly see the unprepossessing hulk of the *Orion* sitting forlornly on the offshore reefs.

There was no time to be lost. Exposed from every side to wind and sea, *Orion* could not hope to survive even a moderate blow. Although it was now almost pitch dark, Cowley brought *Josephine* in as close as he dared, feeling his way with the echo sounder through the "sunkers" — the appropriate name which Newfoundlanders give to underwater reefs and rocks. A quick inspection showed that *Orion* was aground for half her length and that she was open to the sea in at least two of her holds.

Cowley and his salvage foreman, diver Ray Squires, were doubtful that the vessel would have sufficient value left in her, even if she were freed, to meet the salvage costs — but they prepared to do their best. A Lloyd's Open Form agreement was signed by the two captains.

At dawn *Josephine* was eased through the reefs and made fast alongside *Orion*. The salvors, fighting their way through a mob of sheep which had broken out of their pen during the general excitement, and brushing aside an angry flutter of cockerels, began swinging their gear aboard.

Three big gasoline pumps came first, and these were soon discharging streams of black and stinking water over the side. At the same time, two clam buckets were swung out of *Josephine*'s hold and deposited on *Orion*'s deck. Using the casualty's own derricks and winches — she still had steam — these clams were then put to work jettisoning coal out of Numbers 3 and 4 holds in order to lighten the ship.

Simultaneously, fire hoses were run from *Josephine*'s bulk CO_2 tanks to *Orion*'s Number 1 hold, and the fire was soon smothered.

The old vessel's decks had become a scene of thundering, clanging, rattling, baa-a-a-a-ing, and mooing activity.

Jettisoning of coal continued but there was a heavy swell running and *Orion*'s old plates were being steadily crumpled against the reefs. Not even the big eight-inch salvage pumps could lower the water in her holds significantly, and by early afternoon it began to look like a losing battle — so much that the Captain of the *Orion* eventually shrugged his shoulders, made a sweeping gesture which seemed to convey that he was washing his hands of the whole affair, then went ashore — for good.

By 1500 hours the wind had begun to rise out of the west and shortly thereafter *Josephine* had to cast off and feel her way back out to deeper water, where she anchored. Cowley had left his Third Mate, Freddie Squires (Ray Squires's brother), and five salvage men aboard the *Orion*, with twenty or thirty Newfoundland fishermen who had been hired to assist. A dozen of *Orion*'s crew and all the livestock also remained aboard.

Within an hour it was evident that the westerly was going to blow up into a full gale. At this juncture the fishermen politely announced they were going home to Flower Cove while they were able. They climbed into their one-lung motor skiffs and putted away through the surf which was already beginning to break on the nearby reefs. With their departure, as Squires said afterwards, he began to feel a little lonely.

"The gale got up remarkably fast. By seven o'clock it was blowing Force 8 or 9 and the sea was breaking white all around us. We could see *Josephine* was dragging her anchors and was in trouble herself. She got one hook up but the other jammed in the rocks and she finally had to cut the cable and abandon it. Then she steamed out to sea. There was nothing else for her to do. She couldn't have come anywhere near us, drawing the water she did, and to have stayed close to the coast in a howling westerly would have been plain foolishness.

"After she pulled out we felt twice as lonely. We had no boats and anyway ordinary ships' boats couldn't have lived in the sea that was breaking right across the *Orion*.

"The Greeks began to get awfully nervous. They kept asking me to use the radio to call *Josie* back. When I wouldn't, they began to jump up and down and shout. I didn't want to drown any more than they did — but *Josie* couldn't have helped us anyway.

"Buck Dassylva, he was our pumpman aboard, came on deck to tell me the whole bottom was going out of the ship and the engine room was flooding. We hustled down there right quick and put out the fires. All we needed to make things really interesting just about then was a good boiler explosion.

"When we put out the fires, the Greeks seemed to think that was the end, and they started chasing me round and round the ship trying to get me to perform a miracle on the radio.

"I couldn't understand the Greeks very well, but I tell you, I *could* outrun them. Of course there were a lot of obstacles. Every now and again I'd fall over a sheep or goat, and Buck would laugh like hell. I think he was making book on me.

"Meantime Cowley had sent out a general SOS for help, and he got an answer from a Newfoundland revenue cutter, the *Marvita*, which was lying in Flower Cove to shelter from the gale. She was a shallow-draught boat and her skipper, Captain Houndsel, was a real old-time Newfoundlander, the kind that are supposed to be half seal. It was a good thing for us he was around, because he was probably the only man on that whole coast who would have dared to try and get us off the *Orion*.

"About ten o'clock even the Greeks had given up, and none of us thought the future looked very bright. *Orion* was breaking up under us and we figured she couldn't last much longer. Then, all of a sudden, a searchlight cut through the storm, and a blinker light started up.

"I got hold of a flashlight and answered back. It was Houndsel in the *Marvita*, and he signalled that he was going to try and pick his way right through those shoals — they were breaking white as milk — and pick us up.

"He warned us to be ready. 'Will lie alongside for sixty seconds,' he signalled. He wouldn't have dared stay longer, and I don't know yet how he risked putting her alongside *Orion* at all.

"I had everybody lined up at the rail waiting for him when he flashed another signal: 'Don't come empty handed.'

"I knew what he meant. *Orion* had more booze aboard her than Halifax could have drunk in a week. I hustled around and got every man to tuck a couple of bottles into his jacket or his shirt. Sort of passage money you might say. Remembering that *Marvita* was a revenue boat, I only hoped Houndsel had left the revenue officers behind in Flower Cove.

"Houndsel brought the *Marvita* in like a bird. She just touched alongside, and everyone was aboard of her in one jump, and then Houndsel was backing her out to sea. About then some of the bottles just seemed to pop open by themselves.

"When we got clear we made a rough passage around to Flower Cove. As we were going into the harbor, I could hear what sounded like a hundred motor boats starting up. Houndsel switched on the searchlight, and there was every boat in Flower

Cove that had a motor and would float at all, heading out to sea.

"Can you imagine it! A Force 9 gale on a lee shore, and those little skiffs were heading right out into it. I couldn't figure what was going on so I asked Houndsel. He just grinned and said, 'Well, Bye, y'know the *Orion*'s abandoned now.' He didn't need to say another word.

"Next morning the gale had pretty well blown itself out and I went back to the wreck to see about the gear we had left on board. She really *was* a wreck by then. Completely broken, and a total loss — and stripped as clean as a whistle! Those fishermen hadn't left a thing to go to waste — not even the cow.

"I couldn't for the life of me figure how they got the cow off of her. So I asked one of the local boys, as a special favor, to tell me how they managed to get a cow into a skiff in that kind of a storm.

"He said, 'We never put her in no skiff. She'd have sunk it, and us too. We just ties a rope around her horns and kicks her overboard, and when she gets clear of the reefs we picks up the free end of the line and swims her home!' "

While Squires had been involved aboard the *Orion*, a startling encounter had been taking place a thousand miles away to the southeast.

◆

While Josephine *was occupied with* Orion *her smaller sister,* Foundation Lillian, *had been scouring the mid-ocean wastes for the abandoned Liberty ship* Leicester. *That* Leicester *was still afloat when* Lillian *finally found her seemed almost miraculous.*

◆

"As we bore down on her nobody had a word to say. I guess most of the men never thought we'd find her, and some of us had begun to wonder if she existed at all.

"It wasn't just the end of the days and days of uncertainty that got us — it was the look of the ship herself. Nobody aboard *Lillian* had ever seen anything quite like it — and during the war most of us saw plenty of torpedoed derelicts. Torpedoed ships were always low in the water, usually half awash. But this ship stuck up until she looked damn near as big as the *Queen Mary*. She looked to me to be lying flat on her side, and right on top of the water like the great-granddaddy of the biggest whale that ever was.

"She seemed so unnatural — for a ship — that it was indecent. As we closed with her there wasn't a man who wasn't waiting for her to finish her roll and slip away down before our eyes.

"We came up from her starboard side — or maybe I should say from her bottom side, since her bilge keel was a good ten feet out of the water. As we came around her bows so we could see her decks and superstructure, I began to feel as nervous as a kid waiting for the big bang at a fireworks show. We were thinking: what in the name of God is stopping her from going over? She seemed to have about a fifty-degree permanent list, but she was rolling down past seventy degrees. Each time she rolled, the seas ran in over her decks, and some broke clean above the edge of her boat deck. As we came past her port side we could almost look down her funnel.

"When I remembered that this ship had been abandoned at the tag-end of a hurricane more than ten days earlier, and had drifted derelict about six hundred miles to the southeast through three heavy storms and a lot of ordinary bad weather, I knew I was looking at some kind of sea-going miracle. Not the churchy kind, you understand, but the kind ships sometimes seem to be able to pull off on their own, without any help from men or God. This was a ship that didn't want to die."

At 1700 hours Featherstone's secretary finished decoding a message which had been received a few minutes earlier. Featherstone was not exactly hanging over her shoulder — he would not have betrayed his impatience quite so blatantly — but almost as soon as her pencil stopped moving, his big hand closed over the transcript:

FOUNDATION HALIFAX
   LYING OFF CASUALTY HAS 50 DEGREE LIST INCREASING TO 70 DEGREES IN SWELLS STOP DOES NOT APPEAR TO BE MAKING WATER STOP WILL ATTEMPT TO BOARD TONIGHT BUT WILL NOT ATTEMPT TOW TILL EXAMINED CASUALTY STOP WILL WORK WITH JOSEPHINE CONFIRM WHO SHOULD TAKE

TOW STOP NO SIGN RIVAL TUG BUT THINK NEAR AT HAND
— CROWE

Featherstone laid the message down, dug out a cigar and
carefully lit it. His only comment was: "Mmmmm. Damn near
time." But the outthrust jaw no longer looked like the prow of
an icebreaker and the pale blue eyes seemed almost gentle.

In his reply to Crowe, Featherstone was positively garrulous.

> GOOD WORK CONSIDER JOSEPHINE SHOULD TOW AHEAD
> WITH LILLIAN FREE TO GO ON LINE ASTERN TO STEER IF
> NEEDED COWLEY AND YOU HAVE TO DETERMINE BEST
> METHOD BY TRIAL STOP DETERMINE DESTINATION SIMI-
> LARLY BUT CONSIDER BETTER CHANCES FAVOURABLE
> WEATHER TOWARD BERMUDA STOP IMPERATIVE YOU GET
> MEN ABOARD NOW TO AVOID CHANCES RIVAL TUG HOOKING
> UP IN NIGHT — FETER

Crowe and Rose, on *Lillian*'s bridge, read the message together.
A little ruefully Crowe said:

"Feathers has really let himself go, hasn't he? Actually forced
himself to say 'Good work.' Well, let's get on with it."

At exactly 0800 hours on October 3 the way began to come
off *Josephine* and her crew began to shorten up the tow line. As
the little convoy closed with the land, three harbor tugs, their
sirens sounding, came bustling out from the entrance of the
narrows. Leading them was the pilot boat bearing an easily
recognizable Featherstone who was so far forgetting his dignity
as to wave both hands high in the air.

It was a magnificent moment even for the most blasé members
of the rescue tugs; but they had little enough time to savor it.

The pilot boat bumped against *Josephine*'s bulwarks just long
enough for a pilot to leap aboard, then it was off to *Leicester*. The
pause here was a little longer, for Featherstone and the Chief
Pilot both had to be landed on the derelict. Within minutes they
had clambered up the canted deck using the same ropes that had
been fixed in place by the salvage men at sea.

The pilot went directly to the bridge and wedged himself on
the high starboard wing. Featherstone made a rapid tour of the

ship to satisfy himself that all was as he had expected it to be, and that his plans would not be upset by some previously unknown factor. Only then did he join the pilot and give the signal for the tow to carry on.

By this time *Josephine* had shortened up so that there was less than three hundred yards of wire between her and *Leicester*. The Army tug *ST-10* had placed a hawser on *Leicester*'s stern and was falling back into a position from which she could help to steer the unwieldy hulk. The Admiralty tug *Justice* had come alongside on the starboard quarter and was ready to assist. *Lillian* and the second Army tug were standing by.

At 1005 *Josephine* passed between the two buoys marking the entrance to the channel. At that exact moment *Leicester* took a sharp sheer to starboard.

Cowley immediately put the tug's helm hard over; but *Leicester*'s sheer only grew worse. *ST-10* began going full astern but *Leicester* still moved implacably toward the coral reefs which now lay less than a hundred feet away. *Justice*'s Master, sensing the urgency of the moment, did not wait for orders. He cast off his lines and slid his tug forward along *Leicester*'s exposed bottom until she could put her nose against the big ship's starboard bow. Then *Justice*'s screw began to kick the shallowing water into foam.

Slowly, slowly, *Leicester*'s bow began to swing back into the channel, back behind *Josephine*.

With the tow straightened out once more, Cowley discovered he was having trouble keeping *Leicester* moving. Baffled, he called on Gilmour for more power, but the big ship astern continued to hang back as if she were wilfully dragging her heels.

Featherstone and the pilot, glancing astern from *Leicester*'s bridge, saw the clear blue waters going milky white! *Leicester* indeed *was* dragging her heels, or rather her stern, upon the coral bottom.

There was nothing to be done about it. There was no room to turn in order to head her back to deeper water. The only hope was to continue towing and pray she was only running over a small area of spoil which the dredges had somehow neglected to remove.

At every instant Featherstone expected her to take the ground solidly. If that happened, he was convinced she would have rolled right over.

The entrance channel to Murray's Anchorage is two miles long. It took the combined flotilla of tugs just under two hours to ease the *Leicester*, still sheering erratically, still dragging her stern, through those two miles of torment. She was intractable to the last. As Myalls said afterwards, "That was the longest part of the whole damn tow."

But at 1340 hours *Leicester* cleared the inside channel approach, and *Josephine* swung her down the broad South Channel.

At 1406 hours *Leicester* lay securely moored to a battleship mooring buoy in Murray's Anchorage.

Shortly after 1400 hours a flight of four patrol bombers had taken off en route for Tampa, Florida, on a routine training mission. The big aircraft had gone thundering into the air only a few hundred yards above *Leicester* and her attendant tug.

Barely twenty minutes later the flight leader had begun calling his Bermuda base, and what he had to report was of a nature calculated to send the base meteorologists into an immediate flurry of activity. The results of this activity were relayed by telephone to Bermuda Radio, and at 1452 hours the station was transmitting in both code and voice.

Vatcher, who had been ordered by Cowley to remain on listening watch, was almost deafened when the international code began to clatter out of his loudspeaker over 500 kilocycles:

BERMUDA RADIO TO ALL STATIONS EMERGENCY HURRICANE WARNING WEST INDIES HURRICANE CHANGED COURSE EASTWARD HEADING DIRECT BERMUDA ETA BETWEEN 1900 AND 2200 HOURS TAKE IMMEDIATE PRECAUTIONS

Except for the masters of the several vessels lying in Bermuda waters — men who could smell approaching weather without the aid of radio reports — the sudden change in the course of the hurricane caught the islanders off guard. Even after the emergency warning was broadcast, there were many who thought it was probably a false alarm.

They had some reason for their doubts. In order to threaten

the island directly, Hurricane IX would have had to alter its course by nearly 40 degrees, and do so within a matter of an hour or two. It was not really credible that this could have happened.

But it had.

"It was almost as if the damned thing suddenly took a look around from fifteen thousand feet and saw Bermuda off to the east, with the *Leicester* lying there in Murray's Anchorage. If it had been human, or inhuman but sentient, it could hardly have reacted more directly. One minute it was heading into the northeast. The next, it spotted the ship which two previous hurricanes had failed to sink, and it seemed to make up its mind right off the bat, deciding it would finish off the job." This from a meteorologist. This from a scientist — and scientists are not much given to anthropomorphic explanations of natural phenomena.

The Anchorage was no place to be caught by a hurricane. In those constricted, reef-studded waters, totally unprotected from north, west, or southwest winds, and very slightly protected from really heavy seas, a ship's master who chose to remain in so dubious a shelter was pushing his luck to the limit. The alternative, and the only one, assuming that it was impossible to find mooring in St. George's, was to put to sea, get well clear of the reefs, and then steam in such a manner as to keep the body of the island between the ship and the prevailing direction of the hurricane.

Standing on *Leicester*'s bridge, the Salvage Master watched a cruiser, three destroyers, and six merchant vessels, all of which had been peacefully at anchor half an hour earlier, steaming at full speed toward the exit channel. It was not a sight to engender a feeling of complacency. Nevertheless there was nothing Featherstone could do which he had not already done to protect the *Leicester*. She could not be moved towards St. George's Harbour — the hurricane would certainly catch her on the way. She could not be towed out to sea for, even if there was sufficient time for this maneuver, she would stand little chance of weathering the blow outside. All she could do was stay "where she was at," as the Newfoundlanders put it, and trust to her doubled moorings and to the three ten-ton concrete anchors of the battleship buoy.

But this was not *quite* all. She could, if Featherstone and Cowley so decided, also put her trust in *Josephine*.

At 1520, as the motor launch was bucking its way back out to *Leicester* through an increasingly heavy chop, Featherstone boarded *Josephine* and spoke to Cowley.

"The choice is yours, John," he said. "*Josephine* is your vessel and I can't give you orders where her safety's at stake. If you think you ought to go to sea, I'll support you. But if you think it's a reasonable risk to stay alongside, I'll support that too. Frankly, I'd hate to see you go. I'd feel we were abandoning this ship. The power you've got might make the difference whether she rides this one out or whether she goes ashore. If we leave her and she breaks free and drives out to the reefs, that's the end of her. If you stay, and the same thing happens, it might be the end of *Josie* too. But it would have to be one hell of a hurricane to shift the two of you, with those concrete anchors down and your thirty-two-thousand horsepower to ease the strain."

Cowley did not hesitate. He had already thought the matter through and he agreed with Featherstone that it would be little short of cowardice to abandon *Leicester* — even though she was not their vessel, nor even their responsibility now that the salvage contract had been fulfilled.

"We'll stick it out, Cap," he said. "We'll ride it out."

By the time Featherstone regained *Leicester*'s deck, the motor launch was back alongside. She looked as if she had had a rough trip of it, for her "captain" and "engineer" were both busy bailing and pumping, while five of *Josie*'s crew stood by with boathooks to keep her from staving her gunwales in against the tug.

During the preceding half-hour both sea and wind had risen so rapidly that they were now of full storm proportions. Seaward, the swells preceding the hurricane were bursting over the barrier reefs with a roar which could be heard seven miles away in St. George, and with a violence which sent the spray leaping fifty feet into the darkening air.

To the westward the sky had assumed the terrible black mantle of the hurricane bar. Air pressure was dropping so rapidly that no mechanical barometer was needed to indicate the fact — every man was his own barometer, as human organs, sensitized by apprehension, registered the decrease physically. Storm scud was already sweeping in, almost at masthead height, and only a cold grey light filtered vaguely through the roiling cirrus clouds above.

Before the eye of the storm began passing over Bermuda, the cyclone had been blowing from southeast. After the passage of the eye, the raging winds which again burst upon the island did so from the northwest.

When the period of calm began, *Leicester* and *Josephine* were lying bow to bow, facing into the southeast. Consequently when the terrible wind heralding the arrival of the second portion of the hurricane struck, it caught the two vessels from astern.

In any ordinary gale they would have swung in a semicircle with the battleship mooring as a pivot, and would have again presented their bows to the wind. This was no ordinary gale.

"When that unholy terror slammed into us, it was like we'd been rammed by an icebreaker coming up from astern. We never had a chance to swing. The wind pushed us forward right over the battleship mooring.

"I was in *Josie*'s wheelhouse and I could see the buoy — it was a steel drum about twenty feet long and maybe ten in diameter — slide off *Leicester*'s port bow and come down between her and *Josephine*. I could guess what was going to happen when it wedged in between our bow and *Leicester*. As I watched the damn thing, I was so interested I never even opened my mouth. Not that words could have helped us then.

"The buoy fetched up between the two ships with a jolt that nearly shook me off my feet. By the time I got a grip on something and peered out again, I couldn't see the buoy or anything.

"It wasn't the rain coming down that cut visibility to zero, it was the ocean going up. The first gust of wind blew away the hurricane seas as if they'd been made of sawdust. It blew them right into the air and turned them into a kind of salty muck that was too thick to breathe, and too thin to swim in. There wasn't any boundary between sea and air; you couldn't tell where one began and where the other quit.

"We might just as well have been in a submarine for all we could tell of what was happening around us. We couldn't see anything, and the roar of the storm was so bad we couldn't hear anything. It was like living in a silent movie. Cowley, the Squires boys, and three or four others were all in the wheelhouse, and we could see each other's lips moving but you could hardly hear a word unless you stuck your ear right up against the other fellow's mouth.

"We didn't need to hear or see, to know what that buoy was doing. It was jammed between the two ships like a wedge, and both ships were driving down on it as if they were under full power in the open sea. They told us afterwards the wind was supposed to have reached speeds of more than 140 miles an hour — and a wind like that can do some pushing!

"The worst of it was, the buoy had dragged the mooring chain right under *Leicester*'s bottom so she couldn't swing and get her head around into the wind. She was caught almost broadside-to, and not even thirty tons of concrete anchors could have held her broadside against that blow for long.

"Something had to give. Cowley figured the only hope for *Leicester* was for us to let go our lines so the buoy would free itself and let the *Leicester* come round head into it. He rang the engine room for stand-by and then Wally and a couple of deck-hands undertook to go out on deck and cast off the lines.

"They had to crawl on hands and knees, and they damn near suffocated. The wind was so strong you could hardly suck the air into your lungs — and when you did the wind would suck it right back out. Anyway, the stuff you got wasn't air at all — it was salt-water soup.

"Wally reached the starboard forward bitts somehow though, and he saw right away it was impossible to do anything with the lines, except maybe cut them. The tension on them was so great nothing could have slacked them off.

"Our bow mooring was a doubled length of one-and-a-quarter-inch towing wire — the kind old *Foundation Franklin* used to have on her winch, and plenty strong enough to haul a big ship through a winter gale. It was made fast to the bitts or niggerheads, which were of heavy cast iron and bolted right through the deck into the ship's frames. The wire was crossed around them both.

"Wally could only see about five or six feet in front of him — what with the muck that was flying about. He was lying there trying to figure what to do next when he noticed the bitts *start to bend in toward each other*. He didn't believe his eyes at first, but when he looked along the wire to where it went through the bulwarks, he saw that the fairlead — that's an iron casting two inches thick — had broken like a piece of glass and the wire was cutting its way back through the bulwarks.

"He had to wiggle some to get out of the way. By the time he got back to the accommodations, that wire had cut through thirty feet of half-inch steel plating as easy as opening a sardine can. Then the forward bitts snapped off. We never heard them go but we felt the ship give a heavy shudder, and we knew.

"After the bow mooring went, the rest didn't take long to follow. There were steel wires and eight-inch ropes bursting like bits of string all down our starboard side, until we were only held by a single ten-inch manila hawser aft. Someone crawled out on deck to try to cut this with an axe, but before he got to it we had swung right around and smashed our port side against the *Leicester*'s bow, buckling half a dozen shell plates on *Josie* and making a hell of a dint in the *Leicester* as well.

"Then the ten-inch line parted, and we were free.

"Cowley rang for full speed on both engines. We knew we had just one chance — and that was to get *Josie* headed up into the wind and hold her there with the engines. There wasn't much room to play about in either. There were coral reefs on three sides, and the land on the fourth.

"*Josie* had thirty-two hundred horsepower — more than there is in some ocean liners. But even with both engines going at full revs she still wouldn't come up into that wind! She couldn't do it. She kept blowing sideways; and only God knew where she was blowing to.

"Dave Clark was at the wheel — as good a wheelsman as you'd ever find — and he tried every trick he knew to make her head into it — and got nowhere at all. Things were getting right desperate about then, so Cowley sent Wally forward to let go the anchor — we just had one anchor left, we'd lost our second hook on the *Orion* job. Wally crawled out there again, knocked off the brake, and let run about seven shots of chain. The hook caught, and we could feel just a little bit of a jerk and then the chain parted like it was made of mud.

"It was just twenty-five minutes since the wind first hit us, but

I tell you it seemed like twenty-five hours. When the anchor chain broke and we knew we were teetotally out of luck, every minute got as long as a year.

"The wind hadn't let up one bit. Every now and again a real nasty gust would take us on the quarter and lay us right over — the way a man would kick over a beer bottle with his foot.

"We were all straining our ears to catch the roar of breakers on the reefs, but we might as well have tried to hear a tin whistle in the middle of a fiddlers' contest.

"Things weren't so good down below either. We'd taken a lot of damage when we hit the *Leicester* and the pumps were working hard to keep the water down. God only knows what Gilmour and his crowd thought was happening up on deck. If there was any prayerful men amongst them, they must have been working overtime to get a hearing.

"Freddie — the skipper's dog — was in the wheelhouse with us, and I felt real sorry for him. He was getting too old for this sort of stuff. All he wanted to do was find a quiet corner and lay down. But every time he got settled someone would fall over him, or a sea or gust would hit us and heel us over, and he'd go sliding across the deck.

"By this time we all had our life preservers on and we were just standing by — or holding on as you might say — waiting for her to hit. It was going to happen, and nothing on God's green earth could stop it.

"Cowley had told Vatcher to send an SOS, though what good that was going to do I couldn't figure. Maybe it was so if we went down all-standing, someone would have a hint of what had happened. But Vatcher wasn't having any luck with his radio. His aerials had blown away and, as we heard later, even the big steel transmitter towers on the island had blown down too, so he couldn't have talked to the shore stations anyhow.

"The wind had shifted some, but it wasn't steady in any quarter, and we didn't know how far or in what direction we had drifted. There was a chance we might have been blown through the entrance channel, but there was a damned sight better chance we were already in among the reefs.

"We'd been out there banging around like a bird in a paper bag for just twenty-seven minutes when there was a hell of a bump and the old girl keeled over on her side. She straightened up again all right, but from then on it was just one bump after another; like a baby falling down the stairs. Between rolling, bumping, and pitching, you couldn't keep your feet at all.

"Cowley grabbed the phone and tried to get the engine room, and luckily Chandler was on the other end trying to get Cowley. They howled at each other for a couple of seconds, and then Cowley turns to us and hollers that she's filling fast.

"The boys in the engine room just made it up the ladder one jump ahead of the water. Some of them weren't quite fast enough. It was already up to Gilmour's knees before he reached the top rung. Three minutes after we'd hit, *Josie* was a stone-dead ship — no power, no lights, no nothing.

"When *Josie* struck, Ray Squires and Buck Dassylva had been down in the salvage hold checking to see that the gear hadn't started to break loose. The lights went out and there they were in the pitch dark, with the ship sinking under them. Instead of making for the deck, they went all around down there closing the watertight doors, and doing it by feel.

"*Josie* was still moving. Each big sea that lifted her would shove her over a new reef and she'd come down on the coral with a God-almighty jolt.

"A few of us tried to get down to our cabins to rescue some personal belongings, but by this time most of the accommodations were flooded. Vatcher got into his room, which was about half full of water since *Josie* was listing about thirty degrees to starboard by this time, and damned if he didn't find one of the oilers in there with a sick cat. They were both too sick to move. Vatcher had to carry the cat, and kick the oiler, all the way to the saloon.

"Then the saloon started to fill with water so we all crowded into the wheelhouse where Cowley and Wally were trying to decide what the chances were of launching a boat. Four of us went to work on the door to the boat deck, and we could just barely hold it from blowing right off its hinges when we opened it. Cowley went out, with Freddie Squires right behind him, to see what could be done.

"Between them they got the starboard boat cut loose — but they never got to launch it. The wind caught it, and it lifted right off the deck and went flying into the night. After that there didn't seem to be any point in fiddling with the port boat.

"The list wasn't getting any worse, so we figured we were probably hung up on the edge of a reef and being held by the pressure of the wind. What worried us was the chance *Josie* was on one of the outer reefs and might slide off into deep water any minute. If that had happened, she'd have gone down like a stone.

"It was night time now, but that couldn't have made it any darker than it had been before. The air didn't just look black, it *was* black. You could have cut chunks out of it and made a fortune selling the stuff to funeral parlors. The hurricane still wasn't letting up one damn bit. We didn't know if we were glad, or mad, about that. If it didn't let up we'd never know where the hell we were, or have a chance to get away. But if it *did* let up, *Josie* might slip into deep water and take us with her. No man, even with a lifejacket, was going to live more than ten seconds in that sea.

"*Josie* struck at 1945 hours, but it wasn't until nearly 2200 hours that the hurricane began to abate. As soon as we could, we pried open the door to the port wing of the bridge and we carted all our flares and signals out there and started to touch them off. It was a dandy fireworks show. Trouble was, no one ever saw it. The spray and rain was still so thick you couldn't have seen Cape Race Lighthouse if it had been fifty feet away.

"As the wind began to fall out, Cowley thought we ought to have another try at launching a boat; but the port boat was too high up now and we couldn't swing her over — which was probably just as well. Vatcher got busy and cut the Carley Float loose and a couple of the hands were just going to grab hold of it when zip, it got airborne too. Nobody ever did see hide nor hair of it again.

"Vatcher watched it go, and then he says to me: 'By God, if I get out of this I'm going to sea no more!' There weren't many fellows aboard *Josie* right about then who would have give him any argument.

"Buck Dassylva was prowling around on the port side with a boathook, and he kept poking it down into the foam alongside. Nothing ever bothered Buck. He was singing at the top of his lungs:

" 'NO CAN DO . . . NO CAN DO . . . Nobody NOHOW no CAN DO!'

"All of a sudden he stops singing and gives a bellow. The wind was falling fast by now and the sea water that had gone up into the air was dripping back where it belonged, so you could see a little better. Some of us went over beside Buck and we could just make out something looming up hard on the port quarter.

" 'By Gar, I tink dat's land!' says Buck. And sure enough it was.

"An hour later the sky was clear, and the wind was hardly strong enough to sail a dory in. It was what they call a beautiful tropic night. You'd have thought the whole thing had been some kind of rubby-dub's nightmare. Right alongside us was a little island. We shoved the gangplank over to it and everybody walked ashore with dry feet, just as comfortable as if they'd been coming off a P. & O. liner at Southampton.

"The island was joined to the mainland by a narrow neck, and somebody recognized the place. We'd gone ashore on Ferry Point at the south side of Whalebone Bay, not half a mile from where *Josie* and *Leicester* had been moored! So we knew where *we* were, but there wasn't a thing to be seen of *Leicester*.

"Before the hurricane died out, Cowley sent Ray ashore to hoof it cross country to St. George and tell Feathers what had happened. Then he got the rest of the crew settled down in an abandoned gun position on the little island. Later on we salvaged some blankets and the odd mattress out of the wreck, and we brought the bonded liquor supply ashore so it wouldn't get damaged.

"After a while, when we were settled down a bit, Buck starts pacing to and fro.

" 'Wat the matter weeth you fellows, heh? Everybody get dressed and shave to go ashore tonight. Now you *got* ashore all you want to do is sleep! By Gar, I never see such a lazy bunch. I guess I go to town alone!'

"And be damned if he didn't too."

Jumping from the jeep, Featherstone strode over to the tug. His whole attention was concentrated on the stricken ship. For twenty minutes he climbed over her, peering into her holds and accommodations. When he finally came ashore his step was as brisk as ever and his face betrayed no sign of gloom.

"Big job," he said succinctly to the waiting men. "It'll take us a while. Now, what's happened to the *Leicester*?"

There was no immediate answer to that one. The whole sweep of Murray's Anchorage lay open to view, and there was no ship, and no sign of any ship in sight. On the distant reefs there was nothing but the white surf from the failing swells. *Leicester* had apparently vanished. But this was impossible. If she had gone down in those relatively shallow waters, her superstructure, or at least her spars, would have remained in sight. Yet there was nothing to be seen.

It was Ray Squires who solved the mystery. Ray had climbed to the high ground behind the little point where *Josephine* lay skewered, and idly glancing along the shore he saw a ship's topmasts apparently thrusting right out of the cliffs which lay on the north side of Whalebone Bay.

Squires's shout brought everyone up the hill, and a skein of wondering men was soon making its way around the foot of Whalebone Bay and out to the headland on the northern side.

They reached the edge of the cliff and there below them, driven hard ashore for her whole length, lay *Leicester*. She was not four hundred yards from *Josephine*, lying almost high and dry. Tucked comfortably against her shoreward flank was the battleship mooring which, along with its three concrete anchors, she had dragged to this quiet resting place.

At the time *Josephine* was torn away from her, *Leicester* still had one passenger aboard — an elderly colored man who had been hired as night watchman. Now the morning rang to the shouts of the crewmen on the cliff as they tried to rouse some sign of life from the old man.

When their cries brought no response, they took to heaving largish rocks down the cliff and bouncing them off *Leicester*'s plates. Still no response. Reluctantly, they gave the old man up for dead.

Later that morning Featherstone and some of the salvage gang boarded *Leicester* from a boat and proceeded to search the ship for the missing man. They found him — comfortably ensconced in the saloon where he had just made a pot of coffee. The watchman greeted his visitors with a broad smile and offered to share his coffee with them.

Even Featherstone was impressed by such sang-froid. Only it wasn't really sang-froid at all — it was acute deafness which accounted for the old man's casual manner. It was later discovered that he had not even realized he had been living through a hurricane aboard the derelict.

V.

THE
ROCK

FROM

THIS ROCK WITHIN THE SEA, 1968
THE BOAT WHO WOULDN'T FLOAT, 1969

FROM

This Rock Within the Sea

THE ISLAND
AND THE SEA

Newfoundland is of the sea. Poised like a mighty granite stopper over the bell-mouth of the Gulf of St. Lawrence, it turns its back upon the greater continent, barricading itself behind the three-hundred-mile-long rampart that forms its hostile western coast. Its other coasts all face toward the open ocean, and are so slashed and convoluted with bays, inlets, runs, and fiords that they offer more than five thousand miles of shoreline to the sweep of the Atlantic. Everywhere the hidden reefs and rocks (which are called, with dreadful explicitness, "sunkers") wait to rip the bellies of unwary vessels. Nevertheless these coasts are a true seaman's world, for the harbors and havens they offer are numberless.

Until a few generations ago the coasts of the island were all that really mattered. The high, rolling plateaus of the interior, darkly coniferous-wooded to the north but bone-bare to the south, remained an almost unknown hinterland. Newfoundland was then, and it remains, a true sea-province, perhaps akin to that other lost sea-province called Atlantis; but Newfoundland, instead of sinking into the green depths, was somehow blown adrift to fetch up against our shores, and there to remain in unwilling exile, always straining back toward the east. Nor is this pure fantasy, for Newfoundland is the most easterly land in North America, jutting so far out into the Atlantic that its capital, St. John's, lies six hundred miles to the east of Halifax and almost twelve hundred miles east of New York.

Thousands of years ago Newfoundland was over-mastered by a tyranny of ice. Insensate yet implacable, the glacial presence crept out of Labrador, flowing from the northwest toward the southeast across the spine of the peninsula; arming itself with the jagged shards of mountains it had crushed in its inexorable passage. Bridging the narrow Straits of Belle Isle it engulfed the island. Great, tearing granite teeth, embedded in the ice, stripped the living flesh of soil and vegetation from the face of Newfoundland and gashed gigantic furrows in the underlying rock. The mountains of the interior were ground down to form a vast and almost featureless plateau, a realm of utter desolation. When the ice reached the southern coast, which in those times presented a mountain wall to the sea, it slashed a series of immensely deep wounds in the fronting cliffs, wounds that eventually became the fiords of southern Newfoundland.

With the island vanquished, the ice moved on to engage the sea itself in a titanic struggle. It thrust outward from the southeastern shores, forcing the waters back, until its invading snout extended three hundred miles to seaward. This was no superficial conquest: the glacier was a solid entity resting upon the ocean floor hundreds of fathoms down; and its ice-valleys and ice-mountains lay glittering beneath an Arctic sky.

The waters were forced to retreat for perhaps a thousand years before the last ice-age approached its end. Then the sun burned with renewed passion and the congealed surface of the northern seas softened and reliquefied. Illimitable ocean began to eat into the cold invader. The glacier, at bay, could not retreat as the sea had done; it could only stand and die. In death it delivered itself of billions of tons of soil and pulverized rock stolen from the land. This debris sank to the sea floor, where it remains as the vast area of shoal banks, including the Grand Bank of Newfoundland, fringing the southern and eastern coasts of the island of whose substance the banks were formed.

So the ice rotted from the sea and left the sea unmarred. But when it melted from the land it left the island scarified, denuded, a polished and eroded skull. Life crept back upon that bared bone with infinite slowness for, although the glacier itself was gone, the shadow and the influence of the vanished ice remained. Out of the polar seas flowed, and flows still, an Arctic river called the Labrador Current. Sweeping down out of Baffin Bay and Hudson Strait, it chills the shores of Labrador and Newfoundland and, for several months of every year, wraps much of the island in the frigid embrace of drifting Arctic ice.

The polar pack and the polar current are brutal adversaries of all life upon the lands they touch; but life on the coasts of Newfoundland, particularly on the Sou'west Coast, must also endure other inimical influences. One of these is the fog that in spring and summer can shut off the light of the sun for weeks on end. Then there is the wind. Raging unchecked across an unbroken sweep of water stretching to South America, out of the cyclonic cauldron of the Caribbean, come some of the world's most majestic and consuming storms. The south coast of the island lies full across their track; and from September through to May the furious winds seldom rest. The tortured air clamors against the sea-cliffs, driving the salt storm-wrack far inland as the winds scythe on toward the stony highlands of the interior, where only crawling, clinging vegetation can maintain its hold.

The Sou'west Coast is not, and has not been since before the ice-ages, a world hospitable to men who must make their living from the land. Before the coming of Europeans, even the native Beothuk Indians eschewed the Coast except during a few weeks in summer; then they crossed the tundra barrens from the wooded highlands far to the north and visited the shore to make a hurried harvest of sea birds, eggs, and shellfish. The Beothuks hovered on the edge of the sea, at the brink of the vital discovery that it was the sea and not the land which was the key to human occupation of the Sou'west Coast. But the discovery itself was not for them to make since they were not truly a people of the sea.

Yet the very factors which turned this coast into a wasteland were, paradoxically, the factors which created the conditions for a rich and rewarding way of life for men: the surrounding waters. The glacial ice, which turned much of the high plateau into subarctic barrens, created the offshore banks which became the greatest fish pastures in the world. The cold Labrador Current paralyzed the coasts it touched, but produced simultaneously on the banks ideal conditions for the unbelievably fecund proliferation of living things.

After the passing of the glacier, life exploded in the offshore waters. The minute plankton animals and plants formed a veritable soup through which swam, fattened, and spawned untold numbers of fish of innumerable species. At the surface, horizon-filling flocks of sea-fowl fed on small fry and, with their guano, began the slow process of restoring life-conditions to the denuded islands and the bleak sea-cliffs. Millions of pelagic seals came drifting south early each spring to whelp on the pack-ice and feed their young high over the teeming fish life of the Banks. Pods of great whales, in numbers that may never have been equalled in the world's seas, lazed along the sweep of high and rocky coast. Seals invaded the bays and the shallow, sandy lagoons; otters appeared along the tide water; salmon began to re-enter the almost sterile rivers. Lobsters, mussels, winkles, and crabs returned to the shore rocks; and wavering jungles of kelp began to lift above the inshore reefs. And so it went, until the entire infinitely varied world of life within the sea was re-established, but on a vastly expanded scale, around the island mass which itself had hardly begun to be reclaimed by living things.

Life within and on the sea was the key to human life upon the coasts, the key with which to open the rock-ribbed island casket; but this key could only be grasped by men who were truly of the sea.

As the first such voyagers, sailing from European shores, approached the Sou'west Coast, they saw from afar a looming wall of rock rising as much as a thousand feet out of the sea-foam; a forbidding granite wall which, at first sight, must have appeared totally inhospitable to mariners and ships.

With trepidation they ventured closer, the lead swinging steadily and the helmsman ready at a moment's notice to put about for the safety of the open sea. But they found a bold coast — "bold water," seamen call it — offering a deep and secure passage almost to the shoreline. And as they came under the loom of the sea-cliffs they saw that the apparently unbroken wall had many doors. Every few miles a fiord-mouth opened, sometimes as narrow as a knife-wound, sometimes wide enough to admit a dozen ships sailing abreast.

La Poile, Le Moine, Connoir, Bay de Loup, White Bear, Bay

de Vieux, La Hune, Avalon, Chaleur, Facheux, Bay d'Espoir
— all these and more slice into the coastal escarpment for
distances of up to thirty miles. They are sheer-walled and possess
a massive grandeur; but all of them hold inner nooks and coves
where a vessel can anchor or moor right to the rock walls, in
absolute security from any hurricane that ever blew.

At the heads of these great fiords white rivers, highways for
the salmon, roar down off the interior plateau through deep and
twisting gorges which, protected from the eternal winds, have
clothed themselves in pine and spruce, hemlock and birch. The
river-mouths are places where men can build cabins secure from
the fury of the roiling winter seas and the spume-laden gales,
with abundant firewood easily at hand; and where the gorges
provide steep stairways up to the lip of the plateau to the caribou
country where a man can still kill a winter's meat in a single
day. So attractive were these inner sanctuaries that it became the
pattern for early settlers to build "winter houses" in them to
which they could retreat during the most violent months when
fishing from frail open boats had to be abandoned temporarily.

But although the fiords offered a temporary shelter for ships
and a retreat from the worst days of winter for the settlers, they
were not places where many men could hope to build a permanent way of life. The key to human existence on the Sou'west
Coast remained in the seas' keeping; and perforce, men had to
make their real homes hard by the unquiet waters.

Perhaps no other ocean emanates such a disturbing feeling of
sentience as does the North Atlantic. It is not just a realm of
water, it is a veritable presence — one of incalculable moods. It
is seldom still; even in its rare moments of brooding calm, a
long and rhythmic swell rolls under the surface so that it ripples
like the hide of a monster. It is at times like these that men of
the sea distrust the sea most. They view the quiet interludes with
foreboding; "weather breeders" they call such days, and they
prepare for what they know will follow: a passionless and almost inconceivable violence of wind and water.

For those who live by it and upon it, the sea is the ultimate
reality in their existence. They accept it as their master, for they
know that they will never master it. The sea is there. It is their

life: it gives them life and sometimes, in its moments of fury, it gives them death. They do not struggle against its imponderable strength, nor do they stand in braggart's opposition to its powers.

"Ah, me son," a schooner skipper told me once, "we don't be takin' nothin' from the sea. We sneaks up on what we wants — and wiggles it away."

THE HERITAGE

This island was a reality in the consciousness of European men long centuries before the void of darkness obscuring the rest of the Western Hemisphere began to be filled with knowledge. It was a concrete reality to Greenland Norse settlers who saw it first in 987, who tried and failed to colonize it at the turn of the first millenium and called it Vinland. It was an indisputable reality to the wide-ranging seamen of the Basque provinces of Spain and France who whaled along its shores at least a century before Columbus sailed west to immortality. By 1436 it had appeared, if dimly, on European maps as The Land of Stockfish. Well before the end of the fifteenth century Portuguese seamen knew it as Terra de Los Bachalaos; Breton and Norman fishers knew it as Terre-Neuve; Bristol fishermen were seeking it under a name whose origins are now lost to us — The Isle of Brasile — and, on reaching it in 1481, adopted the French name and called it New Land.

Men of ancient centuries, fishing at great distances in time and space from their home ports, had needs that only solid land could satisfy. There was the need to shelter from the great Atlantic storms; the need for snug harbors where ships could water, repair, and take on wood for fuel. Stockfish (dry cod), whether it was preserved with salt or only dried by wind and sun, could only be "made" on shore. The blubber from whales and seals could only be "tried" (rendered into oil) at crude factories constructed on the land. Thus it is certain that from the first days of the fisheries off Newfoundland men were making at least seasonal use of the coasts. Skippers who came back year after year — and many did — had their chosen harbors where permanent structures came into being. Inevitably the owners had to take measures to protect their shore-bases, not so much against the presence of the native Beothuks (who were an inoffensive people), as against the thievery and malicious destruction by crews of other ships of their own and foreign nations.

The only certain way to protect a shore-base was to leave men to winter there; and with the first such successful winterings-over, well before the end of the fifteenth century, the seeds of permanent occupation of these coasts were sown.

It was a short further step to the decision by certain hardy men to "plant" themselves in New Land. The advantages were obvious: a group of men, permanently established in a convenient harbor, near good fishing grounds where they could use small boats, could fish for eight months of the year off the northern coasts and almost year-round off the southern shores.

There was more to settlement than that. During the early centuries of Newfoundland's discovery and occupation, the common man in Europe was in peonage — if not in outright bondage. His very life was forfeit at the whim of those who governed him. The poverty of the damned was the general lot of most except the upper ranks. The hardships and uncertainties of hacking out a free life on the granitic coasts of Newfoundland were no greater than those a man had to face at home in Europe and, in all likelihood, were considerably less. And in Newfoundland, as in no other part of North America, there was only the natural hostility of wilderness with which to deal: the Beothuks made no real effort to resist the alien interlopers, as did their brothers on the continental mainland.

One thing was needed before the slow swirl of Europeans along the Newfoundland shores could begin to clot into real settlements — and that was women. Historians say nothing about where the women came from, but come they assuredly did. In the beginning some were taken forcibly out of the tents of the Beothuks. Others accompanied the fishing ships from Europe. The latter were women without homes, without men to keep them — women who perforce kept themselves the only way they could. Aboard ship they served the dual purpose of entertaining the crew and, in their spare time, slaving at the job of making fish. It cannot be doubted that, given an opportunity, those women would choose to abandon servitude in order to build a life with a free man, even in a remote cove in Newfoundland.

There is a legend (which is still perpetuated by some smug town-dwellers in Newfoundland) to the effect that the men and women who first settled the outports were criminals, outcasts, and fugitives attempting to evade justice and punishment. This is a lie. Many of these people may have been law-breakers according to the oppressive regulations of their times; many of them certainly deserted from ships whose crews were treated little better than galley-slaves; others fled from a European justice so barbarous that it thought nothing of having a man drawn and quartered — but criminals they were not. They were in truth the strongest and bravest of the oppressed; and their only real crime was that they dared risk everything to gain the freedom to live or die by their own efforts.

The birthdate of the first real settlement on the Sou'west Coast is unknown. Written history holds no record of it, for it was not established with great fanfare by some aristocrat intent on building an empire in the new world. But although the Basque peoples of the fifteenth century left no documentary record of their distant venturings, Spanish scholars two hundred years later chronicled a Basque tradition which stated matter-of-factly that their seamen had been whaling off Newfoundland a full century before Columbus sailed. So it could well be that these mysterious and incredibly ancient people provided the Sou'west Coast with its first European inhabitants; and it is surely no mere coincidence that the harbor which is now Newfoundland's navel, and which lies at the western extremity of the Sou'west Coast, still bears the name Port-aux-Basques.

The first documented reference to settlement comes from the Portuguese. It is a fragmentary notice of a voyage made just before 1500. After this date the pattern becomes a little clearer. Until about the middle of the sixteenth century Portuguese, French and Spanish Basques, and Normans and Bretons were almost equally numerous and had together sometimes as many as six hundred ships in Newfoundland waters in any given year, mostly on the southern and eastern coasts. The Portuguese and the Spanish Basques seem to have occupied the Sou'west Coast under a rough and ready *modus vivendi* which gave the French (Bretons, Normans, and French Basques) possession of the remainder of the south coast, from Fortune Bay east to Cape Race.

As the years slipped by, Basque and Portuguese interest and influence in southern Newfoundland declined while those of the French grew. This shift was a continuous one — not a simple replacement of one people by another. Those early settlers who were already established when the French drifted westward remained where they were and blended their blood with that of the newcomers, eventually adopting the French tongue as the general language. The change was slow, spanning most of the seventeenth century.

In the train of the French came a new infusion of Indian blood. Micmacs of Nova Scotia, close allies of the French, were encouraged to migrate to Terre-Neuve, where they found no color bar. White and Indians intermarried freely and lived and worked on a basis of equality.

Thus by the early eighteenth century the Sou'west Coast was home, and had been home for centuries, to a people of mixed Basque-Norman-Breton-Portuguese-Indian heritage. The race — and it was in reality a race — took on further admixtures, for during most of the seventeenth century this was a famous pirate-coast where Dutch, English, and Spanish freebooters made their headquarters secure from interference, since not even France attempted to exercise affective sovereignty over it.

The Sou'west Coast developed and preserved a remarkable degree of freedom from involvement in the wars, skirmishes, and raids that grew out of the bitter, decades-long struggle between France and England for possession of Newfoundland and Canada. It became and remained a neutral zone, bypassed by the warring fleets but visited by peaceful fishermen and honest pirates with profit to themselves and to the inhabitants. In consequence of this continuing freedom both from war and from official interference, the little clusters of families that now inhabited every suitable cove and harbor from Cape Ray to Fortune Bay developed no real sense of allegiance to any European nation. They were a people united within themselves in a society that had no name, no flag, no boundaries. The sea was their common country, and the way of the sea was their community of life. Each outport lived not only in freedom from the turmoil of the outer world but also in freedom from the too-close propinquity even to its neighboring settlements, since each group of human beings in its cliff-girt cove was insulated from all other settlements by the dark wastes of ocean. Nevertheless the coast-dwellers were all as one people, for the sea had made them one.

Through the generations changes came imperceptibly to the coast, though in the main these changes were superficial and did not deeply affect the lives men led. Even the Treaty of Utrecht, in 1713, by which France was forced to cede the whole south coast to England, caused no severe dislocation of the centuries-old way of life. The English sent a naval officer, Capt. Taverner, to cruise the newly acquired coast and to demand an oath of allegiance from the settlers on pain of expulsion if they refused. He met with little if any resistance. The people took the oath. After all, what was a nominal change of allegiance to them? They went on about their age-old business with the sea.

But change in an unpleasant guise was on its way, with the arrival of carpetbaggers representing powerful merchant companies based in southern England and in the Channel Isles. These newcomers seized some of the best harbors and proceeded to introduce the same mercantile system under which outport fishermen in the English parts of Newfoundland (the English had settled the East Coast as early as 1600) had been mercilessly exploited for generations. These merchants controlled all imports, and sold supplies on credit to the outport people to carry them through the next season's fishery; but they demanded exclusive rights to the fishermen's catch to be applied against their debt. If there was a surplus to the fishermen's credit (and the merchant was the sole judge of this since the people were completely illiterate), it could only be "taken up in trade" at the merchant's store. The outport men were no longer allowed to sell fish to visiting ships of English or foreign nationalities, or to buy goods from them.

This system, once established, continued in full force until the 1940's, and is still in effect in at least one outport on the Sou'west Coast today. The profit on goods sold to outport fishermen sometimes exceeded five hundred percent, while the net profit on salt fish taken from them regularly amounted to three or four times the sum credited to the fishermen's accounts.

The arrival of the English and Jersey merchants had yet another result. These companies used indentured labor. Each year their ships brought out cargoes of so-called "youngsters" (men ranging in age from fourteen to sixty years) recruited mostly in the counties of Devon, Dorset, and Somerset and on the island of Jersey.

These "youngsters" were obliged to serve their masters for a period of from three to five years in exchange for their keep; and, if the masters so chose, they were obliged to make a payment of three or four pounds at the termination of the indenture. They were used as crews for the fishing boats owned by the merchants, and as brute labor; and sometimes they were hired out to English entrepreneurs who had established themselves as masters of certain small outports which they ran as minor principalities. Hundreds of the "youngsters" reached the Sou'west Coast in the eighteenth and nineteenth centuries, and few ever returned, or even wished to return, to the starvation lot of the poor in the England of those times. Some served out the full indenture period and then slipped away to take up the outport way of life. A great many others drew the breath of freedom early and ran off to hide themselves in bays and inlets where they too became "livyers" (people who "live here").

Chauvinistic historians have claimed that after Utrecht the French mysteriously vanished from the coast, to be magically replaced by an entire English population. Nothing of the sort occurred. The steady intermarriage of Englishmen with local girls gradually brought about an apparent anglicization of the population — a further extension of the melding process that initially made the south-coast people what they were. The language changed and the surnames of many families were anglicized. But other things did not change. Most of the old names for the bays, the settlements themselves, mountains, and rivers remained, as indeed they still remain. And the pattern of the coast-dwellers' lives did not undergo any essential change.

English officialdom showed little interest in the Sou'west Coast, leaving it to be run as a fiefdom by the great merchant companies whose only real opposition came after 1800 when

Americans from New England began fishing the coast in earnest. In 1818 a treaty between Britain and the United States not only gave the Americans the right to fish the Sou'west Coast in any way they chose, but also allowed them to make use of any "unoccupied" harbors, creeks, or bays. This treaty remained in force for almost one hundred years.

The Americans' freedom to come and go as they pleased (a freedom shared, illegally, by the French fishing fleets operating out of the nearby French islands of St. Pierre and Miquelon) was bitterly resented by the English merchant companies. But it was a blessing to the people of the Coast: it offered them an escape-door, no matter how narrow, from complete servitude to the merchants. They could and did engage in an illegal bait-trade, selling squid and herring to American and French fishing vessels and getting paid in gold. And they could and did engage in an equally illegal trade with St. Pierre and Miquelon, smuggling loads of lumber, fresh caribou meat, and other produce to the French islands — where they bought rum, sugar, flour, clothing, and similar essentials at a fraction of the price charged them by the merchant monopoly on their home coast. American vessels harboring on the Sou'west Coast bought fur and fish from the local people, again for gold, and sold them cheap New England goods, while the merchant princes raged and sent delegation after delegation to England demanding that this poaching on their preserves be stopped by force.

Without the presence of the "foreigners," life on the Sou'west Coast might have become intolerable. For centuries the Coast people had endured adversity, had overcome and thrived on it; but that had been natural adversity. The ruthless exploitation (there is no other word for it) they had to endure under the rule of the English and Jersey merchants strained the fabric of their lives to the breaking-point. It became nearly impossible for a man to obtain or cling to much more than a fingerhold on existence. It became virtually impossible for the population to grow either in numbers or in spirit. Conditions grew worse in the first decade of the twentieth century, when the merchants at last succeeded in persuading the government to cut off the American trade. Left with a free hand, the merchant companies and the smaller independent merchants tightened their grip to such an extent that they very nearly throttled the life out of the Sou'west Coast. These were the years that are still starkly remembered by the old people as The Hard Times. And they were hard indeed. Starvation was a constant spectre. Malnutrition was something men were born to and died of. It is perhaps the surest measure of the qualities of the Coast people that they survived this period at all. They were helped by the two world wars which brought so much prosperity to the fishing business that a little of it managed to spill over from the merchants' grasp, and the people could draw new breath. After 1933, the new colonial government (a Commission established by Great Britain after Newfoundland's merchant princes had run the island into bankruptcy) began to offer help to a forgotten people. Cottage hospitals were built, and a free medical service (even if of a rudimentary nature) was provided. It was little enough help, but by the time the Second World War began, the people were on their feet again. True, the merchants still dominated the scene, but their grip had slackened sufficiently so that life could renew itself.

In the last hours before confederation with Canada became a reality, in 1949, the Coast was a land of vigorous men and women. They were a unique and fascinating breed. They were quick, confident, eminently successful survivors of an evolutionary winnowing-process that few modern races have undergone. As fishermen they were unparalleled. As seamen who had been manning ocean-going sailing ships for centuries, they were unsurpassed. Although their homes were remote from the outer world, they were by no means isolated in thought or in experience. There was hardly a family that had not sent sons, brothers, uncles, and fathers abroad as seamen or as skippers in the great overseas carrying-trade that before the Second World War had made the Newfoundland mercantile fleet one of the largest (in numbers if not in tonnage) in the world. London, Lisbon, and Genoa were names familiar in the mouths of most of the coastal peoples. Nor did they obtain their information about foreigners and foreign lands at second hand. Under-educated and largely illiterate as they may have been, their understanding of and empathy with strange peoples with strange ways was deeper and embraced more tolerance than most of us can claim today.

The Islanders were always much more closely linked to the seaboard peoples of Europe than to those of North America. Until two decades ago they had no real political, little social and cultural, and not even much commercial affiliation with this continent. In 1867, when confederation with Canada was first mooted, Newfoundlanders lustily sang this song:

> *Hurray for our own native land, Newfoundland!*
> *Not a stranger shall hold an inch of her strand.*
> *Her face turns to Britain, her back to the Gulf.*
> *Come near at your peril, Canadian Wolf!*

And they were still singing the same song when Confederation came upon them.

The man who engineered Confederation was Joseph Smallwood, once a labor organizer and once a pig farmer, but always and forever a political animal; combining messianic visions with the essential ruthlessness of an Alexander, or a Huey Long. He became the first premier of Canada's newest province in 1949, and remained its premier for twenty-three years. "King Joey," as he was called (sometimes affectionately, sometimes with bitterness), tried to transform his island kingdom into an industrialized principality, dependent on and imitative of the Admass society of Canada and the United States. "Off with the old and on with the new" was his guiding principle, and he applied it with a vigor and a haste that made no reckoning of the psychic and spiritual havoc it created in the lives of his own people.

The day that Smallwood came to power, the continuity and evolution of the Newfoundland way of life was disrupted, probably forever. Newfoundland turned its back upon the sea which had nurtured her through five centuries. Fishing and fishermen, ships and seamen became obsolete. Progress, so the new policy dictated, demanded the elimination of most of the thirteen hundred outport communities that encircled the island, and the transformation of their people into industrial workers. Progress dictated that the men of the sea forswear their ancient ways of life and move, as rootless migrants, to the alien milieu of industrial and mining towns. The entrepreneurs of the new industries wanted abundant labor and, of course, they preferred it cheap. The outport people had to be induced — and if not induced, then forced — to abandon the ways and the world they knew.

The tactics used combined both methods. The first step was to wither the fisheries and the mercantile marine by withholding the support which would enable them to make the transition into effective economic enterprises of the twentieth century. With their underpinnings knocked out the outports began to totter; but they did not fall, for their intrinsic strength was greater than the politicians had anticipated. The next step was to reduce basic services, or to fail to maintain them in the outports at a level comparable to that available to citizens in the factory towns. Outport schools found they could no longer obtain teachers; those regions (like the Sou'west Coast) whose main communications were by sea, found that the government-owned steamer-service was deteriorating. But the heaviest pressures were brought to bear through reduction in medical services. On the Sou'west Coast many outports found themselves going without a visit from a doctor for as much as ten months at a time, even though two government doctors were resident on the Coast and could call on helicopters and float-planes with which to reach the settlements.

In conjunction with these "deprival tactics" the government devised a centralization plan. Outporters were to be subsidized into moving to a few chosen "growth centers" on the coasts. At first people were offered $500 per family, provided that every family in an outport agreed to move. The size of this "assistance grant" has since been substantially increased, but it still falls far short of compensating the people for their abandoned houses, or for the cost of buying or building new homes in the chosen towns.

Whatever the tactic used, the aim itself is dubious in the extreme. The *raison d'être* for the centralization plan is to create viable new economic and social units. Yet Burgeo, a typical growth center on the coast, has suffered a massive expansion in its population without any increase in ways to provide it with a decent way of life. The one fish-processing plant in the town employs only a fraction of the employable people already living there, and it pays them only minimal and intermittent wages.

Many of the younger men can find work neither at the plant nor on the fish company's ships, and are forced to seek work as far away as central Canada. Burgeo is not a growing community; despite its increase in size, it is a dying community; and it may be that this too is part of the plan, for a people once uprooted can more readily be forced to move again.

The heritage of the outport people at the time of Confederation held a promise for the future — a promise that a strong, venturesome, and viable people could move into our modern world with no loss of their own sources of strength, and perhaps with a great gain to the waning strength of other men elsewhere. It was a promise that had little or no meaning to the apostles of instant change.

I remember a summation of the outport people made to my wife and myself by a woman doctor, an employee of the new government, who held a most responsible position on the Sou'west Coast. We were aboard the coastal steamer as she nosed into Burgeo harbor. The steamer blew a long and lugubrious blast on her whistle and, as the sound echoed amongst the islands, men, women, and children began to appear from the scattered houses and move toward the wharf. The doctor, standing beside us at the rail, gestured toward them: "These people are scum. They are descended from scum, and they are still scum."

But I also remember a stormy evening in February when photographer John de Visser and I sat in the snug kitchen of a fisherman's home in the village of François. Present with us were three men, a woman, and a girl-child. John and I had spent most of the day photographing the men as they hand-lined for cod from dories pitching in a gale of winter wind. Now the time had come for rest and talk. As had been the case during most of the evenings we spent along that coast, the talk ranged wearily over the problems of a people who had no future, of a way of life whose end could not long be postponed.

After a while there was silence; it was the silence of men who, for the first time in their lives and, perhaps, for the first time in the lives of their people, were experiencing the ultimate bewilderment that had come upon them with recognition of the truth that they were completely helpless to save themselves.

The woman brought a pot of fresh tea to the table where we sat and filled our mugs. As she returned to her seat by the stove to begin combing her daughter's hair, her husband broke the silence.

"It's been fine you came to visit us. I hopes your 'snaps' turns out just what you was after, and that you'll make a good voyage out of them — a prosperous voyage, you know. But still and all, I'm wondering could you, maybe, do one thing for we? Could you, do you think, say how it was with us? We wouldn't want it thought, you understand, that we never tried the hardest as was in us to make a go of things. We'd like for everyone to know we never would have left the places we was reared, but . . . we . . . was . . . drove!"

The last word burst into the quiet room with a terrible intensity. The little girl, who had been half-asleep as the comb slipped through her long dark hair, stared up at her father with astonished eyes.

He slowly lowered his head until he was looking with an unseeing gaze at the splayed hands with which he clutched the table-top before him. Unconscious of us all he spoke once more, no louder than the half-heard murmur of the black waters gentling the pilings of the landing stage outside the door.

"Aye Jesus, Jesus God, but we was drove!"

WITHIN
THESE WALLS

The home of an outport Newfoundlander is not the man's castle, it is the woman's. It is at once the core and the boundary of her existence. Once she has come to it as a bride, when she is perhaps no more than sixteen years of age, she rarely leaves it for more than a few hours, not because she is imprisoned in it but because for her it is the area of ultimate reality, the cave of ultimate security. Within these walls she becomes the mistress of her world, accomplished in a score of skills and unconsciously at ease in her fulfilment.

The outport house has evolved to suit its environment as surely as any animal evolves to suit its world. Built four-square, with the flexible strength that belongs to wooden ships, it makes total use of the space its walls enclose. The roof is pitched almost flat, since in this land of winds there is but little chance of its being overloaded with accumulated snow. The ceilings are low and heavily beamed, and the rooms have the snug and comfortable feeling of a vessel's cabin. Essentially the house is a land-berthed ship. Its upper deck contains the bedrooms, usually four in number, and unheated. Big beds — soft-sprung and mattressed with down ticks — almost fill them, for in these homes a bedroom is exactly what its name implies and nothing more. The lower deck may have a parlor and perhaps a bedroom too; but the main cabin is the kitchen, the heart and essence of the house.

The kitchen is the largest room; bright, warm, and welcoming. It always contains at least one "day-bed" (a combination of sofa and single bed) which provides a place for the man to stretch out for a few minutes before his meal; a place for the woman to sit with the children beside her as she knits, sews, or spins; a place for a gaggle of neighbors' children to perch in owl-eyed silence; a place for a grandfather or an aging aunt to rest and reminisce; a place where young lovers come together when the rest of the household lies sleeping.

The stove is central and looms large; it glitters with nickel trim, and its top shines like a black mirror with the accumulated polish of the years. Above it hang thick woollen mittens, socks, children's outer clothing — all swinging and steaming. It is a room where everything is neatly in its place, ship-fashion; and it is kept scrupulously clean. The kitchen is colorful to such a degree that the eyes of a mainlander are dazzled by the brilliance of high-gloss paints upon the walls and by the gleaming, painted linoleum or canvas on the floors.

Not so long ago most of the furniture was hand-made, and well-made, by men who had acquired their competence as carpenters at the intricate work of ship-building. Today the pervasive influence of the mail-order catalogue has made its mark, but has not yet destroyed the aura of the outport kitchen.

The kitchen windows — there are usually two — look out upon the cove and over it to the grey sea beyond. During the long hours when the husband's boat is away at the fishing grounds, the woman's glance is forever reaching out beyond this room, so that the eyes of the house — the salt-streaked eyes of glass — become her eyes as well.

As for the man, he spends so little time in his own house that he sometimes seems to feel slightly uneasy in it. He often leaves it before dawn. If it is a good day, he may be at sea until late afternoon, after which he will be preoccupied at his stage or store until suppertime. On a "leeward day," when the weather "ain't fittin' " and the boats stay in the harbor, he spends most of his time down at the store. The house is where he eats his meals, sleeps, procreates, and occasionally indulges in some special skill — carving ship models, perhaps, or whittling out birch brooms. But it is only when he is very old, "not good for it anymore," that he at last enters fully into the house he built, or that his father's father built before him.

So the house belongs truly to the woman, and she gives of it to her children who are born within its walls; to young lovers; to her husband and to aged relatives; and, as often as circumstances will allow, to the entire settlement. There is no single thing in their lives that outport people value more than what they call a "time."

Almost anything will serve as an excuse to have a time and to fill the house with people. The arrival in the harbor of a fishing vessel from another port, a member of whose crew is perhaps a fifth cousin of some local householder, can spark a time. During the Twelve Days of Christmas (the outports still celebrate both old and new Christmas day and the twelve days between), every night is a time in its own right. Masked and costumed mummers come pounding at every door: "Is mummers allowed in?" Once inside they pound the kitchen floor with sea boots and rubber boots to the shrilling of a fiddle or the whine of an accordion. A time can happen quite spontaneously when three or four neighbors drop in for a "gam" (gossip), or it can be made to happen with the miraculous appearance of a bottle of "white stuff" (pure alcohol), imported without the blessing of the Customs Officer from the off-lying French islands of St. Pierre and Miquelon on foggy nights when the Royal Canadian Mounted Police patrol boats are drowsing at their moorings.

Here there is gaiety. But there is also pain and fear and darkness in the spirit. This is the place where women watch and wait through the interminable night, while the house shivers in the tearing talons of a winter's gale and a boat is too long overdue. It is the place where people sit in silence, but not alone, while in an upstairs room a pulse flickers fitfully and a heartbeat slows. The outport home rejects no man and no emotion. It accepts all that there is of life and death. It provides a place where those who have outworn their flesh can wait the hours down. For them there is no banishment to "a room of one's own," or to an old folks' sterile dying-place where they must endure that pervading chill of death, preceding death, that freezes the spirit of the world's unwanted. Until their last breath fails, those whose present has become their past are nurtured within the haven of these walls. And at the going out at the end of it they pass in dignity and in simplicity. And they are mourned.

Within these walls there is a sustaining certitude that is proof against disaster, against hardship, against the darkest hours of adversity, and against loneliness. Here there is a quality to human sharing, and an unspoken understanding that is proof against the very fates themselves. Here there is a unity that has no name. And here there is quiet at the close.

FROM

The Boat Who Wouldn't Float

◆

The Boat Who Wouldn't Float describes the love-hate relationship between Farley Mowat and a small, ugly fishing schooner he purchased in 1960, and which has owned him at various times in his life ever since.

◆

I have an ingrained fear of auctions dating back to the third year of my life. In that year my father attended an auction as a means of passing an aimless afternoon, and he came away from it the bewildered possessor of thirty hives of bees and all the paraphernalia of an apiarist. Unable to rid himself of his purchase, he became perforce a beekeeper, and for the next two years I lived almost exclusively on a diet of soda biscuits and honey. Then the gods smiled on us and all the bees died of something called foul brood, enabling us to return to some semblance of a normal life.

Auctions remain associated in my subconscious mind with great catastrophes. I normally avoid them like the plague, but one April day not many years ago I too fell victim to the siren call. It happened in a sleepy little Lake Ontario town which once had been a major port for the great fleets of barley schooners that vanished forever shortly after the turn of the century. In that town there lived a ship chandler who refused to accept the coming of steam and the death of sail, and who kept his shop and stock intact for half a century, waiting for the day when a sailorman would again come knocking on his door. None did. He died, and his heirs decided to auction off the old man's junk so they could turn the building into a pool hall.

I happened to be passing through that town on auction day accompanied by a young lady for whom I had conceived a certain passion. However, *her* passion was primarily reserved for auctions. When she saw the auction sign she insisted that we attend. I steeled myself to buy nothing, but as I stood in the dim and ancient store which was still redolent of Stockholm tar, oilskins, and dusty canvas, something snapped within me.

Among the attitudes I acquired from my father was a romantic and Conradian predilection for the sea and ships. Like him I had often found surcease from the miseries I brought upon myself by spending hours immersed in books about the cruises of small boats to far-distant corners of the oceanic world. Ten years before the day of the auction I had anchored myself to a patch of eroded sand hills in central Ontario, about as far from the sea as a man could get. There I had labored to make grass, trees, vegetables, and mine own self take root. My labors had been in vain. Drought killed the grass. Sawflies and rabbits girdled the trees. Wireworms ate the vegetables. Far from rooting me into the Good Earth, a decade of servitude to the mingy soil only served to fuel a spirit of rebellion the intensity of which I had not begun to suspect until I stood in the old ship chandler's store physically surrounded by a world I had previously known only in the imagination.

I bought. I bought and I bought and I bought. I bought enough nautical gear out of another age to fill an outbuilding on my parched little farm. I am my father's son, and so the story of the bees had to repeat itself to an inevitable conclusion.

It happens that I have a friend who is a publisher and who feels much the same way about the book business as I do about dirt farming. Jack McClelland is a romantic, although he blanches at the word and vehemently denies it. During the war he served as skipper of M.T.B.'s (Motor Torpedo Boats) and other such small and dashing craft, and although he returned at war's end to the drabness of the business world, his spirit remained on the bridge of an M.T.B. streaking through the grey Atlantic wastes, guns blazing at the dim specters of German E-boats hopelessly trying to evade their fates. Jack owns a cottage on the Muskoka Lakes and there he keeps an old-fashioned, knife-bowed, mahogany launch which in the dark of the moon sometimes metamorphoses into an M.T.B., to the distress of occasional lovers drifting on the still waters in canoes.

One night a few weeks after I bought the departed chandler's stock, Jack McClelland and I were moored to a bar in Toronto. It was a dismal day in a dismal city so we stayed moored to the bar for several hours. I kept no notes of what was said nor do I recall with clarity how it all came to pass. I know only that before the night ended we were committed to buying ourselves an oceangoing vessel in which to roam the salt seas over.

We decided we should do things the old-fashioned way (we both have something of the Drake and Nelson complex), and this meant buying an old-fashioned boat, the kind of wooden boat that once was sailed by iron men.

The only place we knew where such a boat might be procured was in the remote and foggy island of Newfoundland. Consequently, one morning in early May I flew off to that island's ancient capital, St. John's, where I had arranged to meet a red-bearded, coldly blue-eyed iconoclast named Harold Horwood, who was reputed to know more about Newfoundland's scattered little outport villages than any living man. Despite the fact that I was a mainlander, and Harold abhors mainlanders, he had agreed to help me in my quest. I am not sure why he did so but perhaps the unravelling of this chronicle will provide a hint.

Harold took me to visit scores of tiny fishing villages clinging like cold treacle to the wave-battered cliffs of the great island. He showed me boats ranging from fourteen-foot dories to the rotting majesty of a five-hundred-ton, three-masted schooner. Unfortunately, those vessels that were still sufficiently seaworthy to leave the wharf were not for sale, and those that could be had within my range (Jack had astutely placed a limit of a thousand dollars on the purchase price) were either so old and tired that piss-a-beds (the local name for dandelions) were sprouting from their decks, or they were taking a well-earned rest on the harbor bottom with only their upperworks awash.

Time was drawing on and we were no forwarder. Harold's red beard jutted at an increasingly belligerent angle; his frosty eyes took on a gimlet stare and his temper grew worse and worse. He was not used to being thwarted and he did not like it. He arranged to have a news item printed in the papers describing the arrival of a rich mainlander who was looking for a local schooner.

Two days later he informed me that he had found the perfect vessel. She was, he said, a small two-masted schooner of the type known generally as a jack boat and, more specifically, as a Southern Shore bummer. I can't say that the name enthralled me, but by this time I too was growing desperate, so I agreed to go and look at her.

She lay hauled out at Muddy Hole, a small fishing village on the east coast of the Avalon Peninsula — a coast that is rather inexplicably called the Southern Shore, perhaps because it lies south of St. John's and St. John's is, in its own eyes at least, the center of the universe.

Tourist maps showed Muddy Hole as being connected to St. John's by road. This was a typical Newfoundland "jolly." Muddy Hole was not connected to St. John's at all except by a tenuous trail which, it is believed, was made some centuries ago by a very old caribou who was not only blind but also afflicted with the staggers.

In any event it took us six hours to follow where he had led. It was a typical spring day on the east coast of the island. A full gale was blowing from seaward, hurling slanting rain heavily against the car. The Grand Banks fog, which is forever lurking just off the coast, had driven in over the high headlands and obscured everything from view. Guided by some aboriginal instinct inherited from his seagoing ancestors, Harold somehow kept the course and just before ten o'clock, in impenetrable darkness, we arrived at Muddy Hole.

I had to take his word for it. The twin cones of the headlights revealed nothing but rain and fog. Harold rushed me from the car and a moment later was pounding on an unseen door. It opened to allow us to enter a tiny, brilliantly lighted, steaming-hot kitchen, where I was introduced to the brothers Mike and Paddy Hallohan. Dressed in thick homespun sweaters, heavy rubber boots, and black serge trousers, they looked like a couple of characters out of a smuggling yarn by Robert Louis Stevenson.

Harold introduced me, explaining that I was the "mainland feller" who had come to see their boat.

The brothers wasted no time. Rigging me up in oilskins and a sou'wester they herded me out into the storm.

The rain beat down so heavily that it almost masked the thunder of breakers which seemed to be directly below me, and no great distance away.

" 'Tis a grand night fer a wreck!" Paddy bellowed cheerfully.

It was also a grand night to fall over a cliff and break one's neck, a matter of more immediate concern to me as I followed close on Paddy's heels down a steep path that was so slippery your average goat would have thought twice about attempting it. Paddy's storm lantern, fueled for economy reasons with crude cod-liver oil, gave only a symbolic flicker of light through a dense cloud of rancid smoke. Nevertheless the smoke was useful. It enabled me to keep track of my guide simply by following my nose.

Twenty minutes later I bumped heavily into Paddy and was bumped into as heavily by Mike, who had been following close behind. Paddy thrust the lamp forward and I caught a glimpse of his gnomelike face, streaming with rain and nearly split in two by a maniacal grin.

"Thar she be, Skipper! T'foinest little bummer on t'Southern Shore o' Newfoundland!"

I could see nothing. I put out my hand and touched the flank of something curved and wet. Paddy shoved the lantern forward to reveal reflections from the most repellent shade of green paint I have ever seen. The color reminded me of the naked belly of a long-dead German corpse with whom I once shared a foxhole in Sicily. I snatched my hand away.

Mike roared in my ear. "Now dat you'se seen her, me dear man, us'll nip on back to t'house and have a drop o' tay." Whereupon Mike and Paddy nipped, leaving me stumbling anxiously in their wake.

Safely in the kitchen once more, I found that Harold had never left that warm sanctuary. He later explained that he had felt it would have been an intrusion for him to be present at my first moment of communion with my new love. Harold is such a thoughtful man.

By this time I was soaked, depressed, and very cold, but the Hallohan brothers and their ancient mother, who now appeared from a back room, went to work on me. They began by feeding me a vast plate of salt beef and turnips boiled with salt cod, which in turn engendered within me a monumental thirst. At this juncture the brothers brought out a crock of Screech.

Screech is a drink peculiar to Newfoundland. In times gone by, it was made by pouring boiling water into empty rum barrels to dissolve whatever rummish remains might have lingered there. Molasses and yeast were added to the black, resultant fluid, and this mixture was allowed to ferment for a decent length of time before it was distilled. Sometimes it was aged for a few days in a jar containing a plug of nigger-twist chewing tobacco.

However, the old ways have given way to the new, and Screech is now a different beast. It is the worst conceivable quality of Caribbean rum, bottled by the Newfoundland government under the Screech label, and sold to poor devils who have no great desire to continue living. It is not as powerful as it used to be, but this defect can be, and often is, remedied by the addition of quantities of lemon extract. Screech is usually served mixed with boiling water. In its consequent near-gaseous state the transfer of the alcohol to the bloodstream is instantaneous. Very little is wasted in the digestive tract.

This was my first experience with Screech and nobody had warned me. Harold sat back with an evil glitter in his eye and watched with delight as I tried to quench my thirst. At least I *think* he did. My memories of the balance of that evening are unclear.

At a much later date I was to be accused by Jack of having bought our boat while drunk, or of having bought her sight unseen, or both. The last part of the accusation is certainly not true. As I sat in the overwhelming heat of the kitchen with steam rising to maximum pressure inside my own boilers, the brothers Hallohan drew on the wizardry of their Irish ancestors and conjured up for me a picture of their little schooner with such vivid imagery that I saw her as clearly as if she had been in the kitchen with us. When I eventually threw my arms around Paddy's neck and thrust a bundle of bills into his sharkskintextured hand, I knew with sublime certainty that I had found the perfect vessel.

As we drove back to St. John's the next morning Harold rhapsodized about the simple-hearted, honest, God-fearing Irish fishermen of the Southern Shore.

"They'd give you their shirt as soon as look at you," he said. "Generous? Migod, there's nobody in the whole world like them! You're some lucky they took to you."

In a way I suppose Harold was right. Because if the Hallohans had not taken to me I might have remained in Ontario, where I could conceivably have become a solid citizen. I bear the Hallohans no ill will, but I hope I never again get "took to" the way I was taken to on that memorable night at Muddy Hole.

Two days later I returned to Muddy Hole to do a survey of my vessel and to get my first sober (in the sense of calm, appraising) look at her. Seen from a distance she was indeed a pretty little thing, despite her nauseous color. A true schooner hull in miniature, she measured thirty-one feet on deck with a nine-foot beam and a four-foot draft. But she was rough! On close inspection she looked as though she had been flung together by a band of our paleolithic ancestors — able shipbuilders perhaps, but equipped only with stone adzes.

Her appointments and accommodations left a great deal to be desired. She was flush-decked, with three narrow fishing wells in each of which one man could stand and jig for cod, and with two intervening fishholds in each of which the ghosts of a million long-dead cod tenaciously lingered. Right up in her eyes was a cuddy two feet high, three feet wide, and three feet long, into which one very small man could squeeze if he did not mind assuming the fetal position. There was also an engine room, a dark hole in which lurked the enormous phallus of a single-cylinder, make-and-break (but mostly broke) gasoline engine.

Her rigging also left something to be desired. Her two masts had apparently been manufactured out of a couple of Harry Lauder's walking sticks. They were stayed with lengths of telephone wire and cod line. Her sails were patched like Joseph's coat and seemed to be of equivalent antiquity. Her bowsprit was hardly more than a mop handle tied in place with netting twine.

It did not appear to me that the Hallohans had sailed her very much. I was to hear later that they had *never* sailed her and shared the general conviction of everyone in Muddy Hole that any attempt to do so would probably prove fatal.

She was not a clean little vessel. In truth, she stank. Her bilges had not been cleaned since the day she was built and they were encrusted with a glutinous layer of fish slime, fish blood, and fish gurry to a depth of several inches. This was not because of bad housekeeping. It was done "a-purpose," as the Muddy Holers told me *after* I had spent a solid week trying to clean her out.

"Ye see, Skipper," one of them explained, "dese bummers now, dey be built o' green wood, and when dey dries, dey spreads. Devil a seam can ye keep tight wit' corkin [caulking]. But dey seals dersel's, ye might say, wit' gurry and blood, and dat's what keeps dey tight."

I have never since had reason to doubt his words.

Since the sum the Hallohans had demanded for their vessel was, oddly enough, exactly the sum I had to spend, and since this nameless boat (the Hallohans had never christened her, referring to her only as She, or sometimes as That Bitch) was not yet ready to go to Samoa around Cape Horn, I had to make a serious decision.

The question really was whether to walk away from her forever, telling Jack McClelland a suitable lie about having been waylaid by highwaymen in St. John's, or whether to try and brazen it out and somehow make a vessel out of a sow's ear. Because I am essentially a coward, and anyway Jack is onto my lies, I chose the latter course.

Upon asking the Hallohans where I could find a boatbuilder who could make some necessary changes for me, I was directed to Enarchos Coffin — the very man who had built the boat four years earlier. Enos, as he was called, was a lean, lank, dehydrated stick of a man. In his younger days he had been a master shipwright in Fortune Bay, building vessels for the Grand Banks fishery; but when the Banking fleet faded into glory, he was reduced to building small boats for local fishermen. The boats he built were beautifully designed, but a combination of poverty among his customers, a shortage of decent wood, failing vision, and old age somewhat affected the quality of his workmanship. The Hallohan boat was the last one he had built and was to be the last he would ever build.

When I went to visit him, armed with an appropriate bottle, he was living in a large, ramshackle house in company with his seven unmarried daughters. Enos proved amiable and garrulous. The Southern Shore dialect is almost unintelligible to the ear of an outsider, and when it is delivered at a machine-gun clip it becomes totally incomprehensible. For the first hour or two of our acquaintance I understood not a single word he addressed to me. However, after the first burst of speed had run its course he slowed down a little and I was able to understand quite a lot.

He said he was delighted to hear I had bought the boat; but when he heard what I had paid for her, he was able to cure his attack of apoplexy only by drinking half the bottle of rum, neat.

"Lard livin' Jasus!" he screeched when he got his breath back. "An' I built her for they pirates fer two hunnert dollars!"

At which point I snatched the bottle from him and drank the other half of it, neat.

When we had recovered our breath I asked him if he would undertake repairs, modifications, and a general refit. He willingly agreed. We arranged that he would fit a false keel and outside ballast, a cabin trunk over the fish wells, and bunks, tables, lockers, and other internal essentials; respar and rerig her properly; and do a hundred other smaller but necessary jobs. Enos thought the work would take him about two months to complete.

I returned to St. John's and thence to Ontario in moderately good spirits. I did not worry about the boat's being ready on time since we did not plan on sailing her until midsummer. Occasionally I wrote to Enos (he himself could neither read nor write) and one or other of his strapping daughters would reply with a scrawled postcard, of which this one is typical:

Dear Mister Mote
   Dad say yor boat come fine lots fish
   this month Gert got her baby
                     Nellie Coffin

During the waiting months Jack and I dreamed many a dream and made many a plan. We agreed that I should precede him to Newfoundland near the end of June, taking with me a jeep-load of gear and equipment, and that I would have the few finishing touches to the boat completed so that she would be ready to sail when Jack arrived in mid-July. After that, well, we would see. Bermuda, the Azores, Rio de Janeiro — the world lay waiting!

I have never been able to decide whether I am glad I was not present when Jack arrived at Muddy Hole, or whether my absence should have been a matter for regret. I missed witnessing a scene which has since become part of Southern Shore folklore.

Jack's plane arrived in St. John's at a quarter to one. He disembarked, got my note, and sprang into action. He is like that. He springs into action. On this occasion he did not spring quite as lithely as usual because he had recently put his back "out" and as a consequence was wearing, under his Savile Row sports coat and sharkskin slacks, a fearsome device composed of rubber, steel, and whalebone that would have been the envy of the tightly corseted ladies of the Victorian era.

Nonetheless he sprang to such effect that in less than two hours he was heading for Muddy Hole. Some of the spring went out of him as he drove south, and all of the springs went out of the brand-new, chrome-plated, red-painted convertible Buick which (it was the only such car on the island) he had managed, with his usual ability to overwhelm the better judgment of those he deals with, to rent from St. John's leading garage.

At seven o'clock he arrived at Muddy Hole. The fish plant had just let out, and scores of girls in white aprons and rubber boots, and dozens of men in overalls and rubber boots were pouring out of the stinking building in which they had done their day's servitude. They were stopped in their tracks by the tremendous blare of a tri-tone horn.

At first they thought some strange vessel must be entering the harbor; then one of the girls saw the glint of the setting sun upon a mass of polished chrome poised on the lip of the rocky slope above the settlement.

This was a visitation the likes of which none of the inhabitants of Muddy Hole had ever seen before. As they stared, transfixed, the flame-colored monster on the crest eased forward over the lip of the descent. *That* galvanized them into action. A hundred arms began to wave as hoarse voices were raised in a great shout.

Jack, at the wheel of the red beast, was delighted.

He thought the people were welcoming him to Muddy Hole. He also thought he was still on the ill-defined track which led down the boulder scree to the shore of the cove.

He was wrong on both counts. There was no road, and the inhabitants were trying desperately to warn him of this fact.

"My son!" one of the observers on the scene told me afterwards. "It were a wunnerful sight to see!"

And here I had better explain that in Newfoundland the word "wonderful" still means what it used to mean in older times: full of wonder, full of awe.

The car negotiated the first yards without incident, then the slope abruptly steepened and although Jack, suspecting by now that all was not well, tramped on the brakes, it was too late. Down came the red behemoth, careless of the boulders in its path and heedless of a number of split-stick fences, leaping and bounding with the abandon of a hippopotamus driven mad by hashish. Things flew out of it. Two thirty-gallon, galvanized tin tanks intended for the boat (one for water and one for fuel) that had been insecurely reposing in the back seat, rose up and described glittering parabolas in the evening air. The trunk flew open, and Jack's modest assortment of seagoing gear, five suitcases and some smaller oddments, abandoned ship.

Suddenly it was all over. The car stood still, its shiny face buried in the end wall of a sheep shed. For a long minute none of the watchers moved. Before they could run to the rescue Jack stepped out of the small dust cloud that hung over the battered shed.

As might be expected of a man who, as commander of a motor torpedo boat, once attempted to make a new entrance into St. John's harbor through a four-hundred foot granite cliff, he had lost nothing of his cool. Blithely he made his way down the remainder of the slope. He was as nonchalant as if he were about to board a luxury cruiser moored to the carpeted docks of the Royal Yacht Squadron at Cowes.

Enos nervously stepped forward to meet him. He was completely befuddled by the spectacular nature of Jack's arrival.

Instead of guiding Jack to his house, pouring him a drink, and holding him there until I returned, Enos obediently responded to Jack's imperious demand that he be taken to the boat at once.

Enos conducted the jaunty and resplendent visitor directly to the stage. Jack took three steps out on the oil-soaked poles, stepped on a putrid piece of cod-liver, and his feet went out from under him. Appalled, Enos and three or four other men leapt *at* him, rather than to him, and in their awkward attempts to help him up — they shoved him overboard.

Although years have fled since then, Jack still refuses to talk about this episode. He claims he cannot remember it at all. I suspect his mental blackout resulted from the ministrations he received that evening from Enos and Enos's seven husky daughters. The strain of spending several hours in an overheated kitchen, being force-fed by a clutch of Valkyries while clad only in a corset and inadequately swathed in a blanket, and while attempting to establish human contact with eight people who seemed to speak no known language, is explanation enough.

Obie and I arrived back at Muddy Hole at midnight. Fortunately Jack was asleep by then. It was with a heavy heart and dubious hopes of the morrow that I crawled into my sleeping bag.

I was awakened early. Jack stood by my bed wearing a blanket and an anxious look.

"Hi," he said. Then, tautly, "Where in hell's the bathroom?"

Now it is to be borne in mind that Jack is the product of a very good private school, an old Toronto family, and a life of comfort if not of luxury. He is not one of your rough-and-ready pioneering types. He likes his conveniences. He is used to them and he is unhappy without them.

Muddy Hole homes, however, do not boast many conveniences. There are no indoor toilets and there are no outdoor toilets. Ladies keep porcelain pots under their beds but men do not. This seems unfair and, indeed, downright cruel, until one is inducted into the mystery of male behavior in an outport.

On *my* first visit to Newfoundland it took me several days to resolve this mystery, and I suffered accordingly. However, having become a member of the fraternity, I was able to spare Jack the agonies of having to find out for himself.

"Hello there. Have a good sleep? Yes? Well, you go on down to the stage, you know, the wharf thing made of sticks. And there's a little shack on the shoreward end of it. It's called the fish store and every fisherman has one. You go inside and you'll find a hole just beside the splitting table, where they dump the cod gurry into the water. And, oh yes, better take some paper with you."

Jack's face was a mirror of the struggle taking place within him. I was touched by the pleading look in his eyes, but it was necessary to be firm.

"Look," I said gently, "you don't have any choice. Not unless you want to try sneaking into the girls' room to borrow the pot." (All seven daughters slept in one room in two beds.) Jack flinched. "And as for the great out-of-doors, forget it. You'll find yourself entertaining five or six little boys and as many dogs, all of whom will spring full-blown from nowhere as soon as you think you're alone."

Jack moaned a little, gave me a bleak look, and headed out the door. He was gone a long time and in his absence the girls got up and lit the fire. By the time he returned they were preparing breakfast.

I felt sorry for Jack, truly sorry. I remembered well my own first visit to a fish store when, perched precariously between wind and water, and surrounded by pungent tubs of codfish soaking in brine, I had injudiciously looked down to behold a consortium of flatfish, sculpins, crabs, and eels staring hopefully upward at me out of the shallows.

Traumatic as the experience must have been, Jack managed to rise above it. But he nearly collapsed when the smell of breakfast struck him. He is a gourmet and a delicate eater. Furthermore he has a weak stomach.

He clutched my arm so hard it hurt and whispered hoarsely in my ear.

"*What* in God's name is *that?*"

"That," I explained cheerfully, "is Newfoundland's national dish. A special treat for visitors. It's called fish-and-brewis."

"Never mind the name. What's *in* it?"

"Well, basically it's a mixture. You take hard bread or ship's biscuits and soak them all night to make them soft and to get rid of the weevils. And you take some shore-dried salt fish and soak it all night, 'watering it' is the term. Then you boil the fish and the hard bread and when it's all nice and mushy you pour a cup of spitting hot sowbelly fat over it, and then . . ."

I never finished my explanation. Jack was already on his way back to visit the sculpins and the eels.

Most Southern Shore Newfoundlanders acquire a taste for rum soon after abandoning their mothers' breasts, and by the time they are grown men they have developed a high degree of immunity to it, but it is not total immunity. Up until this day I had been master of the rum situation and had governed the issuing of rations according to the three cardinal tenets of rum drinking in Newfoundland. The first of these is that as soon as a bottle is placed on a table it must be opened. This is done to "let the air get at it and carry off the black vapors." The second tenet is that a bottle, once opened, must never be restoppered, because of the belief that it will then go bad. No bottle of rum has ever gone bad in Newfoundland, but none has ever been restoppered, so there is no way of knowing whether this belief is reasonable. The final tenet is that an open bottle must be drunk as rapidly as possible "before all t'good goes out of it." Having learned these rules I made it a point never to produce more than one bottle at a time.

Unfortunately Jack did not know the rules and I did not have enough foresight to brief him. When he arrived back from St. John's, I was away at the other end of the harbor. He carried the case on board the vessel and lovingly unpacked it, placing all twelve bottles on the saloon table, lined up like twelve little soldiers.

Enos and Obie came below to watch him, and Jack told me later that the ruby glow given off from the bottles, as they sat in a ray of sunshine coming through the forward portlight, was reflected in the oddest manner from the eyes of his two companions.

Jack then went back to the jeep for another load of supplies. When he returned to the boat every bottle was open and the corks had vanished. He went on deck to ask Obie about this phenomenon and Obie, wordless as usual, simply pointed to the water of the cove where twelve corks were floating seaward on the receding tide like a child's flotilla.

It was at this moment I returned and at once I realized we had a crisis. Jack was for recorking the bottles with plugs of toilet paper, in lieu of anything better, until I explained that such a departure from tradition would certainly result in a mutiny and might well get us run out of Muddy Hole. The die was cast. There was no turning back; there was only one thing to be done.

"Look," I said in a whisper I hoped would not carry to the deck, "by afternoon every one of those bottles is going to be empty. That is a fact and you can rely on it. And if Enos and Obie do all the emptying there's going to be damn little work done on the boat in the foreseeable future. We just have to sacrifice ourselves, Jack. Start drinking!"

Neither of us are born Newfoundlanders but we did the best we could.

The unclear events of that unclear day can only be hazily reconstructed but one of them stands out. That was when we went ashore to get the new mainmast which Enos had been shaping upon a pair of sawhorses in his front yard. The mast had to be carried about a quarter of a mile down the slope then out on the rickety stage and finally swung into the air and stepped aboard the boat. In preparation for this Obie and Enos went below and when they came on deck there were only eleven little soldiers left on the table. Then the two of them swaggered up to where the mast lay and picked it up, one at each end.

The weight proved a little too much for Enos — it weighed a good three hundred pounds — so Obie shifted to the middle of it, taking the entire strain on his own shoulder, and began to trot down the slope. Obie is a big man and very powerfully built, but that mast diminished him until he looked like a small child carrying the biggest caber any Scotsman ever hefted.

Jack and I stood stunned and watched him go. He gained momentum with every plunging step. Enos ran along beside him, a sprightly terrier barking encouragement.

They reached the narrow stretch of level ground at the land-wash and Obie's speed did not diminish. Enos stopped encouraging him and began to yell in a rising inflection:

"Fer Jasus's sake, me son, *slow down!*"

It was no good. Gravity and momentum and various other physical laws which I don't understand had taken full control. Obie went thundering out along the stage, which shook and quivered like a spider's web — and he went right off the end.

He and the mast made a fantastic splash and the sound brought the girls and the men at the fish plant running to the wharf to see what had happened. They saw Obie astride the mast, laughing like a gawk — a Newfoundland seabird — and paddling toward shore with his big, splayed hands.

That incident established the mood of the day. A dozen men from the plant abandoned their work and came to lend a hand. They fished the mast and Obie out of the soup and then the whole lot of them plunged into the cabin. When they emerged again there had been a slaughter among the soldiers but the crowd was now good for anything. They hefted the mast into the air, swung it around by main strength, and dropped it onto its step with such enthusiasm that I expected it to go right through the hull of the boat, skewering her forever to the bottom of Muddy Hole harbor. Then they all went back below for a moment, came out on deck again, picked up the foremast and flung *it* into place. Then they all went below again.

Still trying doggedly to implement our plan, Jack and I attempted to get below too but there was no room. When we eventually reached the table there was one bottle still more or less inviolate, so we did our duty.

Happy Adventure sailed an hour after dawn. It was a fine morning, clear and warm, with a good draft of wind out of the nor'west to help us on our way and to keep the fog off shore. We had intended to sail *at* dawn but Enos did not turn up and when we went to look for him his daughters said he had gone off to haul a herring net. We recognized this as a ruse, and so we searched for him in the most likely place. He was savagely disgruntled when we found him, complaining bitterly that a man couldn't even "do his nature" without being followed. Little by little we coaxed him down to the stage, got him aboard and down below, and before he could rally, we cast off the lines.

Happy Adventure made a brave sight as she rolled down the

reach toward the waiting sea. With all sails set and drawing she lay over a little and snored sweetly through the water, actually overtaking and passing two or three belated trap skiffs bound out to the fishing grounds. Their crews grinned cheerfully at us, which is as close to a farewell as a Newfoundland seaman will allow himself. There is bad luck in farewells.

Before we cleared the headlands I celebrated a small ritual that I learned from my father. I poured four stiff glasses of rum. I gave one of these to Enos and one to Jack, and I kept one for myself. The fourth I poured overboard. The Old Man of the Sea is a sailor and he likes his drop of grog. And it is a good thing to be on friendly terms with the Old Man when you venture out upon the grey waters that are his domain.

All that morning we sailed south on a long reach, keeping a two- or three-mile offing from the grim sea cliffs. We came abeam of Cape Ballard and left it behind, then the wind began to fall light and fickle, ghosting for a change. The change came and the wind picked up from sou'east, a dead muzzler right on our bows, bringing the fog in toward us.

Enos began to grow agitated. We were approaching Cape Race, the southeast "corner" of Newfoundland and one of the most feared places in the western ocean. Its peculiar menace lies in the tidal currents that sweep past it. They are totally unpredictable. They can carry an unwary vessel, or one blinded by fog, miles off her true course and so to destruction on the brooding rocks ashore.

In our innocence Jack and I were not much worried, and when Enos insisted that we down sail and start the engine we were inclined to mock him. He did not like this and withdrew into sullen taciturnity, made worse by the fact that I had closed off the rum rations while we were at sea. Finally, to please him, we started the bullgine, or rather Jack did, after a blasphemous half-hour's struggle.

The joys of the day were now all behind us. Somber clouds began closing off the sky; the air grew chill, presaging the coming of the fog; and the thunderous blatting of the unmuffled bullgine deafened us, while the slow strokes of the great piston shook the little boat as an otter shakes a trout.

By four o'clock we still had reasonably good visibility and

were abeam of Cape Race — and there we stuck. The engine thundered and the water boiled under our counter, but we got no farther on our way. Hour after hour the massive highlands behind the cape refused to slip astern. Jack and I finally began to comprehend something of the power of the currents. Although we were making five knots through the water, a leebow tide was running at almost the same speed against us.

The fog was slow in coming but the wall of grey slid inexorably nearer. At six-thirty Jack went below to rustle up some food. An instant later his head appeared in the companionway. The air of casual insouciance, which was as much a part of his seagoing gear as his jaunty yachting cap, had vanished.

"Christ!" he cried, and it was perhaps partly a prayer. "This bloody boat is sinking!"

I jumped to join him and found that he was undeniably right. Water was already sluicing across the floor boards in the main cabin. Spread-eagling the engine for better purchase, Jack began working the handle of the pump as if his life depended on it. It dawned on me his life *did* depend on it, and so did mine.

The next thing I knew Enos had shouldered me aside. Taking one horrified look at the private swimming pool inside *Happy Adventure*, he shrieked:

"Lard Jasus, byes, she's gone!"

It was hardly the remark we needed to restore our faith in him or in his boat. Still yelling, he went on to diagnose the trouble.

He told us the stuffing box had fallen off. This meant that the ocean was free to enter the boat through the large hole in the sternpost that housed the vessel's shaft. And since we could not reach it there was nothing we could do about it.

Enos now retreated into a mental room of his own, a dark hole filled with fatalistic thoughts. However, by giving him a bottle of rum to cherish, I managed to persuade him to take the tiller (the little boat had meanwhile been going in circles) and steer a course for Trepassey Bay, fifteen miles to the eastward, where I thought we might just manage to beach the vessel before she sank.

There was never any question of abandoning her. Our dory, so called, was a little plywood box barely capable of carrying one man. Life preservers would have been useless, because we were in the Labrador Current where the waters are so cold that a man cannot survive immersion in them for more than a few minutes.

By dint of furious pumping, Jack and I found we could almost hold the water level where it was, although we could not gain upon the inflow. And so we pumped. The engine thundered on. We pumped. The minutes stretched into hours and we pumped. The fog held off, which was one minor blessing, and we pumped. The engine roared and the heat became so intense that we were sweating almost as much water back into the bilges as we were pumping out. We pumped. The tidal current slackened and began to help us on our way. We pumped.

Occasionally one of us crawled on deck to breathe and to rest his agonized muscles for a moment. At eight o'clock I stuck my head out of the companionway and saw the massive headland of Mistaken Point a mile or so to leeward. I glanced at Enos. He was staring straight ahead, his eyes half shut and his mouth pursed into a dark pit of despair. He had taken out his dentures, a thing he always did in moments of stress. When I called out to tell him we were nearly holding the leak he gave no sign of hearing but continued staring over the bow as if he beheld some bleak and terrible vision from which he could not take his attention for a moment. Not at all cheered I ducked back into the engine room.

And then the main pump jammed.

That pump was a fool of a thing that had no right to be aboard a boat. Its innards were a complicated mass of springs and valves that could not possibly digest the bits of flotsam, jetsam, and codfish floating in the vessel's bilge. But, fool of a thing or not, it was our only hope.

It was dark by this time, so Jack held a flashlight while I unbolted the pump's faceplate. The thing contained ten small coil springs and all of them leapt for freedom the instant the plate came off. They ricocheted off the cabin sides like a swarm of manic bees and fell to sink below the surface of the water in the bilges.

It does not seem possible, but we found them all. It took

twenty-five or thirty minutes of groping with numbed arms under oily, icy water, but we found them all, reinstalled them, put back the faceplate, and again began to pump.

Meanwhile, the water had gained four inches. It was now over the lower part of the flywheel and less than two inches below the top of the carburetor. The flywheel spun a niagara of spray onto the red-hot exhaust pipe, turning the dark and roaring engine room into a sauna bath. We pumped.

Jack crawled on deck for a breather and immediately gave a frantic yell. For a second I hesitated. I did not think I had the fortitude to face a new calamity — but a second urgent summons brought me out on deck. Enos was frozen at the helm and by the last light of day I could see he was steering straight toward a wall of rock which loomed above us, no more than three hundred yards away.

I leapt for the tiller. Enos did not struggle but meekly moved aside. His expression had changed and had become almost beatific. It may have been the rum that did it — Enos was at peace with himself and with the Fates.

"We'd best run her onto the rocks," he explained mildly, "than be drowned in the cold, cold water."

Jack went back to the pump, and I put the vessel on a course to skirt the threatening cliffs. We were not impossibly far from Trepassey Bay, and there still seemed to be a chance we could reach the harbor and beach the vessel on a nonlethal shore.

At about eleven o'clock I saw a flashing light ahead and steered for it. When I prodded him, Enos confirmed that it might be the buoy marking the entrance to Trepassey harbor. However, before we reached it the fog overtook us and the darkness became total. We felt our way past the light-buoy and across the surrounding shoals with only luck and the Old Man to guide us.

As we entered the black gut which we hoped was the harbor entrance, I did not need Jack's warning shout to tell me that our time had about run out. The bullgine had begun to cough and splutter. The water level had reached her carburetor and, tough as she was, she could not remain alive for long on a mixture of gasoline and salt seawater.

Within Trepassey harbor all was inky black. No lights could be seen on the invisible shore. I steered blindly ahead, knowing that sooner or later we must strike the land. Then the engine coughed, stopped, picked up again, coughed, and stopped for good. Silently, in that black night, the little ship ghosted forward.

Jack came tumbling out on deck, for there was no point in remaining below while the vessel foundered. He had, and I remember this with great clarity, a flashlight in his mouth and a bottle of rum in each hand. . . .

. . . At that moment *Happy Adventure*'s forefoot hit something. She jarred a little, made a strange sucking sound, and the motion went out of her.

"I t'inks," said Enos as he nimbly relieved Jack of one of the bottles, "I t'inks we's run'd ashore!"

Jack believes *Happy Adventure* has a special kind of homing instinct. He may be right. Certainly she is never happier than when she is lying snuggled up against a working fish plant. Perhaps she identifies fish plants with the natal womb, which is not so strange when one remembers she was built in a fish plant yard and that she spent the many months of her refit as a semi-permanent fixture in the fish plant slip at Muddy Hole.

In any event, when she limped into Trepassey she unerringly found her way straight to her spiritual home. Even before we began playing flashlights on our surroundings we knew this was so. The old stench rose all around us in its familiar miasma.

The flashlights revealed that we had run ashore on a gently shelving beach immediately alongside a massively constructed wharf. Further investigation had to be delayed because the tide was falling and the schooner was in danger of keeling over on her bilge. Jack made a jump and managed to scale the face of the wharf. He caught the lines I threw him and we rigged a spider web of ropes from our two masts to the wharf timbers to hold the vessel upright when all the water had drained away from under her.

When she seemed secure I joined Jack on the dock and cautiously we went exploring. The fog was so thick that our lights were nearly useless, and we practically bumped into the first human being we encountered. He was the night watchman for Industrial Seafood Packers, a huge concern to whose dock we were moored. After we had convinced the watchman that we did not have a cargo of fish to unload, but were only mariners in distress, he came aboard.

He seemed genuinely incredulous to find we did not have a radar set. How, he asked, had we found our way into the harbor? How had we missed striking the several draggers anchored in the fairway? And how, in hell's own name (his words), had we found the plant and managed to come alongside the wharf without hitting the L-shaped end where the cod-oil factory stood in lonely grandeur?

Since we could not answer these questions we evaded them, leaving him with the suspicion, which spread rapidly around Trepassey, that we were possessed by an occult power. Witches and warlocks have not yet vanished from the outport scene in Newfoundland.

The watchman was a generous man and he told us we could stay at the wharf as long as we wished. He felt, however, that we might be happier if we moored a hundred feet farther to seaward.

" 'Tis the poipe, ye know; the poipe what carries off the gurry from the plant. Ye've moored hard alongside o'she."

Happy Adventure had come home with a vengeance and, for all I know, it may have *been* vengeance at that.

That was a singularly dreadful night.

We had to begin repairing the leak immediately, while the tide was low. We soon found that Enos's diagnosis had been correct. The outside stuffing box, or gland, had come adrift when both retaining lag screws parted, allowing the box to slip down the shaft until it rested against the propeller.

In order to repair it we had to borrow a big drill from the helpful watchman, drill out the remains of the old lag screws, fair off the dead wood where the shaft had chewed it up, and then screw the gland back into place. Perhaps this does not sound like much of a task, but let me try to paint the scene.

To reach the gland we had to wade knee-deep in black, stinking muck, a composite product consisting of aboriginal slime fortified over the decades by decaying contributions from the fish plant. We worked in darkness except for the light from two poor flashlights which could produce only a dim orange glow in the shroud of bitterly cold fog that enveloped us. We kept dropping things, and the recovery of a wrench or a bolt from the sucking slime brought to mind Hercules at his task in the Augean stables.

By three o'clock the job was done, and just in time because the tide was rising. We waited impatiently for it to float the boat so we could haul her out along the wharf, away from the ominous presence of the "poipe." Half an hour before the plant began operations, the tide was full.

It was not full enough. *Happy Adventure* did not float.

We had run her ashore "on the last of the springs," which is to say, on the highest tide of the month. Enos, who knew all about such things, pointed out to us it would be nearly twenty-eight days before the tide was as high again.

Enos also said he felt it was time for him to leave. He said he did not want to be a bother to us and, considering the cramped accommodation on our little vessel and the fact that we would be making a prolonged visit in Trepassey, he thought it would be better if he went away as soon as the fog thinned. He said he would sacrifice his own comfort and stay with friends ashore until he could find transportation back to Muddy Hole.

I did not attempt to dissuade him but Jack was displeased because, as an old Navy man, he took a dim view of people jumping ship. However, after breakfast Jack found he was able to accept Enos's departure with equanimity.

I cooked that breakfast. It was a hearty one for we were all half-starved. I cut up and fried about three pounds of side bacon. It was fat bacon; it was tough bacon; and it had a rind on it a quarter of an inch thick.

Jack and Enos sat at the saloon table while I served them. What with the layers of muck that coated our clothing, and what with the stench from the fishy flats outside, the atmosphere was not salubrious. However, for once Jack was too tired, too hungry, and too depressed to care about his mealtime surroundings. Grimly he went to work on his bacon while I turned back to the stove to cook my own rashers. Suddenly I heard Jack make a despairing, strangled sound. I spun around.

Jack sat rigid on the bench, his eyes staring glassily from a face that had lost its usual ruddy color and had become grotesquely mottled. He was staring at Enos.

All unaware of the scrutiny, Enos was busy eating his bacon. It had proved too tough for him to deal with while his badly fitting dentures remained in his mouth, so he had removed both plates. He now held them firmly in the angle between thumb and forefinger of his left hand, and he was making them snap open and shut with a dexterity that argued long practice. With his right hand he was passing a strip of bacon between the two sets of grinders. When this remarkable operation had macerated the strip of bacon sufficiently he threw back his head, poised the bacon over his mouth, and gummed it down.

Jack struggled to his feet, pushed his way past me, and vanished out the companion hatch. Before he returned, an hour or so later, Enos had packed his gear and gone ashore. I cannot in all conscience say that either of us was deeply pained to sign him off.

Nothing about our stay at Trepassey provides memories upon which I care to dwell, but the day of Enos's departure was so horrible that even my notes written at the time fail to deal adequately with it.

Enos departs at 7 A.M., the last I hear of him is a grand final expectoration on deck. I hope it is only tobacco juice and spit, not bacon. Jack can't stand much more. . . . At 8 A.M. the sewage tank at the plant got up its first full head of steam and let her rip. The discharge shot ten feet out of the pipe and did not quite clear *H.A.*'s deck. Most of it hit the mainmast and was deflected into the cockpit. Discharge continues about once every hour. Like Big Bertha at the siege of Paris, but Paris never could have stood up to *this* barrage. . . . Out of rum. Last bottle seems to have disappeared. . . . Tide fell and rose again, one foot short of refloating us. . . . Jack offered to sell *H.A.* "as is, where is," to local fisherman for fifty dollars. Was refused. . . . Manager fish plant came along at noon, asked us to move. Said we are interfering with flow from sewage pipe. Jack made highly personal suggestion to manager where he could put sewer pipe. Was refused. . . . Discover no rum available closer than St. John's. Jack beginning to talk longingly of life of book publisher in Toronto. . . . Small boy aboard at 4:30 offers Jack a rusty tin can full of cod's tongues for ten cents. Was refused. . . . Stink in cabin so atrocious Jack opened portlight over his bunk, forgetting next discharge from pipe was due. Failed to get portlight closed in time. . . .

It was a hideous day but the climax came that evening. Just after supper, for which neither of us had any stomach, Jack decided to light the gasoline lantern. This lantern was a piece of equipment we seldom used, preferring to depend on the dim light from two small oil lamps which, we felt, were less likely to ignite the ever-present raw gasoline floating in our bilge. However, this night we needed the big lantern, not only because its garish flare might brighten the general gloom, but also because it would provide much-needed heat which, to some small extent, might dispel the stinking damp that filled the cabin, and that had turned our sleeping bags and clothing into clammy shrouds.

For safety's sake Jack normally took the lantern on deck or ashore before lighting it, but this evening he was not normal. He may even, although he denies it, have had some hope in his subconscious mind that the thing *would* explode and put us out of our misery. Whatever the case, he chose to light it on the saloon table, and when he opened the valve to prime the generator, he opened it too far and left it open too long. When he touched a match to the mantle a three-foot flame leapt into instant life.

Whatever desire for self-immolation may have lurked in the back of Jack's mind, it was no match for his instinct for self-preservation. Thrusting a long wooden spoon (with which I had mixed our codfish stew) under the lantern's handle, he leapt for the companionway, scrambled through it, and disappeared into the night waving his flaming torch and shouting, "Fire!" at the top of his lungs.

There were a great many boats and vessels moored to the wharf that night, including three big, new side-draggers that boasted all sorts of modern equipment, including Foamite fire control systems. Acting on the assumption that it would be quicker to take the fire to the extinguisher than to wait for the

extinguisher to come to him, Jack made straight for these draggers. His path took him between several rows of forty-five-gallon
drums, painted red, and filled with gasoline for the use of the
smaller fishing boats. His urgent bellowing and the great flare
of light that accompanied him alerted all the crews of the
moored boats, and by the time he neared the draggers he had a
large, attentive, and terrified audience.

What the final outcome *might* have been is anybody's guess. I
like to dwell on the possibility that Jack might have succeeded
in boarding one of the draggers bearing his burning offering and
there been received with such a blizzard of CO_2 foam that he
would have been buried alive.

The reality was not quite so dramatic. Before reaching the
first dragger Jack discovered that the wooden spoon had caught
fire and was burning briskly. He knew he was not going to make
it. Reacting with the split-second reflexes for which he is justly
famed, he swerved to the dockside and flung spoon and lantern
into the cold sea. There was a brief final flare as the last of the
gasoline burned on the surface before darkness closed down
upon us all.

By the time Jack fumbled his way back to *Happy Adventure* (he
had been half-blinded by the glare), I had lit the cabin lamps.
We said nothing to each other; we just sat in silence until, half
an hour later, heavy boots clumped on our deck and a gruff voice
asked permission to come below.

Permission being granted, four very large, very muscular fishing skippers crammed their way into the cabin.

They said they had heard we were having trouble refloating
our boat. They said they would deem it an honor (those were
not exactly the words they used) to give us a helping hand. They
said their crews were already rigging wire warps from our bows
to the main winch of the biggest dragger. Would we, they asked,
come on deck and be ready to move our vessel to a much better
mooring at an unoccupied government wharf on the other side
of the harbor, as soon as they had hauled her off the mud?

I thanked them but pointed out that I would never be able to
find the wharf in darkness and in fog and so would prefer to
moor alongside one of their draggers for the night.

They said they understood how I felt, but two of them would

be delighted to pilot us across the harbor. No, they would not come aboard *Happy Adventure* in order to do this; they would pilot us from a motorboat bearing a large light and keeping well out of our way.

The kindliness of Newfoundland fishermen has to be experienced to be appreciated.

VI.
SIBERIA

❖

FROM

SIBIR, or *THE SIBERIANS, 1970*

TCHERSKY

In 1966 and 1969 Mowat made two trips to Siberia, the first with his wife Claire and the second with the photographer John de Visser. This passage from Sibir describes the culmination of the first journey, in Tchersky, at the mouth of the Kolyma River on the coast of the Arctic Ocean in northeastern Siberia.

◆

Shortly after Claire and I reached Yakutsk in 1966 Simeon Danielov asked us if there was any particular place we wanted to visit. Since at that time we did not know the name of a single locality in the republic except Yakutsk itself, this posed a problem.

"I'm sure there must be hundreds of places we'd like to see. However, since you know them and we don't, I'd prefer to leave the choice to you. One thing, though, I'd like to visit a town in a remote northern region."

Simeon merely nodded. During the days that followed, Claire, Kola, Yura, and I saw several northern towns, all of which appeared to be satisfactorily remote. I assumed my request had already been granted until one afternoon Kola announced we would be leaving before dawn the next day for the town of Tchersky.

"And where is Tchersky?" I asked.

Kola, who is a Muscovite, knew as little about Yakutia as I did, shrugged his narrow shoulders, and looked more birdlike than usual.

"Who knows? Somewhere in Siberia. We'll see. One thing you can be sure about. It will have a lot of kindergartens and we will be taken to see every last one of them so we can tickle the dripping little monsters under their fat chins." Kola didn't really dislike children. He had just had enough kindergartens during our trip.

Yura Rytkheu could have given us some idea of where Tchersky was located, but during the 1966 trip Yura was *not* on the wagon; in fact he had apparently determined personally to create an alcoholic drought in Yakutsk. When we met him for dinner that evening he was unable to speak any known language, unless it was his native Chukchee, so he was no help in satisfying our curiosity about the whereabouts of Tchersky.

Kola rousted us out of bed at 2 A.M. Grumpily, and without even the solace of a glass of tea, we clumped into a Volga and were driven to the airport, where, as was to be expected, we found the flight had been delayed "indefinitely." The pilot's room was locked, so we had to join the proletarian masses — masses and *masses* of them, filling every available chair and even sleeping fitfully on the floor.

It was 25 degrees below outside, though somewhat warmer inside. We were exhausted, hungry, irritable, and gradually freezing to death, but I was fascinated by two ancient ladies who had built themselves a lair under a staircase. Here they had a small stove over which a big, black kettle was suspended. The two old girls hovered around it, cackling balefully and occasionally making a sortie into the den of sleepers to slap wet mops as close as possible to the feet, and sometimes the heads, of the unconscious travellers. Kola, whose long nose was dripping and who was shivering uncontrollably, eyed the old dames uneasily.

"I'll bet your William Shakespeare could have done something with that pair of witches!" he said through a clash of chattering teeth.

Truly the world looked dark — *was* dark — and dawn was

many hours away. At 5 A.M. our flight was called and, led by Simeon Danielov, our guide for this expedition, we stumbled onto the pitch black and bitter field to seek our plane — a twin turboprop carrying Polar Aviation markings on its fuselage. Everyone crowded to get inside out of the cutting frost, but the plane had been sitting out all night and the temperature inside was exactly the same as that outside. It was like a dead machine, without even any illumination, except for the dim glow from a tiny bulb over the entrance door.

Must be the wrong plane, I thought. But, no, a few minutes later the crew arrived, big hearty fellows bundled up as if bound out on a real polar exploration. As the pilot shouldered past, breathing out jets of steam, he gave us all a booming: "*Dobroe ootro!*" — "Good morning!" If any of the passengers agreed with this outrageous piece of optimism, none of them said so.

The jovial pilot wound up the engines and away we went. I still did not know where we were going. I had intended to ask Simeon but was too preoccupied keeping Claire and myself from freezing to death to bother. An hour later, when the interior of the plane had warmed up sufficiently to allow us to loosen our fur ear flaps, we began to descend. It was none too soon. Claire had begun to whimper softly, like a dog that urgently needs to be let out.

We landed, still in pitch darkness, and I began pulling oddments of luggage off the racks until Yura stopped me. "Not Tchersky yet! Only stop here for breakfast. Take your time."

"*You* take *your* time!" Claire hissed at him. "Get out of the way or you'll be sorry!"

We had landed at Khandyga, a little-log town in a taiga clearing on the shores of the Aldan River — the greatest of the Lena's tributaries. A pretty girl, bundled up in an immense dog-skin coat, met us at the plane's door and led us to a blissfully warm log hut where all except Claire were served huge plates of mashed potatoes, reindeer meat, and gravy. Claire had vanished into the black night on urgent personal business.

We had almost finished breakfast before she reappeared, pushing her way weakly through the great double doors that guarded against the frost outside, and looking as if she had just escaped from an Arctic version of the nethermost pit. It was some hours before she could bring herself to tell me all the details of what had happened to her.

On the way to the café she asked the pretty guide where the restroom was, and the girl waved an arm in the direction of a towerlike log structure across the road. Claire raced for it, climbed a flight of outside stairs, pushed open a door, and found herself in a large throne room containing nothing but a hole in the middle of the floor. It was a huge hole, black and menacing. Previous visitors had recognized its potential threat and had stayed far enough away from the edge to be reasonably safe. This had resulted in a build-up of ice which increased the dangers and caused still later comers to use even greater caution. When Claire arrived it was hardly safe to step inside the door without risking the possibility of glissading into that gaping hole.

Claire was not about to take such an appalling risk. She stayed where she was, barely inside the doorway . . . and at the critical moment someone else ran up the stairs and seized the outer door of the unlocked — and unlockable — door.

Claire instantly grabbed the handle on her side; forgetting she had taken off her gloves; that the temperature was 40 degrees below zero; and that the latch was made of iron.

She was now faced with a complex problem. She had to try and adjust her clothing with her left hand, while with her right hand she engaged in a tug-of-war with a stranger of unknown sex on the far side of the door. The situation was complicated by the hellish prospect that she might lose her precarious balance, slide down the icy slope, and vanish forever from human ken. She could not give up the struggle with her unseen antagonist because her right hand was frozen to the latch. Her agonized howls for mercy got her nowhere because the stranger knew no English.

Fortunately the door swung outward, else I might never have seen my bride again.

The exasperated customer on the other side gave one mighty heave — the door flew open and Claire was snapped out of her private purgatory like a released elastic band. Her hand came free of the latch in time to let her avoid being trampled underfoot by an irate woman of elephantine build, who had no time to indulge in polite amenities. Claire slunk down the stairs and over to the café, having only lost a little skin from her fingers, but an incalculable amount of dignity.

I think what really hurt her most was the discovery she made when we boarded the plane again . . . a neat, clean little lavatory in the tail section, equipped with a lock that worked.

We departed from Khandyga in the first light of dawn and began to climb steeply into the northeast. I leaned over and asked Simeon where Tchersky was.

"On Kolyma River."

"Yes, but where is that?"

"Across Verkhoyansk Mountains."

"How *far* across?"

He shrugged. "I do not know. Never go there before."

I gave up, looked out the window, and instantly forgot all about Tchersky.

We were climbing steeply but the earth was tilting skyward at almost the same rate. The taiga-covered plateau which I had come to associate with Yakutia had vanished, to be replaced in the dawn light by a stupendous upheaval of snow-dusted rock — a titanic wall at the end of the world, which our plane was laboring to overleap.

I have flown over many great mountain ranges but none as brutally violent, as bleakly hostile in appearance as the ranges of the massif which leaps skyward beyond the Aldan River. I have since crossed these mountains by air several times and have visited some of the rock-trapped little towns in their chill valleys, but these monstrous Arctic peaks remain amongst the most awesome sights in my experience.

The Ilushin-14 whined higher and higher and the peaks, white-hooded now, kept pace until we cleared the first outlying range at an altitude of fifteen thousand feet. Beyond lay a chaos of broken mountains. The one sign of life was a frail fringe of leafless trees at the bottom of the deepest valleys. We flew over the Verkhoyansk Mountains for an hour; then almost impercep-tibly the image began to change, softening into a mountain terrain of less terrifying character. The plane banked to the right and a frozen river came into view in the bottom of a well-wooded valley. Beside a meander in the river several score wooden build-ings smoked blue plumes into the brilliant morning sky.

The copilot came aft and leaned over us. "Oimyakon and the Indigirka River. We just called them on the radio. They have no passengers so we won't stop today. Too bad, because they're having a regular summer morning. It's only minus 56 degrees down there."

I took advantage of the moment. "Excuse me, but just where is Tchersky?"

The young man grinned, winked at Simeon and Yura, and nodded toward the cockpit. "Just up ahead there. Not so far. I'd better get back to my job."

I was beginning to catch on. There was a conspiracy on foot. Nobody was going to tell me where Tchersky was. I did not really care. Beyond the valley of the Indigirka the mountains went savage again, towering even higher than before and so violently jumbled that they seemed like the debris of a stellar explosion. They are known as the Tchersky Range, but they do not deserve such a civilized identity; they are a glimpse into another time than ours, a time of primal tumult beyond anything we, hopefully, will ever know. The eleven-thousand-foot peaks of the Moma Mountains drifted past under a wing and there seemed to be no end to this weird wilderness. I suggested to Claire that our pilot must have gone the wrong way, that this must be Tibet. The idea did not seem so unreasonable.

In all we flew more than six hundred miles in a direct line across the massif, and when the peaks lowered again toward a forested highland, it was not for long. To the eastward new peaks lifted to a white sky, marching beyond the most distant horizon to the ultimate northeastern tip of Asia. This mighty mountain complex represents nearly a quarter of the Siberian landmass, occupying almost the whole region east and northeast of the Lena valley. It is kith and kin with its Alaskan neighbors, but covers twice the area.

The aircraft let down in a gentle descent toward the wind-burnished ice of a big river that emerged from a gap in the mountains and flowed northward into a wide reach of stunted forest.

"Kolyma River!" Yura called to us, pointing down.

Claire jumped to her feet and scampered aft to the ladies room. Once bitten . . . twice shy. She regained her seat just as we came in to land. I reached for the luggage. Yura grinned from ear to ear.

"Not Tchersky yet. Zirianka. Stop for lunch."

Once again we trotted across the snow to a log café, leaving a bevy of robust ladies to refuel the plane. Over bowls of soup and glasses of cognac, I confronted Simeon and Yura.

"Look," I said, "a game's a game. But just where in hell *are* we going, anyway?"

Yura tilted his glass, wiped his lips, and sighed.

"Ah well, it is too late for you to go back now, so I tell truth. Very many times you talk about Siberia for place of exile. So we make special exile just for you. Under Tsars most dangerous political prisoners sent to Tchersky. Nobody ever escape from there. Impossible! But you are very tough Canadian. We give you chance to try. Not necessary walk five thousand miles to Moscow from Tchersky — only you have to walk eight hundred miles east, then show passport to Yankees on Bering Strait."

We flew straight north along the Kolyma valley with the mountains on our right and a plain of drowned taiga widening into the distance on our left.

Two hours later the copilot came back and drew our attention to a brilliant white line on the horizon ahead.

"The polar sea! . . . And there is Tchersky down below."

Beneath us was a haphazard sprawl of buildings. I searched for a stockaded enclosure but could not pick one out. Later, perhaps. The settlement was on a bold point of land jutting into the Kolyma. Beyond it the white and featureless tundra rolled north to the frozen ocean.

We landed on the river ice and taxied toward the town through an assemblage of parked aircraft which included at least thirty fixed-wing planes and a dozen helicopters. Clearly Tchersky did not lack the means of modern transportation. Our plane stopped beside a crowd of fur-clad figures and we descended the steps into the heart of a mob of welcomers, all of them jovially anxious to pump our hands. It was the kind of reception which would have warmed the heart of the most blasé politician. It assuredly warmed ours, and that was good, because the temperature was close to minus 40 degrees.

Our arrival was a real occasion. Claire and I were the first foreigners to visit Tchersky since the Revolution. Claire was the first foreign woman most Tcherskyites had ever seen. On top of that, we were Canadians, and as such were looked upon as being next-door neighbors, despite the fact that our homes were separated by the width of the Arctic Ocean.

A gleaming-eyed Chukchee, Nikolai Tourot (who began life as a reindeer herder and is now Mayor of Tchersky and a delegate to the National Assembly in Moscow) greeted me with a gentle handshake; but the District Party Secretary, Victor Nazarov, a bouncing brute of a man, embraced me with such fervor I gasped for breath. He had his eye on Claire as well, but she was too quick for him and took shelter in the middle of a group of Russian, Evenki, and Chukchee ladies.

Yura rescued me from Victor's grasp and introduced me to Simeon Kerilev, a tiny, sweet little Yukagir poet and novelist whose most recent book, *Son of an Eagle*, had just been published.

It was impossible to register all those who crowded around us. Their ardor was too overwhelming ... but by far the most overwhelming was Victor Nazarov.

Victor is the sort of man who has to be seen and heard to be believed. Born in 1930 of Russian peasant stock near Tobolsk in west Siberia, he went to the Aldan goldfields of Yakutia with his parents after his father had "some difficulties" with the Stalin dictatorship. Following his father's death during the war, Victor helped support the family by becoming a driver-mechanic. This was a job that suited him and one he loved. He wrestled trucks over most of northern Siberia, and in his spare time from *that* activity, he took correspondence courses until he had the credits needed to enter university at Sverdlovsk, from which he graduated with a prize degree in industrial transportation. He joined the Party in 1955 (bearing no grudges for what was past); ran the truck transport network during the building of Mirny; and in 1962 was dispatched to the mouth of the Kolyma to apply his energies to the construction of the new Arctic town of Tchersky.

Moon-faced, tug-voiced, hairy as a mammoth, strong as a cavebear, and utterly and absolutely indefatigable, Victor Nazarov took Claire and me into his ebullient heart with such rampant enthusiasm that he nearly killed us both. I remember him, and always will, as the most generous, ingenuous, and forceful man I have ever met.

Cutting our party out of the crowd of welcomers, he heaved us bodily into his Bobyk, a jeeplike little car (the nickname Bobyk means "little terrier"), and drove us into town over non-existent roads at fifty miles an hour. Not once did he stop bellowing in our ears. He had a lot to tell us and he was not the man to waste a moment. As the Bobyk skidded, leaped, and crashed into and over obstacles, Victor's massive left arm was flung out in a continuing gesture, pointing to half-built structures, piles of mud, holes in the ground, even to white stretches of virgin tundra, and identifying these as: "APARTMENT HOUSE FOR FIFTY FAMILIES GOES THERE ... THAT IS BEGINNING OF BIGGEST SCHOOL IN SIBERIA ... PALACE OF SPORT, WE ARE BUILDING HERE ... POWER STATION OVER THERE. ..."

When he had reduced all four of us, even Yura, to bruised and battered hulks, and deaf ones at that, he suddenly jammed on the brakes, sending poor Kola smashing into the window.

"POOR CLAIRE! I FORGOT MYSELF! MAYBE YOU ARE A LITTLE TIRED? I TAKE YOU TO HOTEL!"

The hotel, of logs ("WE ARE BUILDING NEW ONE RIGHT AWAY — CONCRETE — ONE HUNDRED FIFTY ROOMS"), was simple, but we had a suite of two pleasant rooms which, it appeared, we were going to share with Victor. Having escorted us to our rooms he showed no inclination to depart but pounded over to the window, thrust out his big paw, and began waving at the distant landscape.

"FARLEE! OVER THERE WE MAKE NEW AIRPORT — BIG ENOUGH FOR JET PLANES — AND CLAIRE! LOOK THERE! WE MAKE NEW NURSERY SCHOOL. ..."

Yura intervened. Somehow he maneuvered Victor out the door — though not without a parting bellow.

"NOW YOU HAVE GOOD REST! LATER WE MAKE PLANS!"

The door swung shut and Claire fell on the nearest bed. I was a little shaky myself as I started to take off my boots. It seemed to me I could still hear Victor's foghorn echoing inside my skull.

It was not an echo! It was reality. The door burst open.

"ULCERS ON MY SOUL! I FORGOT SO MUCH! YOU MUST HAVE FOOD! COME QUICK! COME QUICK!"

I tried to tell Victor we were not hungry, just exhausted, but I might as well have been Canute trying to turn back the tide. He swept us out of the room, across the frozen range of muddy mountains which might someday be a road, and into a restaurant presided over by a beautiful young lady by the name of Lydia, whose husband, Anatoly (she quickly told me), was an interior decorator working in the town.

Interior decorator? Here? Claire and I exchanged glances. But it was true enough and later we had a chance to meet Anatoly and to admire his work.

Lydia had prepared a modest snack. Twelve of us (people kept appearing as if out of the woodwork) sat down to it. The appetizer was pickled reindeer tongue. Next came Kamchatka crab, chocolate éclairs, dumpling soup, fish soup, cream puffs, reindeer cutlets, smoked salmon, stewed Ukraine tomatoes, cherry juice, strawberry jam, and tea. The food was not necessarily served in that order, but since there was one bottle of cognac, one of vodka, and one of champagne at *each* person's place, I can be excused if I have somewhat jumbled the sequence.

Victor proved to be the *tamadar* of all the world. He leaped to his feet at least once every three minutes and every toast was bottoms up. It was at this first meal with him that Claire struck back. He insisted on learning a Canadian toast and so she perversely taught him to say "up bottoms." He was delighted and, so he told me when I revisited him three years later, had no idea of its potential English meaning. However, during a visit to Moscow he was called on to help entertain a party of senior dignitaries from Great Britain at an official function. Beaming with affability and delight, he proposed that they should drink his Canadian toast, which he had unwittingly modified to:

"Up your bottoms!"

He told me this story somewhat ruefully, but without rancor. "MOSCOW SEND ME BACK TO TCHERSKY IN DISGRACE! BUT I FORGIVE DEAR CLAIRE! SHE HELPED ME GET OUT QUICK FROM THAT CURSED TOWN!"

The last toast was drunk about 8 P.M. and we were almost literally carried back to our hotel. We were in no condition to resist when all twelve of our dinner companions crowded into our room and Victor sat down at the table, banged it so that it jumped clean off the floor, and announced we would now have a planning conference.

"HOW LONG YOU STAY WITH US? A MONTH? TWO MONTHS?"

He seemed genuinely outraged when I timidly replied that we could not remain more than two weeks. He pounded the table until I was sure it would collapse and then he planned each of our days in the most minute detail—forgetting only to leave time for sleep.

I could see that Claire, who had unwisely allowed herself to get hooked on the spirit, was not going to be with the party much longer; so, in an act of unselfish heroism which she has never properly appreciated, I agreed (actually there was no way I could have refused) to accompany Victor to the makeshift Palace of Sport while he did his nightly workout.

Kola had faded, but Yura was still going strong. Together with the mayor, the newspaper editor, and half a dozen others, we watched the incredible Victor bounce his two-hundred-seventy-pound bulk around while he played two fast games of volleyball, worked for half an hour with the barbells, wrestled a couple of the biggest truck drivers in Tchersky, and then announced:

"I'M HUNGRY! LET'S GO AND HAVE A LITTLE SNACK!"

We drank the snack at the headquarters of the Tchersky Press, a dilapidated log structure out of another age boasting a modern rotary press which had been flown in from Leningrad to print the daily *Kolymskaya Pravda*. We also did a group show on the radio station which was housed in the same building; although since it was then past midnight I doubt if anyone heard us except, perhaps, the polar bears on the Arctic ice a few versts to the northward. I wonder what they made of my wobbly rendition of "The Squid Jigging Grounds."

At 2 A.M. we were back in the hotel, but not to sleep. Someone had decided our winter clothing was inadequate and half the town had been scoured to find proper clothing. Claire was pried out of bed and, eyes still tight shut, was wrapped in an enormous dog-skin coat, hatted with an Evenki reindeer bonnet, booted with embroidered felt boots which went up to her thighs (Victor insisted on fitting these with his own hands), and gloved in sealskin mittens. She claims she has no recollection of the fittings.

During my absence at the Sports Palace the table in our room had miraculously sprouted several bottles of champagne together with baskets of fresh fruit and cream pastries. So we had another little lunch. At 3 A.M. Victor looked at his glittering Slava wristwatch and the voice of authority shivered the hotel.

"TIME NOW FOR BED! GET GOOD SLEEP! TOMORROW WILL BE BUSY DAY!"

Tchersky is at once one of the oldest and the newest of Siberian settlements. In 1644 the Cossack, Semyon Dezhnev, descended the Lena from Yakutsk, somehow navigated his way along the arctic coast to the mouth of the Kolyma, ascended it a few miles, and built an *ostrug*, a tiny, crude wooden fort which came to be known as Nizhniye Kresty. Through the years and centuries it survived as a fur-trade station and one of the most remote and inaccessible outposts of the Russian Empire. From it the Yukagir (then a strong and numerous people), the Evenki, and the Chukchee of the northeast coast were systematically bled for furs even as the Eskimo of North America were bled at a later time.

By the beginning of the twentieth century the fur-bearers had all but disappeared — and so had most of the native people. Nizhniye Kresty remained alive, though barely so, as a place of exile for the most dangerous and desperate political prisoners in the hands of the Tsars.

After the Revolution the ancient settlement almost vanished and human life in the district shrank to a handful of native Russian trappers and fishermen, a few hundred Yukagir reindeer herders, and a score of Chukchee families.

Then, in 1960, Moscow waved her wand and Nizhniye Kresty was born anew.

The justification for the resurrection was gold — unbelievable quantities of it that had been discovered along the upper reaches of the Kolyma and its tributaries; and to the eastward in the Anyuyskiy Mountains of adjacent Chukotka. The decision was taken to develop this region as a valuta center and to begin building it into one of the new far Northern complexes. There was no gold at Nizhniye Kresty but it was ideally placed to become another Lensk — a transportation and administrative center for the region.

In 1961, when the transformation was begun, there were thirty people living in ten ancient wooden houses on the river bank. In 1966, when I first visited it, there were two brand-new sister towns: Tchersky, on the old site, with a population of five thousand people, and, four kilometers to the north, the sea and river port of Green Cape, with six thousand people. Tchersky had become the capital of the entire Kolymsky District, embracing an area the size of Denmark and the Netherlands put together, and it already boasted one of the most productive reindeer farms in the Soviet Union. The port city was receiving oceangoing ships of fifteen-thousand-ton displacement, and the river had become the everyday highway, summer and winter, for a fleet of ships and trucks.

All of this had been accomplished by the unbridled enthusiasm and the unremitting efforts of people like Victor Nazarov — people who were not motivated by the prospect of personal gain so much as by an idea and a belief.

It was my good luck to live for a little while in the midst of Tchersky's atmosphere of sustained excitement, and to see something of the adolescence of a new world abuilding on the shores of the polar ocean.

By exercising iron self-control, Victor managed to stay away from us until 6 A.M.; then the roar of his voice and the thunder of his feet as he pounded up the hotel stairs brought us unwillingly back to consciousness.

"COME ON!" he boomed. "WE GO SEE REINDEER HERD!"

He hustled us across the street to Lydia's. She had prepared a breakfast of hot boiled deer tongues, salad, chocolate cake, meatballs and fried potatoes, vodka, and cognac. She apologized because there was no champagne!

It was still pitch dark and 33 degrees below zero as our Bobyk bounced out to the airport and delivered us to an enormous MIL-

4 helicopter personally piloted by the assistant district chief of Polar Aviation, a big, bony, and handsome man. His crew consisted of a copilot, navigator, radio operator, and engineer, and considering we were about to make a two-hundred-mile flight into the tundra in what was effectively the middle of the night, I did not feel that any one of them was redundant.

Our own party numbered ten, but since everyone was bundled to the eyes in monstrous coats and fur hats, it was difficult to know just who was who. Only Victor was easily recognizable. His was the one voice audible above the roar of the engine as we lifted off.

Shortly before 9 A.M. the sky began to grey and we could see the featureless white ocean of tundra below us. We thundered over it, and just as the sun tipped the edge of the horizon, a black smudge loomed far ahead on the now saffron-tinted snow. It grew and took on form until it became a solidly packed mass of deer, above which hung a silver cloud of glittering frost crystals condensing from the living warmth of this great herd.

We circled once at low altitude and I expected the milling mass of beasts to stampede, but they only flung back their heads so their antlers ranged the sky like a forest shaken in a gust of wind. They were used to helicopters, which visited them at least once a week, bringing mail and supplies for the herdsmen.

A few hundred yards to one side stood three large skin tents — *yarangas*. A handful of people came running toward us as we settled to the tundra.

They were the herders Nikolai Dyatchiv and Mikhail Kimirgin, men in their early thirties; Innokenty Khodyan, the chief herder, a man of fifty; and the wives of Khodyan and Kimirgin. All were Yukagir. They were dressed in ancestral garb, clad from sole to crown in reindeer skins. We were introduced and then with much grinning, shouting, and some impromptu dance steps from Victor, made our way to the Khodyans' yaranga. Our visit was unexpected, but on the tundra hospitality is always waiting.

The tent was constructed of double layers of deer skins with a vestibule for storing gear and to act as a heat-lock. We pushed through the double flaps to enter the Khodyan home and found ourselves in a spacious room, about twenty feet in diameter, with wall-to-wall carpeting of thick, soft reindeer robes. A small sheetmetal stove glowed red in the middle of the room, and beside it stood a table about ten inches high. There were no chairs. Everyone squatted or lay where he pleased.

Victor came in last, dragging a big burlap bag that clinked. Out of it he drew endless bottles and we hoisted a few "sunrisers" while snacking on chips of raw frozen fish. Glasses of heavily sweetened tea completed this second breakfast.

We shared it with Innokenty Khodyan's grandmother who, at the age of one hundred and seven years, refused to stay at home in the comfort of the reindeer breeders' permanent settlement but insisted on continuing to live the nomadic life of the herders. She told us how surprised she was to meet people from another continent — "across the frozen waters" — and she hoped we would remain at least until the spring as her grandson's guests.

Her age-blackened and desiccated face turned toward a little girl who sat solemnly staring at us. The child was named Elizaveta (Elizabeth). She was the old woman's great-great-granddaughter.

"I am too old to travel much anymore, but this little one may someday visit *your* yaranga. It is good for people who are from far away to visit each other," the old lady told us.

While we breakfasted the two young men slipped off to bring the herd closer to the camp. We went outside to find ourselves surrounded by the living host of the reindeer. Nearly three thousand of them stood passively about, staring incuriously at the helicopter, or pawing through the hard snow to snatch a mouthful of moss.

Armed with rawhide lassos, and with several silent, furry little dogs close at their heels, the three herders loped into the middle of the herd, which spread to let them pass and closed in again behind them. Deep in that maze of antlers they were looking for an especially fat deer with which to make a feast to celebrate our coming.

They lassoed several before they found a suitable one. Dumbly it followed them out of the herd. It stood braced against the rope while Khodyan gentled it and then with a flashing movement thrust his knife between its ribs. Slowly the beast sank to its knees, crumpling to the snow.

The men having done their job, the women squatted beside the animal, neatly paunched it, skinned it, and butchered the steaming meat. They worked without gloves despite the searing frost — the body heat of the dead reindeer keeping their hands from freezing.

While the women prepared the meal in another tent, Victor challenged me to a reindeer race. Laughing and shouting in the brittle air, the herdsmen rounded up several "driving deer" and hitched them to the sleds — slight constructions of thin larch planks bound together with rawhide. We drivers were each given a long willow wand, on the very end of which was fastened a tiny bone hammer. Yura explained that this was my accelerator. When I wanted my deer to speed up I had only to tap him under the tail.

"Not too hard!" Yura warned me. "Or he will fly!"

Bellowing like a bison, Victor pulled away while I rather tentatively explored the technique of deer driving. It turned out to be easy enough and because my deer had to pull only about half of Victor's weight, we soon caught up to him and the two sleds went slithering across the barren plain at top speed. On the home stretch I took the lead, beating Victor by two lengths. He looked just a bit downcast but rallied with a booming laugh as the gallery cheered me home. This was the first of several little tests he was to put me through.

"Now you don't need Aeroflot to get you back to Canada," Vasily Amisov, the Yukagir team leader of the farm reindeer section, told me. "If you want, you and your wife can drive home. Ten days' good sledding should take you there."

"I think we'd prefer to stay right here."

It was the proper thing to say. Vasily embraced me, rolled me on the snow, then, putting his Jew's harp in his mouth, led a pied piper procession back to the yaranga.

The main tent bulged. Champagne corks popped incongruously, and, even more incongruously, Yura tuned in on the Voice of America on the Khodyans' portable radio. The announcer was explaining how much better off the Alaskan Eskimo were than their depressed relatives in Siberia. Everyone listened politely, then Vasily proposed a toast to the announcer, suggesting we invite him to Tchersky so he could see for himself how terribly the native people were suffering.

The women now pushed through the flaps bearing iron pots full of steaming reindeer brisket and we got down to work. Because the meat had been so freshly killed it was a little tough, but greasily delicious. We ate with our hands and I noted that Victor could hold a juicy piece between his teeth while slicing off a mouthful with one slash of his sheath knife. I had learned the same trick while living with the Eskimo. It is a procedure best practiced by people with short noses.

In the babble of talk I learned that the camp had to be shifted every two or three days as the herd slowly grazed across the frozen plain. Once a week one of the men would hitch up a team and drive south to timberline for a load of firewood. And once a month helicopters carried out an exchange of herders and their families.

I asked Innokenty Khodyan whether he did not prefer the comfort of the settlement. He was amazed.

"Why should I want that? The best days of my life are here on the tundra with the herds. I am doing good, useful work, and it is work I love."

I remembered what Madame Ovchinnikova had said about the native reindeer herders.

"We are against any attempt to force the nomadic peoples to stay in one place. It is for them to make their own choice. If they choose to remain nomads, we try to make it possible for them to do so but still have the benefits of modern society. They repay us a hundred times. No one can surpass them as reindeer breeders, and without reindeer it would be much harder for us to develop the North as we are doing."

VII.

THE
DEEPS

FROM

A WHALE FOR THE KILLING, 1972

FROM
A Whale for the Killing

Skipper Ro tugged at the whistle lanyard and the *Burgeo*'s throaty voice rang deep and melancholy over the spume-whipped harbor. The lines came in and we backed out into the stream. Once clear of the fairway buoy, the little ship bent to the gale and headed east, holding close in against the looming, snow-hazed land to find what lee there was.

I went below to the old-fashioned dining saloon with its Victorian, leaded glass windows, worn linen tablecloths, and battered but gleaming silverware. Most of the passengers were gathered there, having a mug-up of tea and bread and butter, and yarning companionably, for on the Sou'west Coast everyone knows everyone else, or is at least known to everyone else. Claire was sitting between the owner of a small dragger and his dumpy, jovial wife. I joined them. The nor'easter screamed in the top-hamper and the old reciprocating steam engine thumped its steady, heavy heartbeat underfoot as we listened to the gossip of the coast.

Had we heard that the government was going to close out the settlement of Grey River? The dragger owner snorted into his cup of tea. "Hah! By the Lard Jasus, they fellers in St. John's is goin' to find they needs a full cargo o' dynamite to shift Grey River. Aye, and I don't say as even that'll shift they people!"

Fish landings had been down. "Entirely too starmy all the fall months. Shore fishermen can't hardly git out at all. Even us

275

fellers onto the draggers, we has to spend the best part of our sea time battened down or runnin' for shelter."

But there were compensations. "Niver did see such a toime for caribou. I tell ye, me son, they's thicker'n flies on a fish flake, and coming right down to the landwash to pick away at the kelp. Oh, yiss bye, they's lots o' country meat on the go!"

He smacked his lips and winked at his wife who promptly took up the tale.

"They got the new school open to Ramea, me dears. Yiss, an Lucy Fenelly, belongs to Mosquito Harbour, got a new baby, and her man away working on the mainland these past ten months! And that young student preacher, come just afore you folks went off, he only stayed long enough to christen the child and then he fair flew off the coast. I don't say 'twas his fault entirely. Lucy's got thirteen youngsters now, and they's none of 'em looks no more like her man than I does meself."

Over the third cup of tea, the dragger skipper, as an act of politeness, asked where we had been.

"Europe," I told him, and added with something of the self-conscious pride of a world traveller, "and Russia. Moscow first, and then right through Siberia as far as the Pacific and the Arctic Coast."

"Roosia, eh? Yiss . . . well now, you'll be some glad to be getting home to Burgeo. . . . Me dear man, they's some glut of herring on the coast this winter. Nothin's been seen the like of it for fifty year. . . ."

The little house which had stood empty for six months was as warm and welcoming as if we had never left it. Our delight was also Sim's delight as he sat unobtrusively nursing a glass of rum in front of the Franklin stove. His self-imposed duty was not yet completed. It was now his task to bring us up-to-date on the really vital events which had taken place during our absence.

"They was talk of a strike down to the plant, but the owner, he put an end to it right quick. Said he'd close her up and move clear of Burgeo and leff the people lump it if they didn't care to work to his wish. Don't know where he figured on going, but they's plenty folk here could name a place proper for the likes of he! . . . Curt Bungay, he's bought a new boat, a longliner from down Parsons Harbour way. . . . Your schooner's hauled up clear, and Joe, he found her leak . . . one of 'em anyhow. . . . They's a new nurse to the hospital; Chinee they *says* she is, but she's good for it. Comes out the dirtiest sort of weather to take care of folks. . . . Good run o' fish this winter, but nothin fit to call a price. . . ."

And so it went, in rapid-fire bursts, until, a decent time having been allowed for us to have our dinner and settle in a bit, other visitors began clumping over the porch and unceremoniously letting themselves into the kitchen. A bevy of teen-age girls led the way. They sat in a tidy row on the kitchen day-bed and said nothing; only beamed, giggled, and nodded as we tried to make conversation with them. Then, with familiar uproar, Albert, our big, black water dog, came galumphing into the kitchen bearing a dried codfish as a homecoming present. Close behind him came his, and our, friend, eighty-year-old Uncle Job; gnome-like, ebullient, and grinning thirstily as he spotted the rum bottle on the kitchen table. During our absence Albert had lived with Uncle Job and his wife and, according to what Sim told us later, dog and man had spent most of their time engaged in acrimonious debate as to whether they would, or would not, go fishing, go for a walk, go for a swim, go to bed, or get up in the morning. They were both inveterate argufiers.

"He'll miss that dog some bad," Sim said. "Wuss'n he'd miss his woman. *She* never says a word, and it drives he fair wild when he can't get an argument."

Rather reluctantly Albert delivered over the cod — a fine one it was too, for Uncle Job was one of the few Burgeo people who still knew and practiced the age-old art of drying and salting fish. Albert then sniffed in a perfunctory way at our luggage with its stickers from Irkutsk, Omsk, Tbilisi, and other exotic places, barged into the living room, climbed up on the sofa, grunted once or twice, and went to sleep.

The homecoming was complete.

Most assuredly whales are not fish, although until a century ago most people, including those who knew them best, their hunters, thought they were. Whales and men trace the same ancient lineage through creatures born in the warm waters of the primal oceans who exiled themselves to the precarious environment of the dry land. They continued to share a common ancestry through the long, slow evolution that began with the amphibians and eventually led to the mammals. But whereas our mammalian fathers stayed ashore, about a hundred million years ago the mammalian forebears of the whales chose to return to the mother of all life — the sea. The descendants of the whale forefathers now number about a hundred species which man, the great cataloguer, has divided into the families of the toothed and the baleen whales.

The toothed whales are the more primitive but the most various, for they include all the porpoises and dolphins, the Sperm, Killer, White Whale, and that unicorn of the sea, the Narwhal. Except for the Sperm, which grows to sixty feet, most of the toothed whales are relatively small, some being less than four feet long.

There are only eleven species of baleen whales, but they rank at the top of the whale's evolutionary tree. About eighteen million years ago, when our own ancestors were abandoning the forests to awkwardly start a new way of life as bipeds on the African savannahs, some of the whales began abandoning teeth in favor of fringed, horn-like plates (baleen) that hang from the roof of the mouth to form a sieve with which the owner strains out of the sea water immense quantities of tiny, shrimp-like creatures, or whole schools of little fishes. It seems a paradox that the largest beast in the world should prey on some of the smallest, but the system works surprisingly well. The proof of the pudding is in the eating, for the baleen whales are the most stupendous animals that ever lived. They include fifty-foot Greys and Seis; sixty-foot Rights and Humpbacks; eighty-foot Finners; and the giant of all time, the Blue, which may grow to a hundred and fifteen feet and weigh almost two hundred tons.

Although they bear a superficial resemblance to fishes, whales have little in common with the scaly tribe. When they returned to the sea they brought with them an intelligence of a radically new order — one that had evolved as a direct consequence of the ferocious difficulties which all terrestrial animals must face in order to survive, and which reached its peak in the mammals.

This legacy was shared by the ancestral whales and by the nameless creatures who were to become the progenitors of man.

In the case of *our* forebears, intelligence continued to develop along terrestrial lines in order to cope with the original stringent need which called it forth: the need to survive under competitive and environmental conditions of appalling severity. From this fierce struggle man ultimately emerged with the most highly developed brain of any land animal, and he used it to become the most ruthless and destructive form of life ever to exist. Intellectual supremacy allowed him to dominate all other forms of life, but it also enabled him to escape the restraints — the natural checks and balances — which had prevented any previous species from running hog-wild and becoming a scourge unto life itself.

It was a different story with the whales. When their ancestors returned to the sea it was to an environment which, compared to the land, was positively amiable. Instead of having to scrabble for survival on the dry, restricted, two-dimensional skin of the planet, split as it was into fragments separated by impassable seas, they returned to the wet, three-dimensional and interconnected world of waters which surrounds and isolates the land-islands. Here they were free to go where and when they pleased. They were restored to a womb world where the climate was more stable; where there was no shortage of food; and where there was no need to occupy or defend territory. Because the ancestral whales returned to this water world endowed with the survival skills so hard-won on land, they were as superior to the old, cold-blooded residents of the seas as time-travellers from some point millions of years in the future might be to us.

Pursuing their advantage over other sea-dwellers, the whales underwent a leisurely evolution extending over many millions of years during which they achieved near-perfect adaptation to the sea environment.

On the other hand, the emerging human stock had to battle desperately for survival in a bitterly rigorous environment, not only against an array of other animals which were often physically and functionally superior, but against the organized and war-like competition of their own species. The human stock would surely have been eliminated if it had not used its developing brain to invent ways of redressing the balance. Faced, as he so often was, with an intolerable climate, man learned to build shelters, use fire, and make clothes. Faced with physically superior animals of other species, *and* with deadly competition from his fellows, he made weapons. Faced with the constant spectre of starvation, he made tools with which to cultivate his own food supplies. Bit by bit he stopped relying on natural evolution to keep him alive and in the race, and came to lean more and more heavily on artificial substitutes. He had invented, and had become a slave to, technology.

Whales never needed a technology. Going back to the sea enabled them to survive successfully as natural beings . . . yet they were beings who, like proto-man, were endowed with a great intellectual potential. What did they do with it . . . with their share of our mutual legacy? We simply do not know. Despite our much-vaunted ability to probe the secrets of the universe, we have so far failed to probe the mystery of the mind of the whale.

Such studies as we have made suggest that the more advanced whales have brains comparable to and perhaps even superior to ours, both in complexity and capacity. It is clear that their power to think has steadily increased, even as ours has, over the millennia. There can only be one reasonable assumption from all this: whales must use their minds, and use them fully in some direction, in some manner, for some purpose which evades our comprehension. For it is an immutable law of nature that any organ, capability, or function which is not kept well honed by constant use will atrophy and disappear . . . and the brain of the whale has certainly not atrophied.

So whales and men diverged from the common ancestry, one to become the most lordly form of life in the oceans, and the other to become the dominant animal on the land. The day came when the two would meet. The meeting was not a peaceful one, in mutual recognition of each other's worth. As usual, it was man who set the terms — and he chose battle. It was a one-sided battle where man wielded the weapons, and the whales did the dying.

Why is it that, if whales have such large and well-developed brains, they have not been able to avoid destruction at man's

hands? The answer seems obvious. The whales never dabbled in
the arcane arts of technology and so had no defense against that
most deadly plague. In time they might have evolved a defense,
but we gave them no time. The answer raises a counter question:
Why is it, if man has such a remarkable intelligence, *he* has been
unable to avoid an almost continuous acceleration of the pro-
cesses of self-destruction? Why, if he *is* the most advanced of
beings, has he become a threat to the survival of all life on
earth?

After supper on Thursday two fishermen from Smalls Island
walked into our kitchen bearing gifts of cod tongues and a huge
slab of halibut. They sat on the day-bed and we talked for a
while about the state of the fishery, the weather, and other usual
topics of Burgeo life. It was not until they were leaving that the
real reason for the visit came out.

"I suppose, Skipper, you knows about the whale?"

"You mean the Finners in The Ha Ha?"

"No, Skipper, I mean the one down in Aldridges Pond. Big
feller. Been in there quite a time."

"What the devil would a whale be doing in there?" I asked
incredulously. "What kind of a whale is it?"

He was vague. "Don't rightly know. Black, like; with a girt
big fin. They says it can't get clear. . . . Well, goodnight to you,
Missus, Skipper."

And with that they vanished.

Sim Spencer was alone in his little store, laboriously working
up his accounts. Rather reluctantly, it seemed to me, he admitted
to having heard something about the Aldridges whale. When I
asked him why he hadn't told me before, knowing how interested
I was in anything to do with whales, he was embarrassed.

"Well," he said, fumbling for words. "They's been a lot of
foolishness . . . a shame what some folks does . . . wouldn't want
to bother you with the likes of that . . . but now as you knows,
I thinks 'tis just as well."

The implications of this escaped me at the time, but soon
became clear enough. The reason I had not been told about the
whale was that many of the people were ashamed of what was

happening and did not want to talk about it with outsiders; and even after five years I was still something of a newcomer in their midst.

Sim took me to see the Hanns. They were reticent at first but they did describe the whale in fair detail; and I now realized there was an excellent if almost unbelievable chance it might turn out to be one of the great rorquals. Having seen Aldridges Pond in the past, I knew it to be an almost perfect natural aquarium, quite large enough to contain even a Blue Whale in some kind of comfort.

The prospect that, for the first time in history, so far as I knew, it might be possible to come to close quarters with the mystery of one of the mighty lords of Ocean, was wildly exciting. I was in such a hurry to rush home and tell Claire about it that Kenneth Hann's concluding words did not quite sink in.

"They says," he warned, "some fellers been shooting at it. It could get hurted, Skipper, an' they keeps it up."

Probably some damn fool has been taking pot shots at it with a .22, I thought, and put the warning out of mind. As I hurried across Messers bridge in the gathering darkness, my thoughts were fixed on tomorrow, and my imagination was beginning to run away as I contemplated what could happen if the trapped whale indeed turned out to be one of the giants of the seas.

Early next morning I telephoned Danny Green, a lean, sardonic, and highly intelligent man in his middle thirties who had been the high-lining skipper of a dragger but had given that up to become skipper, mate, and crew of the little Royal Canadian Mounted Police motor launch. Danny not only knew — and was happy to comment on — everything of importance that happened on the Sou'west Coast, he was also familiar with and interested in whales. What he had to tell me brought my excitement to fever pitch.

"I'm pretty sure 'tis one of the big ones, Farley. Can't say what kind. Haven't seen it meself but it might be a Humpback, a Finner, or even a Sulphur." He paused a moment. "What's left of it. The sports have been blasting hell out of it this past week."

As Danny gave me further details of what had been happening, I was at first appalled, then furious.

"Are they bloody well crazy? This is a chance in a million. If that whale lives, Burgeo'll be famous all over the world. *Shooting* at it! What the hell's the matter with the constable?"

Danny explained that our one policeman was a temporary replacement for the regular constable, who was away on leave. The new man, Constable Murdoch, was from New Brunswick. He knew nothing about Burgeo and not much about Newfoundland. He was hesitant to interfere in local matters unless he received an official complaint.

At my request, Danny put him on the phone.

"Whoever's doing that shooting is breaking the game laws, you know," I told him. "It's forbidden to take rifles into the country. Can't you put a stop to it?"

Murdoch was apologetic and cooperative. Not only did he undertake to investigate the shooting, he offered to make a patrol to Aldridges Pond and take me with him. However, Claire and I had already made other arrangements with two Messers fishermen, Curt Bungay and Wash Pink, who fished together in Curt's new boat. They were an oddly assorted pair. Young, and newly married, Curt was one of those people about whom the single adjective, "round," says it all. His crimson-hued face was a perfect circle, with round blue eyes, a round little nose, and a circular mouth. Although he was not fat, his body was a cylinder supported on legs as round and heavy as mill logs. Wash Pink was almost the complete opposite. A much older man, who had known hard times in a distant outport, he was lean, desiccated, and angular. And whereas Curt was a born talker and storyteller, Wash seldom opened his mouth except in moments of singular stress.

A few minutes after talking to Murdoch, Claire and I were under way in Curt's longliner. I was dithering between hope that we would find a great whale in the Pond, alive and well, and the possibility that it might have escaped or, even worse, have succumbed to the shooting. Claire kept her usual cool head, as her notes testify:

"It was blowing about 40 miles an hour from the northwest,"

she wrote, "and I hesitated to go along. But Farley said I would regret it all my life if I didn't. Burgeo being Burgeo, it wouldn't have surprised me if the 'giant whale' had turned out to be a porpoise. It was rough and icy cold crossing Short Reach but we got to Aldridges all right and sidled cautiously through the narrow channel. It was several hours from high tide and there was only five feet of water, which made Curt very nervous for the safety of his brand-new boat.

"We slid into the pretty little Pond under a dash of watery sunlight. It was a beautifully protected natural harbour ringed with rocky cliffs that ran up to the 300-foot crest of Richards Head. Little clumps of dwarfed black spruce clung in the hollows here and there along the shore.

"There was nobody and nothing to be seen except a few gulls soaring high overhead. We looked eagerly for signs of the whale, half expecting it to come charging out of nowhere and send us scurrying for the exit. There was no sign of it and I personally concluded it had left — if it had ever been in the Pond at all.

"I was ready to go below and try to get warm when somebody cried out that they saw something. We all looked and saw a long, black shape that looked like a giant sea-serpent, curving quietly out of the water, and slipping along from head to fin, and then down again and out of sight.

"We just stared, speechless and unbelieving, at this vast monster. Then there was a frenzy of talk.

" 'It's a *whale* of a whale! . . . Must be fifty, sixty feet long! . . . That's no Pothead, not that one . . .'

"Indeed, it was no Pothead but an utterly immense, solitary and lonely monster, trapped, Heaven knew how, in this rocky prison.

"We chugged to the middle of the Pond just as the R.C.M.P. launch entered and headed for us. Farley called to Danny Green and they agreed to anchor the two boats in deep water near the south end of the Pond and stop the engines.

"Then began a long, long watch during which the hours went by like minutes. It was endlessly fascinating to watch the almost serpentine coming and going of this huge beast. It would surface about every four or five minutes as it followed a circular path around and around the Pond. At first the circles took it well away from us but as time passed, and everyone kept perfectly still, the circles narrowed, coming closer and closer to the boats.

"Twice the immense head came lunging out of the water high into the air. It was as big as a small house, glistening black on top and fish-white underneath. Then down would go the nose, and the blowhole would break surface, and then the long, broad back, looking like the bottom of an overturned ship, would slip into our sight. Finally the fin would appear, at least four feet tall, and then a boiling up of water from the flukes and the whale was gone again.

"Farley identified it as a Fin Whale, the second largest animal ever to live on earth. We could see the marks of bullets — holes and slashes — across the back from the blowhole to the fin. It was just beyond me to even begin to understand the mentality of men who would amuse themselves filling such a majestic creature full of bullets. Why *try* to kill it? There is no mink or fox farm here to use the meat. None of the people would eat it. No, there is no motive of food or profit; only a lust to kill. But then I wonder, is it any different than the killer's lust that makes the mainland sportsmen go out in their big cars to slaughter rabbits or ground-hogs? It just seems so much more terrible to kill a whale!

"We could trace its progress even under water by the smooth, swirling tide its flukes left behind. It appeared to be swimming only about six feet deep and it kept getting closer to us so we began to catch glimpses of it under the surface, its white underparts appearing pale aqua-green against the darker background of deep water.

"The undulations on the surface came closer and closer until the whale was surfacing within twenty feet of the boats. It seemed to deliberately look at us from time to time as if trying to decide whether we were dangerous. Oddly, the thought never crossed my mind that *it* might be dangerous to us. Later on I asked some of the others if they had been afraid of this, the mightiest animal any of us was ever likely to meet in all our lives, and nobody had felt any fear at all. We were too enthralled to be afraid.

"Apparently the whale decided we were not dangerous. It made another sweep and this time that mighty head passed right under the Mounties' boat. They pointed and waved and we stared down too. Along came the head, like a submarine, but much more beautiful, slipping along under us no more than six feet away. Just then Danny shouted: 'Here's his tail! Here's his tail!'

"The tail was just passing under the police launch while the head was under *our* boat, and the two boats were a good seventy feet apart! The flippers, each as long as a dory, showed green beneath us, then the whole unbelievable length of the body flowed under the boat, silently, with just a faint slick swirl of water on the surface from the flukes. It was almost impossible to believe what we were seeing! This incredibly vast being, perhaps eighty tons in weight, so Farley guessed, swimming below us with the ease and smoothness of a salmon.

"Danny told me later the whale could have smashed up both our boats as easily as we would smash a couple of eggs. Considering what people had done to it, why didn't it take revenge? Or is it only mankind that takes revenge?"

Once she accepted the fact that our presence boded her no harm, the whale showed a strange interest in us, almost as if she took pleasure in being close to our two 40-foot boats, whose undersides may have looked faintly whale-like in shape. Not only did she pass directly under us several times but she also passed between the two boats, carefully threading her way between our anchor cables. We had the distinct impression she was lonely — an impression shared by the Hann brothers when she hung close to their small boat. Claire went so far as to suggest the whale was seeking help, but how could we know about that?

I was greatly concerned about the effects of the gunning but, apart from a multitude of bullet holes, none of which showed signs of bleeding, she appeared to be in good health. Her movements were sure and powerful and there was no bloody discoloration in her blow. Because I so much wished to believe it, I concluded that the bullets had done no more than superficial damage and that, with luck, the great animal would be none the worse for her ordeal by fire.

At dusk we reluctantly left the Pond. Our communion with the whale had left all of us half hypnotized. We had almost nothing to say to each other until the R.C.M.P. launch pulled alongside and Constable Murdoch shouted:

"There'll be no more shooting. I guarantee you that. Danny and me'll patrol every day from now on, and twice a day if we have to."

Murdoch's words brought me my first definite awareness of a decision which I must already have arrived at below — or perhaps above — the limited levels of conscious thought. As we headed back to Messers, I knew I was committed to the saving of that whale, as passionately as I had ever been committed to anything in my life. I still do not know why I felt such an instantaneous compulsion. Later it was possible to think of a dozen reasons, but these were afterthoughts — not reasons at the time. If I were a mystic, I might explain it by saying I had heard a call, and that may not be such a mad explanation after all. In the light of what ensued, it is not easy to dismiss the possibility that, in some incomprehensible way, alien flesh had reached out to alien flesh . . . cried out for help in a wordless and primordial appeal which could not be refused.

Darkness had fallen by this time, and the house shook and shuddered in a snow-filled gale. The devils of self-doubt began to stalk me. Perhaps I *was* a little mad — deluded anyway — in thinking I might save the whale. Perhaps the battle was already lost. Perhaps I *had* no business meddling in a tragedy which was essentially a natural one . . . but then I saw again the whale herself, as we had watched her slipping through the green void beneath Curt Bungay's boat. That vision routed the devils instantly. That lost leviathan was one of the last of a disappearing race, and I knew she had to be saved if only because contact with her, though it lasted no more than a few brief weeks, might narrow the immense psychic gap between our two species; might alter, in at least some degree, the remote and awesome image which whales have always projected onto the inner human eye. And if, through this opportunity for intimate contact, that image could be changed enough to let men, to *force* men, to see these secret and mysterious beings with the compassion we have always denied them, it might help bring an end to the relentless slaughter of their kind.

This thought, combined with the effect of the rejections from those whose help I had thus far sought, began to make me fighting mad. I decided that if those who ought to have displayed some interest in the whale refused to do so, I would make them. And, by God, I thought I knew how to do just that.

"Claire," I told my wife, "I'm going to give the story to the press. The *whole* story. About the shooting. There'll be plenty of people who'll react to that. They'll surely make enough fuss, raise enough hell, to force someone out there to act. Burgeo won't like it. It could get damned unpleasant around here. What do you say?"

Claire was very much in love with Burgeo. This was where she had made her first home as a married woman. She understood the delicate nature of our acceptance in the place and she had a woman's shrewd ability to see the possible implications of this decision. Her voice, in reply, seemed very small against the cacophony of the storm.

"If you must . . . oh, Farley, I don't want that whale to die either . . . but you'll be hurting Burgeo . . . the people you like won't understand . . . but I guess . . . I guess it's what you have to do."

Burgeo winter weather often seemed to consist of six days of storm followed by a seventh when all was forgiven, and the seventh day was almost always a Sunday. I once discussed this interesting phenomenon with the Anglican minister but he decently refused to take any credit for it.

Sunday, January 29th, was no exception. It almost seemed as if spring had come. The sun flared in a cloudless sky; there was not a breath of wind; the sea was still and the temperature soared.

Early in the morning Onie Stickland and I went off to Aldridges in his dory. We took grub and a tea kettle since I expected to spend the entire day observing the whale and noting her behavior for the record. I hoped Onie and I would be alone with her, but there were already a number of boats moored to the rocks at the outer end of the channel when we arrived, and two or three dozen people were clustered on the ridge overlooking the Pond. I saw with relief that nobody was carrying a rifle.

We joined the watchers, among whom were several fishermen I knew, and found them seemingly content just to stand and watch the slow, steady circling of the whale. I used the opportunity to spread some propaganda about Burgeo's good luck in being host to such a beast, and how its continued well-being would help in drawing the attention of faraway government officials to a community which had been resolutely neglected for many years.

The men listened politely but they were sceptical. It was hard for them to believe that anyone outside Burgeo would be much interested in a whale. Nevertheless, there did seem to be a feeling that the whale should not be further tormented.

"They's no call for that sort of foolishness," said Harvey Ingram, a lanky, sharp-featured fisherman, originally from Red Island. "Lave it be, says I. 'Tis doing harm to none."

Some of the others nodded in agreement and I began to wonder whether — if no help came from outside — it might be possible to rouse sufficient interest in the whale, yes, and sympathy for her, so we could take care of her ourselves.

"Poor creature has trouble enough," said one of the men who fished The Ha Ha. But then he took me down again by adding:

"Pond was full of herring first day she come in. Now we sees hardly none at all. When we first see the whale, 'twas some fat, some sleek. Now it looks poorly. Getting razor-backed, I'd say."

We were interrupted by the arrival, in a flurry of spray and whining power, of a big outboard speedboat, purchased through the catalogue by one of the young men who spent their summers on the Great Lakes freighters. He was accompanied by several of his pals, all of them sporting colorful nylon windbreakers of the sort that are almost uniforms for the habitués of small-town poolrooms on the mainland. They came ashore, but stood apart from our soberly dressed group, talking among themselves in tones deliberately pitched high enough to reach our ears.

"We'd a had it kilt by now," said one narrow-faced youth, with a sidelong glance in my direction, "only for someone putting the Mountie onto we!"

"And that's the truth!" replied one of his companions. "Them people from away better 'tend their own business. Got no call to interfere with we." He spat in the snow to emphasize his remark.

"What we standing here for?" another asked loudly. "We's not afeared of any goddamn whale. Let's take a run onto the Pond. Might be some sport into it yet."

They ambled back to their powerboat and when the youths

had clambered aboard, one of the men standing near me said quietly:

"Don't pay no heed, skipper. They's muck floats up in every place. Floats to the top and stinks, but don't mean nothin'."

It was kindly said, and I appreciated it.

By this time a steady stream of boats was converging on the Pond from Short Reach, The Harbour, and from further west. There were power dories, skiffs, longliners, and even a few rowboats with youngsters at the oars. Burgeo was making the most of the fine weather to come and see its whale.

The majority of the newcomers seemed content to moor their boats with the growing armada out in the entrance cove, but several came through the channel into the Pond, following the lead of the mail-order speedboat. At first the boats which entered the Pond kept close to shore, leaving the open water to the whale. Their occupants were obviously awed by the immense bulk of the creature, and were timid about approaching anywhere near her. But by noon, by which time some thirty boats, bearing at least a hundred people, had arrived, the mood began to change.

There was now a big crowd around the south and southwest shore of the Pond. In full awareness of this audience, and fortified by lots of beer, a number of young men (and some not so young) now felt ready to show their mettle. The powerful boat which had been the first to enter suddenly accelerated to full speed and roared directly across the Pond only a few yards behind the whale as she submerged. Some of the people standing along the shore raised a kind of ragged cheer, and within minutes the atmosphere had completely — and frighteningly — altered.

More and more boats started up their engines and nosed into the Pond. Five or six of the fastest left the security of the shores and darted out into the middle. The reverberation of many engines began to merge into a sustained roar, a baleful and ferocious sound, intensified by the echoes from the surrounding cliffs. The leading powerboat became more daring and snarled across the whale's wake at close to twenty knots, dragging a high rooster-tail of spray.

The whale was now no longer moving leisurely in great circles, coming up to breathe at intervals of five or ten minutes. She had begun to swim much faster and more erratically as she attempted to avoid the several boats which were chivvying her. The swirls of water from her flukes became much more agitated as she veered sharply from side to side. She was no longer able to clear her lungs with the usual two or three blows after every dive, but barely had time to suck in a single breath before being driven down again. Her hurried surfacings consequently became more and more frequent even as the sportsmen, gathering courage because the whale showed no sign of retaliation, grew braver and braver. Two of the fastest boats began to circle her at full throttle, like a pair of malevolent water beetles.

Meanwhile, something rather terrible was taking place in the emotions of many of the watchers ringing the Pond. The mood of passive curiosity had dissipated, to be replaced by one of hungry anticipation. Looking into the faces around me, I recognized the same avid air of expectation which contorts the faces of a prizefight audience into primal masks.

At this juncture the blue hull of the R.C.M.P. launch appeared in the entrance cove. Onie and I jumped aboard the dory and intercepted her. I pleaded with Constable Murdoch for help.

"Some of these people have gone wild! They're going to drive the whale ashore if they don't drown her first. You have to put a stop to it . . . order them out of the Pond!"

The constable shook his head apologetically.

"Sorry. I can't do that. They aren't breaking any law, you know. I can't do anything unless the local authorities ask me to. But we'll take the launch inside and anchor in the middle of the Pond. Maybe that'll discourage them a bit."

He was a nice young man but out of his element and determined not to do anything which wasn't "in the book." He was well within his rights; and I certainly overstepped mine when, in my distress, I intimated that he was acting like a coward. He made no reply, but quietly told Danny to take the police boat in.

Onie and I followed them through the channel, then we turned along the southwest shore where I hailed several men in boats, pleading with them to leave the whale alone. Some made no response. One of them, a middle-aged merchant, gave me a derisive grin and deliberately accelerated his engine to drown out my voice. Even the elder fishermen standing on shore now seemed more embarrassed by my attitude than sympathetic. I was slow to realize it but the people gathered at Aldridges Pond had sensed that a moment of high drama was approaching and, if it was to be a tragic drama, so much the better.

Having discovered that there was nothing to fear either from the whale or from the police, the speedboat sportsmen began to make concerted efforts to herd the great beast into the shallow easterly portion of the Pond. Three boats succeeded in cornering her in a small bight, and when she turned violently to avoid them, she grounded for half her length on a shelf of rock.

There followed a stupendous flurry of white water as her immense flukes lifted clear and beat upon the surface. She reared forward, raising her whole head into view, then turned on her side so that one huge flipper pointed skyward. I had my binoculars on her and for a moment could see all of her lower belly, and the certain proof that she was female. Then slowly and, it seemed, painfully, she rolled clear of the rock.

As she slid free, there was a hubbub from the crowd on shore, a sound amounting almost to a roar, that was audible even over the snarl of engines. It held a note of insensate fury that seemed to inflame the boatmen to even more vicious attacks upon the now panic-stricken whale.

Making no attempt to submerge, she fled straight across the Pond in the direction of the eastern shallows where there were, at that moment, no boats or people. The speedboats raced close beside her, preventing her from changing course. She seemed to make a supreme effort to outrun them and then, with horrifying suddenness, she hit the muddy shoals and drove over them until she was aground for her whole length.

The Pond erupted in pandemonium. Running and yelling people leapt into boats of all shapes and sizes and these began converging on the stranded animal. I recognized the doctor team — the deputy mayor of Burgeo and his councillor wife — aboard one small longliner. I told Onie to lay the dory alongside them and I scrambled over the longliner's rail while she was still under way. By this time I was so enraged as to be almost inarticulate. Furiously I *ordered* the deputy mayor to tell the constable to clear the Pond.

He was a man with a very small endowment of personal dignity. I had outraged what dignity he did possess. He pursed his soft, red lips and replied:

"What would be the use of that? The whale is going to die anyway. Why should I interfere?" He turned his back and busied himself recording the whale's "last moments" with his expensive movie camera.

The exchange had been overheard, for the boats were now packed tightly into the cul-de-sac and people were scrambling from boat to boat, or along the shore itself, to gain a better view. There was a murmur of approval for the doctor and then someone yelled, gloatingly:

"Dat whale is finished, byes! It be ashore for certain now! Good riddance is what I says!"

Indeed, the whale's case looked hopeless. She was aground in less than twelve feet of water; and the whole incredible length of her, from the small of the tail almost to her nose, was exposed to view. The tide was on the ebb and if she remained where she was for even as little as half an hour, she would be doomed to die where she lay. Yet she was not struggling. Now that no boats were tormenting her, she seemed to ignore the human beings who fringed the shore not twenty feet away. I had the sickening conviction that she had given up; that the struggle for survival had become too much.

My anguish was so profound that when I saw three men step out into the shallows and begin heaving rocks at her half-submerged head, I went berserk. Scrambling to the top of the long-liner's deckhouse, I screamed imprecations at them. Faces turned toward me and, having temporarily focused attention on myself, I launched into a wild tirade.

This was a *female* whale, I cried. She might be and probably was pregnant. This attack on her was a monstrous, despicable act of cruelty. If, I threatened, everyone did not instantly get to hell out of Aldridges Pond and leave the whale be, I would make it my business to blacken Burgeo's name from one end of Canada to the other.

Calming down a little, I went on to promise that if the whale survived she would make Burgeo famous. "You'll get your damned highway!" I remember yelling. "Television and all the rest of it. . . ." God knows what else I might have said or promised if the whale had not herself intervened.

Somebody shouted in surprise; and we all looked. She was moving.

She was turning — infinitely slowly — sculling with her flippers and gently agitating her flukes. We Lilliputians watched silent and incredulous as the vast Gulliver inched around until she was facing out into the Pond. Then slowly, slowly, almost imperceptibly, she drifted off the shoals and slid from sight beneath the glittering surface.

I now realize that she had not been in danger of stranding herself permanently. On the contrary, she had taken the one course open to her and had deliberately sought out the shallows where she could quite literally catch her breath, free from the harassment of the motorboats. But, at the time, her escape from what appeared to be mortal danger almost seemed to savor of the miraculous. Also, as if by another miracle, it radically altered the attitude of the crowd, suddenly subduing the mood of feverish excitement. People began to climb quietly back into their boats. One by one the boats moved off toward the south channel, and within twenty minutes Aldridges Pond was empty of all human beings except Onie and me.

It was an extraordinary exodus. Nobody seemed to be speaking to anybody else . . . and not one word was said to me. Some people averted their eyes as they passed our dory. I do not think this was because of any guilt they may have felt — and many of them *did* feel guilty — it was because *I* had shamed *them*, as a group, as a community, as a people . . . and had done so publicly. The stranger in their midst had spoken his heart and displayed his rage and scorn. We could no longer pretend we understood each other. We had become strangers, one to the other.

My journal notes, written late that night, reflect my bewilderment and my sense of loss.

". . . they are essentially good people. I know that, but what sickens me is their simple failure to resist the impulse of savagery . . . they seem to be just as capable of being utterly loathesome as the bastards from the cities with their high-powered rifles and telescopic sights and their mindless compulsion to slaughter everything alive, from squirrels to elephants . . . I admired them so much because I saw them as a natural people, living in at least some degree of harmony with the natural world. Now they seem nauseatingly anxious to renounce all that and throw themselves into the stinking quagmire of our society which has perverted everything natural within itself, and is now busy destroying everything natural outside itself. How can they be so bloody stupid? How could *I* have been so bloody stupid?"

Bitter words . . . bitter, and unfair; but I had lost my capacity for objectivity and was ruled, now, by irrational emotions. I was no longer willing, or perhaps not able, to understand the people of Burgeo; to comprehend them as they really were, as men and women who were also victims of forces and circumstances of whose effects they remained unconscious. I had withdrawn my compassion from them, in hurt and ignorance. Now I bestowed it all upon the whale.

The whale was not alone in being trapped. We were all trapped with her. If the natural patterns of her life had been disrupted, then so had ours. An awesome mystery had intruded into the closely circumscribed order of our lives; one that we terrestrial bipeds could not fathom, and one, therefore, that we would react against with instinctive fear, violence, and hatred. This riddle from the deeps was the measure of humanity's unquenchable ignorance of life. This impenetrable secret, which had become the core of our own existence in this place, was a mirror in which we saw our own distempered faces . . . and they were ugly.

VIII.

THE ICE

FROM

WAKE OF THE GREAT SEALERS, 1973

Off the coasts of Newfoundland and in the Gulf of St. Lawrence men have for centuries been harvesting the skins and the fat of harp seals. This passage from Wake of the Great Sealers *recounts events, partly in Mowat's own voice, and partly as though told by the sealers themselves.*

B y 1900 the seal fishery was in the hands of only a few St. John's merchants, of whom the most famous — or infamous, depending on your point of view — were A.J. Harvey and Company, Bowring Brothers Ltd., Job Brothers and Company, and Baine, Johnson and Company. These four set the rules of the game, decided the price of fat, and took the lion's share of the profits; but with the continuing decline in the seal herds, each was constantly seeking a means of gaining an advantage over its rivals.

In 1906 Harveys jumped into the lead by building a steel ship for the sealing. The S.S. *Adventure* was a wonder for her time: an 800-tonner with a 200-horsepower engine, specially designed for the ice to a new and daring plan. Her forefoot was cut away so that, instead of trying to split, or butt the pans aside, she could ride right up onto them, breaking and separating them with her weight and her momentum.

At first the old sealing hands, including the directors of the rival companies, thought Harveys had gone mad. "A steel ship like that," they scoffed, "will be crushed in the ice like a sardine can. There's no give to her plates. It'd be suicide, sure, to go to the pack in her!"

This belief was so widespread that Harveys had a job to get a crew for the *Adventure* and she was forced to sail with less than half the men she could have carried. But once in the ice she soon proved herself. She was twice as handy and twice as fast as any of the old wooden walls. She could get along through ice where none of them could follow, and she made a bumper voyage. When she sailed back through the Notch into St. John's harbor, there were some glum faces at Bowrings and Jobs, for she had made it clear that the days of the wooden walls were now numbered.

By 1909 Harveys, well satisfied, had built two more steel steamers, the *Bonaventure* and the *Bellaventure* — 500-tonners with 300-horsepower engines. Striving to catch up, Bowrings built the 2,000-ton, 450-horsepower *Florizel*, and Jobs commissioned the *Beothic*, of the same class as the *Bell* and the *Bon*. In 1912 Jobs added the 1,000-ton *Nascopie*, but Bowrings topped all competition with the 2,100-ton, 600-horsepower *Stephano*. All of these ships were intended to serve as sealers in the spring but as passenger vessels or freighters for the balance of the year.

The coming of the steel fleet brought competition for the remaining seals to a new and frantic pitch. Risks were taken with men and ships that startled sealers who had been going to the ice for half a century. This was especially true with the old wooden walls who, though they were now badly outclassed, still outnumbered the steel steamers. What had been foolhardy daring by captains in the past now became suicidal daring as the skippers of the wooden walls tried desperately to make good showings. By 1914 the competition at the ice had become a kind of madness and events leading up to the spring of that year did nothing to restore sanity. Rumors of war sent the value of seal fat skyrocketing, with the result that the Water Street crowd dispatched to the ice every vessel they could find, seaworthy or not, and crammed them to the hatches with men who had been told this was the El Dorado spring — *this* time they were bound to go home with their pockets stuffed with gold.

That spring, as for many years previously, the honorary commodore of the fleet was Captain Abraham Kean — legendary seal-killer who, before he gave it up in 1934, was to boast of having killed one million seals. He was a hard man, a driving man, and an obsessed man. His ship, the marvellous new *Stephano*, was the unquestioned queen of the fleet, and Kean was determined to fill her up — to bring in the greatest load of fat ever to enter St. John's harbor. With Captain Abe setting the pace it was a certainty that the other captains would risk heaven and earth in order not to be left too far behind in the race for the little silk flag which was the worthless but fiercely coveted prize given by the St. John's Chamber of Commerce to the highlining sealing skipper of the year.

One of those who sailed to the front in the spring of 1914 was my father's shipmate, Skipper Llewelyn Kean. Skipper Lew was from Greenspond but was no relation to Captain Abraham Kean. Although he held his master's papers, he was unable to get a vessel of his own that year and so he shipped as a bridgemaster. That was a common thing, for in those years there were always more captains than there were sealing ships for them to command.

"That was the first spring ever I sailed in one of the new steel ships. I had the luck to get a berth with Captain Billy Winsor in the *Beothic*; a smart little vessel she was too. Billy Winsor was a smart man himself, a devil-may-care lad, all for the seals and a great hand for taking chances with his ship and his men if it would get him the fat.

"That year all the skippers, and the men too, were dead keen. Word had gone round that fat would fetch the highest price for forty years, and all hands looked to make a big bill if we found the patches.

"The old wooden ships put to sea on March 10th, every last one of them as was still afloat — *Bloodhound, Kite, Diana, Newfoundland, Terra Nova, Eagle, Thetis, Neptune, Ranger*, and *Southern Cross*. Some was bound to the front, but most, like the *Cross*, were going to try their luck in the Gulf. Because the steel ships were so much faster and abler in the ice, it was agreed they would give the wooden walls a start, so we didn't sail from St. John's until March 14th. All the steel steamers were bound for the front, for that is where the main patch lies. It was a grand sight they made, steaming out the Notch all in a line: the big *Stephano* in the lead; the *Florizel* and *Nascopie*, and then the smaller ships: the *Bell*, *Bon*, *Adventure*, *Beothic*, *Seal*, and *Sagona*.

"Most of them stuck close to old Abe Kean in the *Stephano*, dogging the Old Man; but Billy Winsor was never a man to follow another skipper's course. When the fleet struck heavy ice off the Funks, and Captain Kean cut in for land to run inside toward St. Anthony, Billy cut north instead into the heavy stuff. My, how he drove that ship! Times I thought sure he'd tear the bows out of her, but in two days we was into the south corner of the main patch and not another ship in sight.

"It looked to be the finest kind of spring. By March 20th almost the whole fleet, wooden walls and all, were into the main patch along of we and killing seals for a pastime. The patch was long and narrow — I'd guess it to be fifty miles long and five or six wide. Right from the first we were high-liner, and Captain Abraham was in a fine fret because we were well up on him. By March 29th we had twenty thousand stowed below and another five thousand panned; but the Old Man had only eighteen thousand altogether. Still and all, every ship was doing very well except the *Newfoundland*. Somehow or other, Captain Wes Kean, old Abe's youngest son, had gone astray and got his ship jammed into the worst sort of heavy ice about seven or eight miles from the whelping pans. Try what he would, he couldn't get clear, and his men were taking no seals at all.

"There were plenty of seals, but conditions weren't the best. One morning, the 23rd I think it was, we was working a patch when Skipper Billy, from the barrel, saw another big patch way off to the westward. He took back aboard two watches — a hundred men — including the one I was in, steamed out to the new patch, and put us on ice while he went back to pick up the panned pelts and the rest of the crowd. Then the weather closed in, thick and wet, and when he started back he couldn't find us.

"We didn't think to take much harm, because there were two or three other ships in the vicinity and we expected we could get aboard one of those if we was put to it. The *Florizel*, with Captain Joe Kean (another of the Old Man's sons), came handy to us to pick up some of his own men, and we started for her, but she veered off and went away full speed and was soon out of sight in the murk. Captain Joe saw us well enough but supposed our ship would pick us up.

"Dark come on with wind and wet snow, and it was not the best. The ice where we was, was going abroad and was soft anyway. The scattered fellow was falling in and when we'd haul him out he'd have to take off his boots and stockings and trousers, wring out the salt water, and pull them on again. He'd be so chilled the life was near out of him.

"The drift got so heavy a man could hardly see his chum even before it come full darkness. We'd been on ice all day, every day, for about a week, and we were all beat-out. A good many of the men began to lose heart. There seemed to be no ships near us by then, though if there was, it would have been a job to find them anyway.

"Sid and Willis White, belonged to Greenspond, came up to me and Willy said: 'Lew, we got to get clear of this crowd. There'll be nary one of them alive tomorrow morning.' I agreed we should branch off and try to find some tight ice and straighten away for the night. There was nine in my lot and we went off on our own. We found some good ice where there was still some live seals and a good many carcasses, and we set to work to build a circular shelter out of ice blocks and dead seals to keep away the wind.

"Now while we was at all this, Skipper Billy was still searching for us. He contacted the *Florizel* on the Marconi and asked had she seen any of his men. Skipper Joe come back and said he had, and Billy asked him to pick them up for the night. Joe agreed to try and, between the jigs and the reels, he did find the main crowd and took them aboard . . . and none too soon for some of them. But he never found us, and we never saw nor heard the ship.

"Never mind that, we was all right. We had about thirty seal carcasses at our 'door.' We tore up our tarred tow ropes and frizzed them out for to light a fire. We fed it with shavings from our gaffs and poles until it was hot enough to melt seal fat and after that we kept it fair roaring with carcasses. They burned like a furnace and gave us all the hot roasted meat we had a mind to eat.

"Every man went and got himself a live young seal and this is what we sat on all night. The seals didn't seem to mind. Every now and again they would open their eyes, look around, and go back to sleep. By morning they weren't white any more . . . they was just as black with soot and smoke as all the rest of us.

"Morning came and the wind veered west, very strong and freezing cold. About midmorning, in the midst of a heavy squall, we heard a voice yell out: 'HARD A STARBOARD!' — and there was the *Beothic* pretty near alongside our pan. Her lookouts had smelled the burning fat — 'tis a terrible strong stink — and she'd steamed up on it until they saw our fire.

"I tell you, we had a good time when we got aboard. Skipper Billy gave all hands a big drink of whiskey. I never minded being out that night — we was comfortable enough. But Sid White told me afterwards he never thought any of us would come through. It seems just before he come to me on the small ice, he and some other fellows were a bit apart when out of the drift there was the loom of something.

" 'Looked to I like a big kind of beast with long, sharp horns,' Sid told me. 'The snow gusted up in a minute, and it was gone when the squall cleared. A fearful bad sign, according to the old folk, for they says if you sees one of them ice spirits it foretells the death of a good many poor fellows.'

"Perhaps that's all a pack of nonsense, but all the same, what happened to us out there that time was well known right through the fleet, because of the Marconi; and I used to wonder afterwards whether the skippers took proper account of it. Certainly, Captain Wes Kean on the *Newfoundland* was the only man who never heard the news, for his was the only ship without a wireless.

"I know one thing, though. Skipper Billy was right heedful where he put his men after that, and we were just as heedful to stay handy to our ship."

By Monday, March 29th, all the ships, with one exception, had been into the fat for ten days or more. Only the *Newfoundland* — the largest and most powerful of the wooden walls — was still out of it, still jammed fast in heavy, raftered ice, about eight miles southeast of the main patch where, in the light whelping ice, the rest of the ships were free to move about almost at will.

Captain Wes Kean's frustration and fury at having put his ship into such a situation had mounted to an explosive pitch by Monday night. At dawn on Tuesday the visibility was exceptional and when he climbed to the barrel he could see several ships on the northern icescape. Although unable to talk to them by wireless, he was sure they must be in the seals. He swung his glasses to the nearest one, the *Stephano*, commanded by his father, and saw that her after-derrick was hoisted vertically. This was a signal agreed upon between father and sons to show that the Old Man was working a good patch of seals. The sight was too much for the young skipper. Only twenty-nine years old, he had been made master of the *Newfoundland* four years earlier, largely because his father had pushed him up with Harveys. In order to refute the charge of favoritism, he had to bring in a good load of fat each spring. Now, the way things looked in this most important of all springs, he stood a good chance of having to come home almost clean. That was an intolerable prospect. Peering from the barrel into the beckoning northern wastes, he made up his mind. If the *Newfoundland* could not reach the seals, her men would have to go to the seals on their own feet.

Shortly before 7 A.M. all four watches, totalling 179 men, were ordered over the *Newfoundland*'s side under the leadership of thirty-three-year-old George Tuff, the vessel's second-in-command.

" 'Tis a long haul and damned rough ice, Jarge," Wes Kean told Tuff, "but the seals is there in t'ousands, sure. Go straight for the *Stephano* and report to Father. He'll put you onto the patches and tell you what to do. Doubtless he'll keep you aboard his ship tonight, and when the ice slacks off I'll steam over and pick up the men and the seals you've panned."

If Tuff had doubts about the wisdom of the plan he gave no sign; but doubts he must have had because, at the age of seventeen, he had been one of the survivors of the *Greenland* disaster. It had taken him months to recover physically from that experience and for years afterwards he had been plagued by frightful nightmares in which dead companions, frozen rigid, implored him to let them into his warm little house at Newtown.

The weather was extraordinarily fine that Tuesday morning — too fine, too warm, too calm by far, so thought some of the men who had heard from the bosun that the barometer was falling. " 'Twas a weather-breeder, certainly!" one of them remembered; and many were aware of a vague sense of unease as the long black column began snaking its way through the chaos of pressure ridges and raftered ice toward the tiny shape of the *Stephano*, hull-down to the north.

The going was even harder than Wes Kean had predicted. "I never saw worse ice in all my time," George Tuff remembered. After three hours of exhausting travel the attenuated column had only gone three miles from the *Newfoundland*. Those in the lead now came upon a scattered handful of whitecoats, and all the men halted gratefully while these were clubbed and sculped. When the long line moved on again it was incomplete. Some fifty men had detached themselves from it and, in startling defiance of the ingrained habits of obedience *and* amid shouts of "yellowbelly" and "coward" from their companions, had stubbornly turned about and headed back for their own ship.

When they reached the *Newfoundland* they were met by an infuriated Captain Kean who as good as accused them of mutiny and threatened them with the loss of their shares in the voyage. Subdued, strangely silent, they remained on the ice until his rage had run its course then, muttering something about "bad weather," they came quietly aboard and went below. Not one of them cared to tell Wes Kean the true reason for their return.

" 'Twas a bright, sunny morning when we left the *Newfoundland*. They was no reason to see nothing as wasn't there. But some of we saw something as had no right to be on the ice or anywhere at all on God's mortal earth! We come round a high pinnacle, and there it was. . . . a giant of a man it looked to be, covered all over, face and all, in a black, hairy coat. It stood there, big as ary bear; blocking our way. . . . Go forward in the face of that? No, me son! Not for all the gold as lies buried in the world!"

It took nearly five hours of exhausting struggle before the remaining 126 men from the *Newfoundland* reached the high steel sides of the *Stephano*, which had stopped to let them come aboard. They had seen no more seals and a heavy haze had clouded the sky. A few glittering flakes of snow were already beginning to fall. The fine day was quickly coming to an end.

"Before we got to the *Stephano* 'twas clear enough there was dirty weather on the go, and they warn't a man of we expected to go back on ice that day. We was certain sure the *Stephano* would be our boardinghouse. While most of the crowd went below for a mug of tea and a bit of hard bread, George Tuff went aft to see Captain Abraham Kean and get his orders.

"The *Stephano* got under way again, and about twenty minutes later we was called back on deck. The snow was coming thicker, but the Old Man was up on the bridge waving his arms and bawling: '*Newfoundland* men, over the side!' Oh yiss, I can hear him yet. 'Hurry up now, byes! Get out and get your seals!'

"We hardly knew what to think about it, but most of us supposed we was just going for a little rally, handy to the ship, and would be back aboard soon enough. But we was hardly clear of her when the *Stephano* swung hard around, showed us her stern, and drove off full steam ahead to the nor'ard. Young Jobbie Easton was along of me and there was a quare look on his face.

"'That one's not coming back for we. She's gone for good!' Those as heard him began to crowd around George Tuff. 'That's a lie now, ain't it, Jarge?' some fellow asked.

"'No, me sons,' says George very low. 'Captain Abraham's orders is for us to go and work a patch of swiles sou'west from here about a mile, pan the pelts, and then strike out for our own ship. He says as he's got men and seals of his own to look out for.'

"The snow was getting thicker by the minute, and any man who'd ever been on ice before knew what our chances was of finding the *Newfoundland* that night. Uncle Ezra Melendy pipes up and says: 'Us'll never do it, Jarge. 'Twill be the *Greenland* all over again.' Then there was proper hell to pay. Some was calling on George to lead us back to the *Stephano* or chase after she. John Howlett stuck his chin out and told Tuff to stop wasting time and to start for the *Newfoundland*. 'God damn it, Jarge. This is no weather to be killing swiles!' Then John turned to us. 'Byes,' he says, ' 'tis time for we to give up this and go for our own ship!'

"It come near to blows, but there was no changing George's mind. He had his orders from the Old Man and bedamned if he'd fly in the face of them. So off we went to find them seals and, afore we knowed it, the starm was on full blast."

On Tuesday morning, March 31st, one of the most savage storms of the year swept in over the southeastern approaches to Newfoundland and overwhelmed the island. Within a few hours the city of St. John's lay paralyzed beneath a tremendous snowfall, buffeted by hurricane winds. Ocean-going freighters labored through towering seas offshore, seeking shelter, or lay hove-to, head to the gale, trying to ride it out.

During the afternoon the storm swept out over the northern ice and that vast plain became a faceless wilderness given over to whirling snow devils that obliterated everything from view. The storm caught nearly a hundred of Captain Abraham Kean's men far from their ship, for he had refused to believe the evidence of his senses, or of the plunging barometer, and had stubbornly continued to pile up seal pelts as if there was nothing else in life of any import. His men were lucky. The *Florizel* appeared, as if by magic, close to the *Stephano*'s men and, thankfully, they scrambled aboard. But the storm also caught one hundred and twenty-six of the *Newfoundland*'s men on ice . . . and there was no luck left for them.

Adrift in that raging chaos, on ice that began to heave and grind and shatter as the storm swell lifted under it, they were at least seven miles from their own jammed and helpless ship. What was more ominous, *nobody knew they were adrift*. Aboard the *Newfoundland*, Captain Wes Kean ate a good hot supper and went to his bunk, content in the belief that his men were safe aboard the *Stephano*. On the *Stephano*, the Old Man was preoccupied with wondering whether or not the storm would prevent him from overtaking that young upstart, Billy Winsor, and getting

enough whitecoats to make him high-liner once again. If he gave
any thought to the *Newfoundland*'s men, it was to assume they had
reached their own ship. After all, that is where he had *ordered*
them to go.

There was no way for anyone to discover the truth. Although
all the other ships were fitted with wireless and could commu-
nicate with one another, the *Newfoundland*'s wireless had been
removed before she sailed, by orders of her owners, A. J. Harvey
and Company. As one of their directors was to testify later: "It
did not pay to keep it aboard." Harveys did not feel that its
presence added to the profits from the seal fishery. They were
wrong. Its absence that spring was to deprive the company of
considerable profit.

" 'Twas terrible . . . terrible, my son! After the starm came
on I never saw a better chance for a disaster. . . . We started back
for the *Newfoundland* 'bout one o'clock, in a gale of wind, with
the snow so thick and wet it was enough to choke a man. We
struck east-sou'east looking for our outward track and found it,
but 'twas too late by then. The ice was wheeling so bad the track
was all broke up and there was swatches of open water everywhere. The snow was so heavy it lay thick on the water and 'twas
a job to tell it from good ice. Before dark six or seven of the men
had fell through and was lost. . . . 'Twas no use to go on. . . .
The men gathered round about on two or three of the biggest
pans they could find, and they was none too big at that, and
built up shelters out of clumpers of ice. Then the snow changed
to freezing rain, driving like shot till we was all drenched to the
skin, but at least it warn't too frosty. I prayed 'twould keep
raining, for if the wind backed to nor'ard and brought the frost,
I knowed we'd no chance at all. . . ."

Lew Kean was safe aboard the *Beothic* that night and, as he
said: "Thankful to God for it. . . ."

"I never saw worse weather at the front. I dare say there were
few enough managed to sleep sound that night. The grinding
and the roaring of the ice was enough to put the fear of the Lord
into any man. Wild? I went on deck a time or two, and I don't

know the words to tell what it was like. It was all a man could do to keep his feet, and the sleet cut into you like shot.

"In the morning it was still blowing a living starm, and then it come on to snow again and the wind veered to nor'west and brought the white frost with it. That killed them altogether! The shelters those poor fellows had built was straight — like a wall — and no good at all when the wind come round. There was no seals where they was to, and they had nothing left to burn. Their clothes was pitiful poor, for it was a warm morning when they left their ship, and the most of them left their oilskins behind, counting to be aboard the *Stephano* for the night. For grub there was nothing but a bit of oatmeal or a pick of hard bread in the bottom of some fellows' nunny bags. A few had little bottles of Radway's Ready Relief — supposed to be a pain killer but, if the truth was out, only flavored alcohol — good enough stuff, but there wasn't more than a glutch for every man.

"Same as a good many sealers, they were mortal feared to lay down and take some rest. Believed they'd never wake again. That was pure foolishness . . . of the worst kind! They spent the whole night on their feet, marching about like sojers, running around, pounding each other to keep awake . . . and they beat themselves right out. In the morning, when the frost took them, they were so done in they began to fall dead on their feet. Some even froze to death standing up.

"About noon the snow let up and the sky cleared, but the wind was sharper and frostier than ever and the ground drift was like a cloud. If a man climbed to the top of the pinnacle he would be in clear air, with the sun shining on him, but on the ice he was near blind with the drift. In breaks in the storm, the few fellows as had the strength to climb the pinnacles could see some of the ships . . . the *Florizel* away to the nor'ard; the *Stephano* under way, and trying to pick up pans far off to the nor'east. Once the *Bell* come straight for them, close as three or four miles. Six men set out to walk to her, but they all perished, and the *Bell*, never seeing them, turned and steamed away. That took the heart out of the men as was left, like it was cut out with a sculping knife.

"The devil of it was that not a one of we on any of the other ships knew they was lost. I tell you, when Harveys took that

wireless out of the *Newfoundland* they killed those men better than
bullets could have done.

"Before dark come on, things was so desperate that George
Tuff, with three of the master watches and a few other fellows,
undertook somehow to get across that heaving mass of broken
ice and reach their own ship. George had spied a glimpse of the
Newfoundland from a pinnacle. She'd finally got clear of the jam
and started steaming toward the *Stephano*, intending, I suppose,
to pick up her men as Wes Kean thought was on his father's
ship. When George saw her she was jammed again, but a lot
closer to the men than before. Those fellows pretty near got to
her, though how they stood up to it, the Lord knows. They was
coming up toward her lee side . . . but all hands aboard her was
looking out to windward where the *Stephano* lay. And then she
burst out of the jam and hauled away for the *Stephano*, and those
fellows just had to watch her go. That finished them entirely.
They crawled into a hole in a pile of clumpers as night come
down, freezing bitter cold and blowing a whole gale again.

"Back on the two floes where most of the men still was, it was
even worse. The stories them poor fellows as lived through it
had to tell was enough to freeze your blood."

". . . The weather was near zero and the snow blowing like a
whirlwind . . . you could look up sometimes through the drift
and see the stars up there . . . down on the ice the men was dying
. . . my first cousin, and my best chum, he lay down to die but
I wouldn't let him do it. I punched him and hauled him about
and jumped on his feet . . . that's how he lost his feet, I suppose.
I got them all broken up, jumping on them. 'Bye,' I said to him,
'Don't you die out here! Don't you give it to them at home to say
you died out here on this ice!' But I had to go on kicking him
. . . I nearly killed that poor fellow to make him live. . . .

"Some went crazy at the end of it, yelling and squalling and
wandering off and never seen again. More died quiet, sitting or
lying there, most likely dreaming of being home again. . . . They
saw strange things. One fellow come over to me and says: 'Come
in to the house now, me son. We'll have a scoff. The woman's
just cooking up a pot of soup.' I never saw him after. His eyes
was froze shut with the ice caked on his face. . . .

"Uncle Ezra Melendy, as had lived through the *Greenland* disaster, was an old fellow but he wouldn't give it up. His legs was froze solid to the hips and he was crawling over the ice trying to keep close to we. He'd lost his mittens and his hands was froze hard like claws. He crawled up to me and says: 'Me hands is some cold, byes.' I went along his back trail a bit and found his mitts, but I couldn't pull them on his hands, all crooked up like they was. So I slit them with me knife and put them on that way. 'That's good now,' he says and crawls off. His body was never found afterwards. . . .

"Freddie Hunt never had his cap, and his boots was gone right off his feet. He had only a poor jacket of cotton made from a flour bag, but he was some determined not to die. Wednesday he started to take the jacket off a dead man, but the corpse rolled over and says: 'Don't ye do it, Freddie. I aren't dead yet!. . . .'

"The worst thing I seen was when I tried to go to another pan and I fell over a clumper. Only it warn't no clumper. 'Twas Reuben Crewe and his son, froze together, and the old fellow's arms tight around the lad, and the lad's head buried under his father's jacket . . . I recall the drift eased off about then and it seemed light as day and I looked around me and 'twas like being in a graveyard full of awful white statues . . . dead men all around. . . ."

At the crack of dawn on Thursday morning Captain Wes Kean climbed to the barrel on the *Newfoundland*'s mainmast. The weather had moderated; the wind had dropped out and visibility was good. For some time he anxiously watched the *Stephano*, which was also jammed now but less than a mile distant to the east. He was looking for his absent men who should have been leaving the big steel ship to return to their own vessel. As yet there was no sign of life aboard the *Stephano* so he swung his glasses to the west to see if there were any seals in sight. He was electrified to see a small group of men staggering across the ice toward him in the pale half-light and, with sick comprehension, he knew what had happened. Kean very nearly fell from the shrouds in his haste to gain the deck, and when he reached it he was close to hysteria.

Half an hour later George Tuff and three others were being helped aboard their ship by a rescue party of horrified shipmates.

These survivors of the lost party looked more like walking dead than living men. Tuff stood before his captain weaving from side to side and barely able to mumble through cracked and bleeding lips.

"This is all the men you got left, Cap'n. The rest of them is gone. . . ."

At about the same time Tuff regained his ship, the barrelman of the *Bellaventure*, which was then steaming about looking for lost pans some miles to the northwest, saw what he took to be a small party of sealers belonging to some other ship. As he watched, he realized there was something wrong with them. "They looked right queer . . . like they was drunk, crawling and falling about." He called his skipper, Captain Robert Randell, and in a few minutes the *Bell* was crashing through the pack toward them under forced draft. Two of the figures were much closer than the others and at 9 P.M. the wireless began to crackle.

CAPTAIN SS BELLAVENTURE TO CAPTAIN SS STEPHANO.
  TWO NEWFOUNDLAND MEN IN PRETTY BAD SHAPE GOT
ABOARD US THIS MORNING. REPORTED ON ICE SINCE TUES-
DAY AND SEVERAL MEN PERISHED.

This report was picked up by almost every ship in the fleet and all those in the vicinity began to converge on the *Bell*. Soon hundreds of sealers were scattering across the pack laden with stretchers, food, and rum, searching for the lost party. By nightfall the *Bell*, magnificently handled by Captain Randell, had found and taken aboard thirty-five survivors, all frightfully frostbitten, including several who were thought to be beyond saving. The other ships had found nine more . . . *and that was all of the lost party ever to be found alive.*

At dusk the *Stephano*, *Bellaventure*, and *Florizel* came together alongside the stricken *Newfoundland*. The death ship's roll was read and the appalling scope of the disaster was finally revealed. Then the dead, the dying, and those who would survive, although crippled and disfigured for life, were all placed aboard the *Bellaventure* and she prepared to leave the ice for home. It appeared that she would be the first ship back to St. John's that year, but for her there would be no cheers from the crowded quay, no bellow of gunfire from Signal Hill. Below decks she

313

carried the sculps of many thousands of prime seals — a fortune for her owners. On deck, twisted and contorted into ghastly postures, she carried the frozen bodies of seventy men who would go to the ice no more. Nine others of the lost party remained behind, already buried in the darkness of the icy sea.

So the *Bellaventure* departed . . . alone. Orders from the owners of the remaining ships had been received by radio. They were to continue sealing. Many of the men on those other ships had lost cousins, brothers, even fathers in the disaster and now they came as close to violence as their natures would allow. When Captain Billy Winsor, whose ship was already log-loaded, tried to put his men on ice they flatly refused orders. "No, Cap'n," their spokesman told him. "Us aren't goin' swilin' in that graveyard. Not for the king hisself!"

One by one the captains gave up and took the cut for home . . . all save one. Captain Abraham Kean stayed out. He was implacably determined to better Billy Winsor's catch, and even when his own men mutinied he kept the *Stephano* in the ice.

"I seen him on the bridge when the *Bell* pulled away," one of his crew remembered. "Never had no eyes for her. He was spyin' to nor'ard on the lookout for swiles. More like a devil than a man, he looked up there. No doubt 'tis a lie, but they was some aboard was sayin' the Old Man'd think nothin' of runnin' the winches on one side takin' up sculps while he was runnin' 'em on t'other side takin' dead men off the ice."

So ended the spring of 1914. The merchant princes of Water Street were the richer by the profits from 233,000 seal pelts. And the ordinary people of Newfoundland were the poorer by the deaths of two hundred and fifty-five of their best men.

"One time every man, woman, and child as could walk would be on the docks and the cliffs to cheer the sealing ships back from the ice fields. This time 'twas all different. The people was there right enough, but they was quiet . . . some of them watching and waiting for a ship, and for men, as would never come home again. It seems to me as something broke in the heart of our old island that spring of 1914, and never rightly healed again in after times."

IX.

THE
HANDS OF
THE DEAD

FROM

THE SNOW WALKER, 1975

FROM
The Snow Walker

❖

"The White Canoe" is one of Mowat's rare short stories, written in the nineteen-fifties and revised in 1975 for inclusion in The Snow Walker. *In its intimations of the proper harmony between man and natural forces, it seems appropriate to end with.*

❖

Desolation enveloped the tundra. The treeless plains stretching to an illimitable horizon all around me seemed neither land nor water but a nebulous blend of both. No birds flew in the overcast skies and no beasts moved on the dun-colored waste of bog. A grey cloud scud driving low over gravel ridges bore the chill of snow. All visible life seemed to have fled, as I too was fleeing, before the thrust of approaching winter.

I had already been travelling for three weeks down the River and had seen no sign of any other human beings. Fear that I might never escape from this uninhabited wilderness grew as my battered canoe leapt and writhed in the torrent as if afflicted with its own panic. The River was one long sequence of roaring white water that had early taken toll. My rifle, pack, and winter clothing together with most of my grub had been lost in the first furious rapids four hundred miles to the westward.

Half starved, with no more than a few handfuls of wet flour remaining for my body's sustenance, and soaked by spume and spray, I was sinking into apathy from which, on some wild rapid still to come, I might not be able to rouse myself in time.

The River whipped me around one of its angled bends to face a mighty ridge rising powerfully out of the sodden tundra like an island in a frozen sea. It should have been visible from many miles upstream yet I had seen nothing of it until the current flung me up against its flank. I had an overwhelming desire to feel its solid stone beneath my feet. Thrusting my paddle against the oily muscles of the current, I came panting to the shore.

When I reached the top of that great mound, I halted abruptly. Before me lay an immense white canoe upended on a bed of frost-shattered granite and shining like a monument of quartz. It had been so placed to leave a narrow opening between the gunwale and the bed rock. Kneeling, I peered into the gloom and could just make out the outlines of many shapes and bundles. Joyfully I thought, and perhaps spoke aloud, "It's got to be a cache!" My strength was just sufficient to lift the gunwale a few more inches and wedge it up with a fragment of rock so I could reach one arm underneath.

The first thing I touched and drew toward me was a .50 Sharps rifle swathed in rotted deerskins and so well coated in hardened tallow that there was not a speck of rust on it. Further scrabbling produced two boxes of shells, their brass cases green with verdigris, but their powder dry; a gill net complete with floats and sinkers; and a bleached wooden box holding several pounds of tea and half a dozen plugs of tobacco. There were also fish spears, steel traps, snowknives, cooking pots, and other implements of an Eskimo household, together with a number of nameless packages which seemed to have succumbed to mildew and decay and which I assumed held bedding and clothing of caribou and musk-ox fur.

I had no hesitation in taking the things I needed. It seemed clear enough that the Eskimo who had made this cache had done so long ago and had never returned to it nor ever would.

The gifts of the white canoe included the knowledge that my escape from the void of the barrenland plains was now reasonably certain. Where this great craft, coming inland from the coast, had been able to ascent against the River, there my canoe could surely descend. The sea — deliverance — *must* be close. Yet when I walked to the eastern end of the ridge and looked eagerly beyond it, I could see nothing except the cold undulations of that same sodden plain in which I had been imprisoned for so long. Escape still lay somewhere beyond a grey horizon blurring into darkness under an onslaught of driven rain.

I carted my loot back to the river edge, set the net in a backwater, and returned to shore to make a little fire of willow twigs on which to brew up a huge pail of tea. As I sat by the minute flames, I mused upon the presence of the white canoe, invisible now in the darkness looming over me.

That it had lain on the ridge for decades past I could not doubt. The decay beneath it, and the way the meager lichens had grown around it, proved this must be so. Yet the canoe itself seemed to have denied the years. Its flanks were smooth, unmarred by summer rains or winter gales. Its wood was sound and as dry and hard as iron. It was of a sea-going type built especially for the Hudson's Bay Company trade and much favored by Eskimos along the Arctic coasts. But what was it doing here?

Rain hissed over the roiling waters and winked out my fire. I crawled into my robes, pulled a canvas tarp over me, and went to sleep.

In the icy dawn I lifted the net and found it heavy with trout and grayling. After cooking my first real meal in many days, I committed myself to the River again.

For five more days I travelled down that watery slope, portaging or running rapids, always straining toward the sea. On the first day I saw a lone caribou on the bank, a straggler left behind by the southbound migrating herds. The old Sharps roared like the voice of doom, nearly knocking me out of the canoe; and that night I gorged on fresh and bloody meat.

On the evening of the fifth day, the River slowed and widened into a long lake. There was a low, rocky island in its center, upon whose shores two deerskin tents squatted like miniature volcanic cones upon a long-dead lava bed.

I made toward them and a mob of dogs broke into a furious uproar, bringing a handful of people tumbling out of the tents. The men waded into the icy shallows to the top of their waterproof skin boots and drew my canoe to shore. We were all overcome with a childlike shyness.

Although I had lived with Eskimos in the past, it had been

weeks since I had spoken to any other human being; and coming as I did from the uninhabited plains to the west, my appearance must have seemed as inexplicable to these people as any shooting star across the midnight sky.

They were six in number. There was an old man, Katalak, whose face had been corroded by the long years into a gargoyle mask; and his wife, Salak, also withered with age but still sharp-eyed and alert. There was their stolid middle-aged son, Haluk; his plump wife, Petuk, and their two children, Okak and Akoomik.

They escorted me into Katalak's tent and, while the women lit a willow fire outside and brought a pot of deer tongues to the boil, we three men sat on a pile of skins and smoked. They asked no questions although their curiosity about me must have been intense.

After we had fed and drunk a gallon or so of tea, I explained that I had come down the River from its source, which I had reached after a twenty-day journey north from timberline. They told me that none of their people had ever lived or travelled that far to the west except for one who had gone that way a long, long time ago and never returned.

"Perhaps I know something of him," I said, and I told of finding the cache under the white canoe and how the things I had taken from it had probably saved my life.

A silence followed, during which Katalak carefully filled the soapstone bowl of his pipe, lit it, puffed once, then passed it to his wife. Eventually he spoke.

"The white canoe is no man's cache. It is the spirit home of Kakut, who was my father and who is the father of us all."

I was appalled by my own stupidity, for I had known that, in death, pagan Eskimos take with them the things they have found necessary during their earthly lives. I knew now that instead of borrowing from a cache, I had robbed a grave.

Katalak sensed my distress. He stretched out his hand and laid it lightly on my shoulder. The expression on his seamed and desiccated face was reassuring.

"You did no wrong," he said gently. "Had Kakut wished otherwise, you would have travelled past the hill called Kinetua and seen nothing. You took from his grave only what he was glad to give."

He reloaded the pipe and when it was lit he passed it to me. Darkness had fallen and Salak brought a small tin can filled with caribou fat into which a wick of wild cotton had been inserted. This lamp produced a meager, reddish flame that wavered beneath a pennant of black smoke. In that flickering and faint illumination I could just see the old man's face, shadowed but intent. He looked slowly at each in turn, until his gaze rested on me.

"You are *Kablunait*, a white man. We are *Innuit*, the People. But tonight we are as one. None of us would be here if Kakut had not wished it so. We live, all of us, because of gifts made by dead hands. There is a story to tell about that."

In the time long ago, I lived by the River, and my father was Kakut, and his name was known along the sea coast and up all the rivers far into the plains that belonged to the deer, the musk-ox, and the great brown bear. Many mysteries were known to Kakut — mysteries that belonged to the Woman in the days when she made Men. Kakut spoke with the spirits. His hunting fed entire camps during bad times, and hunger never came into the tents and snowhouses where he lived. *Ai-ee!* He was a man who knew how to give the spirits their due.

He was such a powerful man that I lived under his shadow, and because of that I was not content. In my sixteenth summer I accompanied my family to the coast for the yearly trading, but when they went back up the River I did not go with them for I had begun to listen to other voices. There were new Gods in the land who spoke through the black-bearded white men you call priests. One of these had built an igloo of wood near the trader and, during our visit, he spoke often to me and told me many strange things. He also talked to the trader, asking him to give me work for the winter so I could stay in that place and learn the ways and the thoughts of the white men.

The trader was uneasy about that because he knew the power of Kakut and had no wish to anger him. So I went to my father and told him what I desired. He did not stand in my way. "The young wolf runs where he runs," was all he said.

I stayed for two years with the white men and learned to speak a new language. But my blood still remembered the old tongues, and when Salak came down to the coast during my eighteenth summer, the old tongues out-shouted the new. I wished her to become my woman and stay with me and learn white men's ways. We would possess ourselves, I told her, of the many good things white men have, and live in a wooden igloo and be always warm and well fed. Salak agreed to become my woman and she came to live with me but she would not agree to stay at the coast. In the autumn she moved into the tent of my father and his family and prepared to return up the River with them. She said that our child-to-be was of the Innuit, not of the Kablunait, and he must be born in his own land among his own people. I was angry with her but, also, I loved her very much and so, against my desires, I gave up the life at the coast and went with my family and my wife.

That winter I thought my own thoughts but did not speak them aloud. It was not until the dark days of mid-winter, when my mother died and they made ready to place her under the rocks with the tools, clothing, and ornaments which were hers, that I could no longer be quiet.

Then I spoke out against the foolishness of burying all those good things with the dead. I told those who sat about in my father's snowhouse it was evil to take the wealth that comes so hard to our people and place it on the windswept rocks to bleach and blow into decay. The women moaned and bent their bodies, and the men turned from me and would not look in my direction. All save Kakut.

His face alone did not change when I spoke against the ways of my people; and he replied in a voice that was as soft as the whisper of the white owl's wings.

"*Eeee* . . . those are words you have said. Perhaps they are the words of one who has darkness in front of his eyes. Men become blind when they travel over new snow on a day when there is a haze over the sun, and that happens because they deny the powers that lie in the wind and the snow and the sky and the sun. That is one kind of darkness. There is another. It comes when men deny or forget what their fathers' fathers knew. We must pity you, Katalak, for you are blind."

After that, I found I could no longer remain in the camps of my people. One day I harnessed my dogs and I took Salak and forced her onto my sled and drove my sled east to the coast and back to the place where the white men lived. Salak made no complaint but did her woman's work while I worked for the trader and became almost his right hand. In the spring, when the snow geese returned to the ponds by the coast, she gave birth.

So did we live until three years after my Haluk was born. That summer, when the families who made up the camp of my father arrived as usual at the coast, I saw that one canoe was missing. It was the great white canoe that belonged to my father.

I went to the camp of the newcomers, and I knew all of the people. They gave me greetings and I waited, as is the custom, for them to tell what was new. They were slow to speak and I grew impatient and asked a straight question, which was a rude thing to do. Someone answered, "It is true. Kakut is dead."

Then I spoke words whose memory will shame me forever.

"Well, then . . . if my father is dead, where is his canoe? Where are his rifles and the many fine things which were his? I am Katalak, his son, and it is just that the son should have those things, for the son is alive and has mouths to feed."

Those people gave me no answer. They spoke of the hard winter, of the shortage of white foxes, of many things which did not concern me, but of my father's possessions they would not speak.

That night I talked to Salak. I told her we would borrow the trader's canoe and engine — he had the first engine ever seen in the country — and we would go back up the River and find the grave of my father. Then I would have those things which the priest and the trader said were rightfully mine, and I would use them and not leave them to rot over the bones of a man who no longer could have any needs.

Salak replied that I would do what I would do but, as for her, she wanted nothing nor did she think she and I and Haluk, and the child who was soon to be born, wanted for anything. She was content, she said, and it would be well if we were all content. But I would not listen to the words of a woman for to have done so would have shamed me in the eyes of the white men.

We began our journey next day. The River was deserted in that season because the people had all come down the coast to trade, to escape the flies and to fish. We had a good eighteen-foot canoe and the little engine, and for a while all went well.

We climbed slowly westward up the white waters. Then the engine broke down and I did not know how to fix it. The flies became a black plague such as I had never known before. The deer, which should have been travelling with their fawns in small companies all over the tundra, seemed to have vanished, and we ran out of food. We had to track the canoe up the rapids for Haluk was too young to help and Salak too pregnant and I could not portage it alone.

But I would not give up. And so we came at last to the camp where I had been born and found no sign of the grave of Kakut. I left Haluk and Salak there, scraping moss off the rocks in order to eat, and went westward on foot. I walked for three days by the banks of the River and found nothing.

When I got back to the camp Salak was sick. We turned back toward the sea, but before we came to the coast Salak gave birth to a dead child — a son it was — and she buried the body in the old way, under some rocks by the shore. I said nothing when she took tea and tobacco and wrapped these things in her own parka and placed them on top of the grave.

That journey should have ended the matter and perhaps it would have done so, but during the following winter a stranger came to the trading post. He was of the *Padliermiut* who dwell far to the northwest and seldom come out to the coast. This man had made the long journey to try and buy ammunition, for his people were out of powder and lead and were starving. His had been a very hard journey and he had been forced to kill most of his dogs. Finally he became lost in strange country and was so weak from hunger he could not go on.

Then, so he told us, he saw a mountain appear high and black on the bleak plains where, before, he had seen nothing. On its crest he saw something white. Although he was afraid, for he was sure this was a vision of the kind men see when death is upon them, he approached and saw a big white canoe. When he went near it, he found the fat carcass of an autumn-killed deer lying on the windswept ridge, its body untouched by foxes or wolves. He took that meat and fed himself and his two remaining dogs, and then followed the frozen path of the River east to the coast.

When he told his story some people talked of the helping

spirits. I paid them no heed, but when the stranger spoke of the great white canoe, I listened. He described where it lay and where the mountain was. Then I thought he was lying, for in my search I had walked far up the River and had seen no mountain. Even so, I was sure he had found the grave of my father and would return to it on his way back to his own people and take from it the goods which were mine.

That evening I hitched up the post dogs and set off on the stranger's back trail. There was need for haste because the first gale would cover his tracks, so I drove the dogs and myself without mercy. Strangely, the weather stayed calm for a week and the tracks left by the sled of the stranger remained as clear as when he made them.

It was after dark when I came to the place where he said he had seen the great ridge. I waited for dawn, but before it could come a blizzard began to blow out of the north. It blew for five days, keeping me trapped in a hole I had dug in the drift, with no heat and no light and my food almost gone.

On the fifth day the wind changed and blew hard enough from the west to cover the land with ground drift so that nothing could be seen. I was driven east out of the plains as a puff of water is driven out of a whale's head when he spouts.

When I got back to the settlement, the trader was angry because I had gone away without his permission and because the post dogs were starved and their feet cut to pieces. He called me a fool. He said the rich grave of my father did not really exist — that it was no more than a story invented to hide from me the fact that the rifles and traps, the nets and the tools of Kakut, had been stolen as soon as he died. The priest said the same thing, adding these words, "Your people are liars and thieves. They are pagans, and cannot be believed. Only when God has come into their hearts will you get back what is rightfully yours."

I believed what the white men said and for years my heart was bitter against my own people. Whenever they came to the post I would make an opportunity to examine their gear. Although I never recognized anything which had belonged to my father, this meant to me only that the people feared discovery and had left the stolen things cached in the country when they came to the coast.

For ten more years I lived with the white men, doing their work and trying to be like them. I tried hard to forget the ways of my people. I thought each new year would be the one when I would cease to be of the Innuit and become truly one of the Kablunait — for this was what they had promised would come to pass if I remained with them and did as they wished.

But the years drew on, and Haluk was growing toward manhood, and Salak bore no more children and there was no change in my life. The people who came to trade at the post treated me distantly, as if I was one of the white men; but the white men did not treat me as one of themselves. Sometimes it seemed that Salak and Haluk and I were alone in the world, and I began to have very bad dreams. I dreamt I was alone in a deserted place where no birds sang, no wolves howled, nothing moved except me, and the sky was growing darker and darker, and I knew that when the night came it would never be followed by another dawn.

I began to grow silent and I did not laugh, and my wife was afraid for me. One day she took courage and spoke.

"My husband, let us go away from this place and return to the River and to the people. For laughter is there, and the deer walk the land, and fish swim in the waters."

Her words were very painful to me so I took my dog whip and struck her across the face with the butt of it, and she was silent.

The months passed and my heart was rotting within me, but I would not turn my face to the River for I could not go back to the people who had stolen what was mine. Yet sometimes, after I dreamt the terrible dreams, I saw their faces in the darkness and they were smiling and their lips shaped words of welcome that I could not hear.

One day the priest came to the wooden shanty in which we lived.

"Katalak," he said, "you have long wished to be one of us — of the Kablunait — now the time is coming. When the trading ship arrives in the summer it will take your son, Haluk, away in it and he will go to the world where all men are white men. He will stay there many years and will learn many things, and when he returns to this land he will be a God-man and like a Kablunait, and so, through him, you will become one of us too."

So he spoke, but instead of bringing me peace his words filled me with despair. Something swelled in my chest and almost throttled me. A shrieking voice swept through my mind. I picked up my snowknife, swung it high over my head and ran at him, shouting: "This you shall not do! You have had *my* life! It is enough! You will not have Haluk's too!"

The priest fled, but in a little while he came back accompanied by the trader. Both carried rifles, and the trader pointed his rifle at my belly and told me he was going to lock me in the dark cellar where we kept the walrus meat for the dogs. He called me a murderer and told me the police would come in the summer and I would be punished for a long time. He was so angry, spit fell from his mouth. But I was even angrier. I reached again for the snowknife, and then he fired and the bullet went into me just under my ribs.

After that there is a space of many days I do not remember. When I came to myself I was in my cousin Powaktuk's canoe. With me was my son and my wife and Powaktuk's family. I was lying on some deerskin robes. I could only raise my head a little but I could see over the gunwales and I knew where we were. We were going up the River. I was being carried to the place of my people.

When they saw I was awake they smiled at me and nodded their heads, and my cousin said, "It comes to pass. On the day Kakut died he spoke, saying that after his eyes became blind forever the eyes of his son would see again."

It had taken a long time for my father's words to begin to come true.

As we continued up the River we stopped at many camps and everywhere I was welcomed back to the land. At each camp people gave me things. Some gave me dogs, some gave me traps, one gave me a good rifle. Another gave me a sled, another a set of harness, and yet another gave Salak a fine meat tray. So it went until by the time we reached this island and prepared to make our own camp, Salak and Haluk and I wanted for nothing with which to begin the old life again.

My cousin and his family camped with us and everyone took such good care of me that I was able to walk before the first snows came. The deer arrived in greater numbers than anyone could remember and we cached enough meat and fat to keep us and the dogs well fed until spring. We set our traps and there were many foxes, and life was good in this place.

One night when the blizzard thundered, I sat in my cousin's snowhouse and spoke to him of certain things which had lain within me for a long time.

"I am a man whose liver is eaten by shame," I told him. "Through all the years since Kakut died I believed the people had taken for themselves the things which were my father's. Now I know they only kept those things against the day of my return. Shame has eaten my liver, yet there is one thing I would like to know. Where is Kakut's great canoe? When the ice goes from the River I will have need of a canoe of my own."

My cousin looked at me strangely.

"*Eeee*, Katalak, the blindness has not yet left your inner eye; otherwise you would have seen that of all the things that you have in your snowhouse, none is familiar from your father's time. You have forgotten, perhaps, that what one of us has belongs to all of us in time of need. These things are true gifts made to you in your time of need. As for the white canoe, it lies where it has lain since Kakut's death — over his bones and over all the things he had in life and which he may have need of in the place beyond."

When I heard this I was more ashamed than ever, yet I felt better inside myself too, for now there was no one else to blame for the mistake I had made when I abandoned my people. There was only myself left to be angry with. And why should a man be angry with himself?

Throughout that winter I slowly learned to live without anger, and it was the best winter of my life. All the people in that camp were as one, and I was again part of that one. Sometimes people from other camps came to visit with us, and sometimes we drove down the River to visit them. There were song-feasts and there was story telling and much eating of good meat. Then in the middle of winter Salak began to grow big with child. It seemed to me that at last I had everything a man could want, and the memory of the years when I had wished to be one of the Kablunait began to grow dim, like the spirit lights in the northern sky fading into the brightness as the spring returns to the land.

When the sun began to climb high over the horizon and the snows started to soften, we finished with our trapping and made ready to receive the returning deer herds.

This island where we sit is a fine place for deer hunting because it is like a stepping stone in the middle of the long lake. In the autumn the deer herds heading south swim to it and rest before continuing on their way. Heading north in the spring, they cross over to it on the ice, for they remember it and take the same path they used in the autumn. Also the island has stands of willows to provide us with fuel, so it is a good place to camp. But in the spring when the ice grows black and rotten and the River begins to break up, we must leave it for then sometimes the island is flooded. It is our custom to camp on the mainland shore at that time of the year until we can begin our voyage down to the coast by canoe.

In the spring that I speak of, the winter snows lay very thick on the land; and when the thaws started, the water flowed everywhere across the rocks and swamps as if the land itself was melting. My cousin and I saw it would be a year of big floods so one day we sledded his canoe over to the mainland shore and cached it at a safe height above the still-frozen surface of the river. Then we returned to the island intending to take all the people and goods ashore on the sleds the following day.

That was our plan, but during the night the spirits sent us such a storm as I do not ever remember seeing. It began with a fall of wet snow, then the wind rose and the snow turned to rain that poured out of the night as if Sredna, Mistress of the Waters, had turned her world upside down. Our snowhouse crumbled and when I tried to stretch caribou hides over the holes the wind was so strong it brought me to my knees. Then the howl of the wind was lost in a shuddering thunder that shook the roots of the island. We knew what it was. Swollen with the flood from the land, the River had risen and burst free of the ice. Swirling floes, thicker than the height of a man, were being flung out over the rotten surface ice of the lake, crushing our road to the shore.

I shouted for my cousin but my voice was snatched away by the wind and lost in the roaring as the islands of ice beat each other to pieces. Salak and Haluk and I fought our way toward a high drift in whose lee my cousin's snowhouse had stood. We met him and his family crawling toward us. His house had collapsed. We all managed to burrow into the back of the soaking-wet drift, and there we stayed until dawn.

It came grey and ugly, whipped by a rain that seemed to grow steadily worse. We knew the rain on the half-melted snows would make the River swell ever faster. Yet with the return of the daylight, our courage came back. We gathered most of our things on the highest part of the island and set up a tent. We had plenty of food, and we believed the lake could hardly rise high enough to submerge the whole island. We believed we had only to wait four or five days for the flooding to end, then we would find some way to escape.

All day we sat in the low tent around a small, smoky fire of wet willow and caribou fat, and we were not frightened. It is not the way of the people to worry when trouble comes. We laughed at our plight, and told stories. Haluk was wild with excitement for he was hardly more than a boy and this was an adventure he would remember through the long years ahead.

It was Haluk who brought the bad news. During a lull in the rain he had gone to the head of the island to watch the floes spinning past. In a little while he was back, running as hard as he could and shouting, "Come quick! Come quick! The island is sinking!"

When we hurried down to the shore we found the lake waters rising so fast they had already covered the slope where the dogs were tethered, and the beasts were up to their bellies, frantically pulling against their leads. We waded in and freed them, but the water continued to rise so swiftly that we were bewildered, not understanding why the water was rising so fast. It was my cousin who guessed the answer.

"It must be the rapids at the foot of the lake," he said. "They have held the pack ice. The gorge must be plugged and now the River has nowhere to go!"

Then we knew we had little time. If the gorge stayed blocked the lake would rise until the island vanished beneath those cold waters.

The women made haste to pack all our important possessions into small bundles after which they placed the heavy things, traps, cooking pots and such, in a hole over which they rolled big rocks. As for my cousin and me, our thoughts were racing, but we could think of no way to flee from the island. Our people do not swim, and in any case no swimmer could have escaped being crushed by the pounding fragments of ice. Nor could we ride the ice pans as one would a raft, for the turmoil was so great and the wind so strong that not even the largest floes were safe from upsetting or being overswept by other floes. I wondered if we might build an *umiak*, a woman's boat of the kind sometimes used by the coastal people, out of willow branches and caribou skins, but I knew there was no time for that.

It seemed we could do nothing but hope that the dam in the gorge would soon burst. I stood on the highest place and saw that the waters had already swallowed more than half the island.

Then it was as if I became two persons. I was a man of my people, but standing beside me was another self. It was a very strange thing that happened. One of my beings was calm, feeling no fear, and this was one who had come back to his own place. The other was panic-stricken, mouthing the prayers he had been taught by the priest.

I was two beings who struggled against each other; and it was the man of the people who won. He felt such a contempt for that other that he flung him away, and he vanished into the cold ice-mist that swirled over the lake. Then I was alone and I looked about me at the world that had harbored my people since time before memory, and I was content to be there even though I believed the waters must soon make an end of us all. I thought of Kakut, and inside myself I asked him to take me back.

These are true things I am speaking; and it is a true thing that when I lifted my eyes to look westward toward the place where my father lay, I saw his canoe.

I saw that great canoe, whiter than the ice around it, breasting the heaving waters and driving down upon the island's head.

I was still watching as if it was something seen in a dream when Haluk ran up the slope and seized my arm. His young voice was shrill and it pierced into the quiet places in my mind. He yelled at me and pulled hard on my arm, and my vision cleared and I went with him.

My cousin and the rest of the people were also running toward the head of the island, everyone burdened with bundles and surrounded by the half-crazy dogs. We were ready when the great canoe grounded. Everything was swiftly loaded. Everyone climbed aboard and there was still room to spare, for Kakut's canoe was a mighty one.

The crossing to the mainland was not easily made and there were times when it seemed certain the canoe would be crushed and all of us drowned. But it was not crushed, and we escaped from the island.

The old man ceased telling his story. Haluk's wife, Petuk, went outside, blew up the embers of the fire, and began to boil another pail of tea. After a while I went down to where my canoe lay. I took from it the rifle, the remaining shells, the net and the tea and tobacco and brought them back to the tent. Katalak looked up as I lifted the flap ... he looked up and after a moment he smiled so broadly it seemed all the years had lifted from his face. Then they were all laughing. Katalak reached over and poked me in the ribs.

"One time I saw a wolf that looked as hungry as you, all bones and a bit of dry skin. He lost his teeth somehow. *Eh!* I think you lost your teeth on the River. Well, Kakut gave them back and you had better keep them until you get to the coast. Leave them there with Anyala, my daughter, if you wish. We will return them to Kakut when the winter snows come."

The amusement faded from his voice.

"*Eeee.* We will take them back, as we took back the great canoe and placed it where it belongs ... where it will always remain, so long as the people remain by the River and live in this land."

BIBLIOGRAPHY

UNITED STATES
AND CANADA

BOOKS BY FARLEY MOWAT

(arranged in chronological order)

People of the Deer. Boston: Atlantic–Little, Brown, 1952 [0-316-58642-0], published simultaneously in Canada by McClelland and Stewart Limited; London: Michael Joseph, 1953; Berlin: Seven Seas Books, 1962. Revised edition, Toronto: McClelland and Stewart, 1975 [0-7710-6589-2 (cloth), 0-7710-6590-6 (soft cover)]. (This soft-cover edition was also issued with *The Desperate People* in a boxed set, titled *Death of a People.*)

Paperback editions: Toronto: Canadian Best Seller Library (McClelland and Stewart), 1965; London: Sphere, 1967; New York: Pyramid, 1968; Toronto: Seal, 1980; New York: Bantam, 1980.

Other editions: Excerpted in *The Atlantic Monthly,* Boston, Jan.–Mar. 1952. Book condensation in *Reader's Digest* international editions, Jan. 1953. Readers' Union edition, London, England, 1954; Talking Books Edition (Braille), U.S.A., 1965.

A large number of foreign translations of this book have been published, including French and Swedish editions, two German editions (1954 and 1956), two Italian editions (1954 and 1977), Norwegian, Yugoslavian, Russian, Polish, Rumanian, Dutch, and Japanese editions.

The Regiment. Toronto: McClelland and Stewart, 1955. Also issued in "illustrated edition" (Toronto: McClelland and Stewart, 1955). Revised edition, Toronto: McClelland and Stewart, 1973 [0-7710-6575-2 (cloth), 0-7710-6571-X (soft cover)].

Paperback edition: Toronto: Canadian Best Seller Library (McClelland and Stewart), 1967. Italian edition: *Il Reggimento.* Milan: Longanesi, 1976.

Lost in the Barrens. Boston: Atlantic–Little, Brown, 1956 [0-316-58638-2], published simultaneously in Canada by Little, Brown & Company (Canada) Limited. Also issued in a "trade paperback edition" (Toronto: McClelland and Stewart, 1974 [0-7710-6640-6] and a soft-cover "school edition" with notes and activities (Toronto: McClelland and Stewart, 1974 [0-7710-6639-2]). London: Macmillan, 1957.

Paperback editions: Toronto: Chariot Literature Texts (McClelland and Stewart), 1962 (with notes and questions); New York: Scholastic Book Services, 1960, new ed. 1968 (as *Two Against the North*); London: Pan (Piccolo), 1978.

Other editions: Many editions of *Lost in the Barrens* have been published in translation, including German, Czech (two editions), Japanese (two editions), Portuguese, Yugoslavian, French, Dutch, Polish, Hebrew, Ukrainian, and Danish editions. A Canadian French-language edition is being issued by the Montreal publisher Le Cercle du livre de France in 1980.

The Dog Who Wouldn't Be. Boston, Toronto: Atlantic–Little, Brown, 1957 [0-316-58636-6]; London: Michael Joseph, 1958.

Paperback editions: New York: Pyramid, 1959; New York: Willow, 1965; New York: Jove/HBJ Books, 1977 [0-515-02333-7]; London: Pan, 1977; Toronto: Seal, 1980 [0-7704-1578-4]; New York: Bantam, 1980.

Other editions: Condensation in *Reader's Digest*, Jan. 1958. German, Italian, Japanese (two editions), Dutch, and Polish editions have also been published.

Coppermine Journey: An Account of a Great Adventure, Selected from the Journals of Samuel Hearne by Farley Mowat. Toronto: McClelland and Stewart, 1958; Boston: Atlantic–Little, Brown, 1958.

Miscellaneous: Serialized in *True*, 1959.

The Grey Seas Under. Boston: Atlantic–Little, Brown, 1958 [0-316-58637-4]; Toronto: McClelland and Stewart, 1958; London: Michael Joseph, 1959.

Paperback editions: New York: Ballantine, 1958 [0-345-23784-6]; London: Pan, 1977.

Miscellaneous: Serialized in *Atlantic*, Sept.–Oct., 1958.

The Desperate People. Boston, Toronto: Atlantic–Little, Brown, 1959 [0-316-58635-8]. London: Michael Joseph, 1960.

Revised edition: Toronto: McClelland and Stewart, 1975 [0-7710-6591-4 (cloth), 0-7710-6592-2 (soft cover)]. (This soft-cover edition was also issued with *People of the Deer* in a boxed set titled *Death of a People*.)

Other editions: German, Russian, Hungarian, Polish, and Czech editions have been published.

Ordeal By Ice. Toronto: McClelland and Stewart, 1960; Boston: Atlantic–Little, Brown, 1961; London: Michael Joseph, 1961. (Excerpts from accounts of

Arctic voyages up to the mid-nineteenth century, selected and edited by
Farley Mowat.)

Revised edition: Toronto: McClelland and Stewart, 1973 [0-7710-6577-9
(cloth), 0-7710-6626-0 (soft cover)]. This soft-cover edition was also issued
with *The Polar Passion* and *Tundra* in a boxed set, titled *The Top of the World
Trilogy* (Toronto: McClelland and Stewart, 1973 [0-7710-6585-X]).

Other editions: Published in Russian translation by Progress Publishing
House, Moscow, 1966.

Owls in the Family. Boston: Atlantic–Little, Brown, 1961 [0-316-58641-2]; Toronto: McClelland and Stewart, 1961; London: Macmillan, 1963.

Also issued by McClelland and Stewart in the Chariot Literature Texts
series (1969), in a "trade paperback edition" (1970) [0-7710-6647-3] and a
"school edition" with study aids (1970) [0-7710-6625-2]. Also published by
Xerox (Waltham, Mass.), 1969. Abridged edition: Chicago: Science Research
Associates, 1963.

Paperback edition: London: Pan (Piccolo), 1971.

Other editions: A Japanese and two German translations have been published. Le Cercle du livre de France, Montreal, plans a French-language
edition for 1980. Available on tape: Toronto: Canadian National Institute
for the Blind, 1975.

The Serpent's Coil. Toronto: McClelland and Stewart, 1961; Boston: Atlantic–
Little, Brown, 1961 [0-316-58643-9]; London: Michael Joseph, 1962.

Paperback editions: New York: Ballantine, 1964 [0-345-23828-1]; London:
Pan, 1977 [0-330-25367-0].

Other editions: A condensation published in Calcutta, 1962; Czech and
French translations.

The Black Joke. Toronto: McClelland and Stewart, 1963; Boston: Atlantic–
Little, Brown, 1963 [0-316-58631-5]. London: Macmillan, 1964.

Also issued by McClelland and Stewart in a "trade paperback" edition
(1973) [0-7710-6649-X] and a school edition (1974), with notes and activities
[0-7710-6648-1].

Paperback edition: London: Pan (Piccolo), 1978.

Other editions: German and Hebrew translations; to be published in French
translation by Le Cercle du livre de France, Montreal, 1980.

Never Cry Wolf. Toronto: McClelland and Stewart, 1963; Boston: Atlantic–
Little, Brown, 1963 [0-316-58639-0]; London: Martin Secker and Warburg,
1964.

Revised edition: Toronto: McClelland and Stewart, 1973 [0-7710-6584-1
(cloth), 0-7710-6582-5 (soft-cover school edition)].

Other English language editions: New York: Franklin Watts, 1969 ("large
type edition").

Paperback editions: New York: Dell, 1965 [0-440-36299-7]; London: Ballantine, 1971 [0-345-09702-5]; London: Pan, 1978 [0-330-25606-8]; Toronto: Seal, 1979 [0-7704-1593-8]; New York: Bantam, 1979 [0-553-13301-2].

Miscellaneous: Foreign-language editions published in Swedish, Czech, Dutch, Russian, Japanese, German (two editions), French, Hebrew, Hungarian, Norwegian, Italian, Portuguese, Finnish, and Polish. Serialized in publications in Poland, Holland, and Israel. Film production: Lewis Allen Productions (New York) for Walt Disney Studio, 1980.

Westviking: The Ancient Norse in Greenland and North America. Illus. by Claire Wheeler. Toronto: McClelland and Stewart, 1965; Boston: Atlantic–Little, Brown, 1965; London: Martin Secker and Warburg, 1966; New York: Funk and Wagnalls, 1968.

Reissued by McClelland and Stewart in soft-cover edition, 1973 [0-7710-6579-5].

Miscellaneous: This was a selection of the Canadian division of The Book-of-the-Month Club in 1965. A Polish translation was published in Warsaw in 1972.

The Curse of the Viking Grave. Toronto: McClelland and Stewart, 1966; Boston: Atlantic–Little, Brown, 1966 [0-316-58633-1].

Reissued by McClelland and Stewart in "trade paperback" edition, 1973 [0-7710-6642-2], and soft-cover school edition, 1973, with notes and activities [0-7710-6641-4].

Paperback editions: London: Pan (Piccolo), 1978 [0-330-25633-5].

Other editions: Czech, Russian, Japanese, Polish, Hebrew, and two Danish editions have been published. Le Cercle du livre de France, Montreal, is bringing out a French-language edition in 1980.

Canada North. Toronto: McClelland and Stewart (Canadian Illustrated Library), 1967; Boston: Atlantic–Little, Brown, 1968 [0-316-58647-1].

The Polar Passion: The Quest for the North Pole. (Excerpts from Arctic journals, edited by Farley Mowat.) Toronto: McClelland and Stewart (Illustrated Books Division), 1967. Boston: Atlantic–Little, Brown, 1968.

Revised edition: Toronto: McClelland and Stewart, 1973 [0-7710-6621-X (cloth), 0-7710-6622-8 (soft cover)]. This soft-cover edition was also issued in a boxed set with *Ordeal by Ice* and *Tundra*, entitled *The Top of the World Trilogy* (Toronto: McClelland and Stewart, 1973 [0-7710-6585-X].

Other editions: Czech and German translations have been published. Available on tape: Toronto: Canadian National Institute for the Blind, 1975.

This Rock within the Sea: A Heritage Lost. (Photography by John de Visser.) Toronto: McClelland and Stewart, 1968; Boston: Atlantic–Little, Brown, 1968.

Reissued by McClelland and Stewart, 1976 [0-7710-6632-5].

The Boat Who Wouldn't Float. Toronto: McClelland and Stewart, 1969; Boston: Atlantic-Little, Brown, 1970 [0-316-58650-1]; London: Heinemann, 1971 [0-434-47985-3]. In 1973 McClelland and Stewart issued a "school edition," and a "special edition for Newfoundland."

New edition: Toronto: McClelland and Stewart, 1974 [0-7710-6586-8 (cloth), 0-7710-6587-6 (soft cover)]. Issued in the "Standard Mowat Series" by McClelland and Stewart in 1976 [0-7710-6623-6].

Miscellaneous: French, Polish, Dutch, German, Japanese, and Bulgarian editions have been published. The book has been serialized in Norwegian and Russian publications. Available on tape: Toronto: Canadian National Institute for the Blind, 1974.

Sibir: My Discovery of Siberia. Toronto: McClelland and Stewart, 1970 [0-7710-6580-9]; Boston: Atlantic-Little, Brown, 1971 (as *The Siberians*) [0-316-58690-0]; London: Heinemann, 1972 (as *The Siberians*) [0-434-47986-1].

Revised edition: Toronto: McClelland and Stewart, 1973 [0-7710-6576-0 (cloth), 0-7710-6581-7 (soft cover)].

Paperback edition: Baltimore: Penguin Books, 1972 [0-14-003456-0].

Miscellaneous: A selection of the Book-of-the Month Club (Canada), 1970, (as *Sibir*) and of the Readers' Union, London, 1973 (as *The Siberians*). German, Dutch, and Japanese translations have been published. Serialized in Norwegian and Russian publications.

A Whale for the Killing. Toronto: McClelland and Stewart, 1972 [0-7710-6570-1]; Boston: Atlantic-Little, Brown, 1972 [0-316-58691-9]; London: Heinemann, 1973. Also issued by McClelland and Stewart in a "standard edition" (1973) and a soft-cover "school edition" in 1976.

New edition: Toronto: McClelland and Stewart, 1977 [0-7710-6600-7].

Paperback editions: Baltimore, Maryland: Penguin Books, 1973 [0-14-003728-4]; London: Quartet, 1974; New York: Viking, 1975; New York: Bantam, 1977; Toronto: Seal, 1978 [0-7704-1523-0]; London: Pan, 1979.

Miscellaneous: A selection of The Book-of-the-Month Club (Toronto and New York), 1972. Translated into German, Italian, Russian, and Hungarian. Serialized in *Zyveda*, Leningrad, 1976, and excerpted in *Weekend*, Montreal, Sept. 1972. Condensed in *Reader's Digest*, international editions, Feb. 1973. Also available on phonotape: Toronto: Canadian National Institute for the Blind, 1975.

Tundra: Selections from the Great Accounts of Arctic Land Voyages. (Compiled and edited by Farley Mowat.) Toronto: McClelland and Stewart, 1973 [0-7710-6627-9 (cloth), 0-7710-6628-7 (soft cover)].

Miscellaneous: A selection of The Book-of-the-Month Club, Toronto, 1973. Soft-cover edition issued with *Ordeal by Ice* and *The Polar Passion* in boxed set entitled *The Top of the World Trilogy* (McClelland and Stewart, 1973) [0-7710-6585-X].

Wake of the Great Sealers. (Text by Farley Mowat; prints and drawings by David Blackwood.) Toronto: McClelland and Stewart, 1973 [0-7710-1527-5]; Boston: Atlantic–Little, Brown, 1974 [0-316-58692-7].

The Snow Walker. Toronto: McClelland and Stewart, 1975 [0-7710-6630-9]; Boston: Atlantic–Little, Brown, 1976 [0-316-58693-5]; London: Heinemann, 1977 [0-434-47988-8].
Paperback editions: London: Pan, 1977 [0-330-25605-X]; Toronto: Seal, 1977 [0-7704-1565-2]; New York: Bantam, 1977 [0-553-10399-7].
Other editions: Also published in German and Czech translations.

Canada North Now: The Great Betrayal. (With photographs by Shin Sugino.) Toronto: McClelland and Stewart, 1976 [0-7710-6596-5].
This soft-cover, revised version of *Canada North*, with revised text and new illustrations, was also published by Atlantic–Little, Brown in a soft-cover edition under the title *The Great Betrayal* (Boston: Atlantic–Little, Brown, 1976 [0-316-58694-3]). A Bulgarian translation was published in Sofia in 1979.

And No Birds Sang. Toronto: McClelland and Stewart, 1979 [0-7710-6618-X]; Boston: Atlantic–Little, Brown, 1980.
Paperback editions: Toronto: Seal, 1980; New York: Bantam, 1981
Miscellaneous: A selection of The Book-of-the-Month Club, Toronto, 1980.